THE LIFE
JOHN NEWTON

THE LIFE OF
JOHN NEWTON

Josiah Bull

THE BANNER OF TRUTH TRUST

THE BANNER OF TRUTH TRUST
3 Murrayfield Road, Edinburgh EH12 6EL, UK
P.O. Box 621, Carlisle, PA 17013, USA

*

First published 1868
First published by the Banner of Truth Trust as
But Now I See: The Life of John Newton, 1998
This reset edition first published 2007

*

ISBN-13: 978 0 85151 967 8

*

Typeset in 11/15 Adobe Caslon Pro at
the Banner of Truth Trust, Edinburgh

Printed in the U.S.A. by
Versa Press, Inc.,
East Peoria, IL

CONTENTS

PART TWO

CURATE OF OLNEY

Contents

PART THREE

RECTOR OF ST MARY WOOLNOTH

PREFACE

Several memoirs of John Newton have already appeared. Why, it may be asked, publish another? It may be replied that, without disparaging unduly former biographies, the life of Newton has yet to be written; for this reason, amongst others, that the materials for an adequate memoir have only recently been accessible. They include a diary unknown to previous biographers, covering a period of fifty-seven years, and a very large correspondence, together with other documents of great value and interest, the greater part of which have never yet been published. These, together with the inheritance of traditions handed down from the friends and contemporaries of Newton himself, have come into our possession, and throw light upon many periods in the life of Newton which were previously obscure, and correct false statements and prejudices which have hitherto been current in many quarters. Hence this attempt to give a more complete history of a life so well worthy of a careful record. It may be added that Mr Newton is here made to speak as much as possible in his own person, so that the memoir is in great part an *Autobiography.**

The presentation of such a life as Newton's is not inopportune at the present time. He is a very striking example of one who thoroughly understood and uniformly illustrated in his life, ministry, and writings, the great doctrines of the gospel, who had a wise discernment of the relative value of the mere forms of religion and its fundamental truths, and who possessed that spirit of true

* Newton published anonymously *An Authentic Narrative of Some Remarkable and Interesting Particulars in the Life of ——, Communicated, in a Series of Letters, to the Rev. T. Haweis*, in 1764. This is referred to in what follows simply as the *Narrative*.

charity, which, unmindful of the lesser distinctions of party, recognises all the true disciples of Christ as such, and seeks fellowship with them.

There is considerable diversity of opinion as to the propriety of making public the contents of a diary and of private correspondence. It is thought by some to be an entrance into those secret chambers of the soul which ought to be sacred from all intrusion. It is alleged by others that diaries do not really give the true exposition of a man's inner life. Without discussing these points, it may suffice to say that we have the virtual authority of Mr Newton himself for quoting from his diary. He evidently thought it might be read by other eyes than his own at some future time. It has many blanks, initials, and shorthand characters, indicating such a possibility. But chiefly we refer to expressions to be found in the body of this work, in which he utters the prayer that his experience, as thus recorded, may be blessed to the use of any who in God's providence shall be led to peruse his history.

Considerable difficulty has been found in dealing judiciously with this important document. In drawing the line between that which is trivial and unimportant and those details which give reality and impressiveness to the story; in presenting some statements which illustrate character, and excluding others which ought never to meet the public eye; in avoiding those repetitions of thought and language which necessarily occur in a mental transcript of so many years; there can scarcely fail to be some imperfections and faults.

One other remark may be added as to the use made of matters already in print. Published works have been quoted from only so far as they contain necessary information, or furnish statements illustrating the various opinions of Mr Newton. Thus there are some repetitions from the *Memorials of the Rev. W. Bull*. Had the design of this Memoir been entertained when that volume was compiled, these materials might have been kept in reserve. The *Narrative* has been abbreviated as much as a distinct record of its interesting facts would allow.

The work we have attempted will be, we trust, in some sort a worthy monument to the memory of John Newton, a volume of interest to all lovers of evangelical truth, and a means of healthful stimulus to those who desire to consecrate themselves to the Master's service as he did.

All that remains for us to do is to commit this effort to the Divine blessing, and to express our obligations to all who have kindly aided us in our undertaking. Our best thanks are especially due to Mrs Janson for the use of the missing volume of the diary; to A. C. Hobart Seymour, Esq., for several valuable illustrative documents; to Dr A. Macaulay; to the Rev. C. Bingham; to Mr. T. W. Coffin, and other friends.

Josiah Bull
Newport Pagnell
1868

PART ONE

MR NEWTON'S EARLY LIFE AND RESIDENCE AT LIVERPOOL

PART ONE

1: FROM THE BIRTH OF MR NEWTON TO HIS MARRIAGE
(1725-50)

Birth – Parentage – His mother's teaching – Her death – Goes to sea, and falls into bad habits – Reformation – Meets with Shaftesbury's *Characteristics* – Miss Catlett – Voyage to Venice – Remarkable dream – Pressed on board the *Harwich* – Evil associations there – Deserts, is arrested and degraded – Exchanged into a Guinea vessel – Miseries on the coast of Africa – His rescue – Peril at sea – His 'Great Deliverance' – In England – Sails again to the coast of Africa – Wonderful escape – Return home.

We are unwilling to believe that the name of John Newton has lost its charm, or that the Christian public has forgotten his writings. There are those, we are sure, to whom his memory is still dear, and who, spite of various attractions elsewhere, yet love to linger over the pages which contain the many wise and pleasant things which flowed from his prolific pen. From such readers we may confidently look for a welcome, and we indulge the hope that others less familiar with his character and his writings will not turn away from this fuller illustration of the life of a man whose 'remains' are really a very precious legacy to the Church.

The account of Mr Newton's early years is a story of adventure and of marvellous providential interpositions which has few parallels. Equally striking in this history are the amazing contrasts between its earlier and later periods. Most beautiful too and instructive is the illustration it affords of the priceless value of a Christian mother's early training, and of her ardent prayers; for after many days those

3

instructions brought forth fruit, and those prayers, laid up before God, were answered when the mother had passed into the skies.

To begin with the 'Narrative' of his early years. John Newton was born in London, July, 1725. His father was for many years master of a ship in the Mediterranean trade, and in 1748 went out as Governor of York Fort, Hudson's Bay, where he died in the year 1750. His son says of him, 'There was a sternness and severity about my father's manner, arising from the effect of his training at a Jesuit College in Spain, which induced a feeling of fear rather than of love, and which overawed and broke my spirit.' May not this in a measure account for the subsequent outbreaks and restlessness under authority, which so characterized the early career of his son? 'Yet,' says the subject of our memoir, 'I am persuaded that my father loved me, though he seemed not willing that I should know it.'

Very interesting is the account Mr Newton gives of his mother. 'I was born,' he says, 'as it were, in the house of God, and dedicated to Him in my infancy. My mother (as I have heard from many) was a pious, experienced Christian. She was a dissenter, in communion with the church of the late Dr Jennings. I was her only child, and almost her whole employment was the care of my education.'

At four years of age he could read with facility, and his mind was stored with many portions of Scripture. He was able to repeat not only the answers in Watts's Smaller Catechisms, but even those of the Assembly's Shorter Catechism, with the proofs. He had little inclination, he tells us, to the noisy sports of children, and was most happy in his mother's company, being as willing to learn as she was to teach him. She observed his early progress with peculiar pleasure, and intended from the first to bring him up to the ministry, if the Lord should so incline his heart. But before her son was seven years old this good woman was taken to a better world.

The elder Mr Newton married again; and, though the son was treated with kindness, his further religious training was little cared for. He was allowed to mingle with idle and ungodly children, and soon began to learn their ways. He was sent to school, where he made some progress in Latin, but remained there only two years. When he was eleven years of age his father took him to sea, and before he had reached his fifteenth year young Newton had made several voyages. He was then placed at Alicante, in Spain. His prospects were good, but his 'unsettled behaviour and impatience of restraint rendered the design abortive.'

During this period old impressions of religion would sometimes revive, but they passed away, and he learned to curse and blaspheme, and was exceedingly wicked. From this state he was aroused by an accident which happened to himself, and which proved nearly fatal, and again by the sudden death of an intimate companion. And thus before he was sixteen years of age, he tells us, he took up and laid down a religious profession three or four different times. His last reform, however, was the most remarkable. Of this period, he says, 'After the strictest sect of our religion I lived a Pharisee!' He read the Scriptures, meditated and prayed through the greater part of the day, fasted often, and abstained from all animal food for three months, almost renounced society, scarcely spoke lest he should speak amiss, and in short became an ascetic. Thus he went about to establish his own righteousness, and so continued for more than two years.

While Mr Newton was in this frame of mind he met with the *Characteristics* of Lord Shaftesbury. The style of the book greatly pleased him, and at first he was not aware of the pernicious character of its matter. His heart was beguiled. He read it till he could very nearly repeat the Rhapsody (the second piece) verbatim from beginning to end. No immediate effect was produced, but it operated like a slow poison, and prepared the way for all that followed.

In December 1742, Mr Newton's father, not intending to go to sea again, was anxious to settle his son; and a Mr Manesty, a merchant at Liverpool, made an offer to send him out to Jamaica, and to take care of his future welfare. To this the son willingly consented. But a circumstance occurred to defeat the project, and which was to influence the whole of his future history. He had some distant relatives in Kent, the particular friends of his mother. They, knowing he was coming into their neighbourhood on business, requested he would visit them. He tells us he was very indifferent about going, but he went, and was most kindly received. In this family were two daughters; the eldest, Mary Catlett, had from the very time of her birth been considered, both by her mother and by his, as a future wife for Newton.

This he was told some years afterwards. Almost at the first sight of this girl (she was then under fourteen), he says, 'I was impressed with an affection for her which never abated or lost its influence over me. None of the scenes of misery and wickedness I afterwards experienced ever banished her for an hour together from my waking thoughts for the seven following years.' Very many years afterwards, Mr Newton being at the house of a lady at Blackheath (probably Mrs Wilberforce), stood at a window which had a prospect of Shooter's Hill. 'Ah!' said he to Mr Cecil, 'I remember the many journeys I took from London to stand at the top of that hill, in order to look towards the place where Mrs Newton then lived, not that I could see the spot itself, for she lived several miles beyond, but it gratified me to look *towards* it. This I always did once, and sometimes twice a week.'

To go to Jamaica, and to be absent four or five years, was now felt to be something intolerable. Newton determined he would not go, and yet he knew not how to acquaint his father with this alteration of his purpose. But he stayed in Kent for three weeks instead of three days, supposing (as it proved) that the ship in which he was to embark would have sailed, and so the opportunity be lost. His father, though greatly displeased, became reconciled to him, and in a short time we find him going on board a vessel bound for Venice. Here he fell a prey to evil companionship. Still he did not become so wholly abandoned as at a future period. He tells us that a strong impression was made upon him by the following remarkable dream:

'The scene presented to my imagination was the harbour of Venice, where we had lately been. I thought it was night and my watch upon the deck, and that as I was walking to and fro a person came to me, and brought me a ring, with an express charge to keep it safely, assuring me that while I preserved that ring I should be happy and successful, but if I lost or parted with it I must expect nothing but trouble and misery. I accepted the present and the terms willingly, not in the least doubting my own care to preserve it, and highly satisfied to have my happiness in my own keeping.

'I was engaged in these thoughts when a second person came to me, and observing the ring on my finger, took occasion to ask me some questions concerning it. I readily told him its virtues. He expressed surprise at my weakness, reasoned with me upon the impossibility of the thing, and at length urged me in direct terms to throw it away. I was at first shocked at the proposal, but his insinuations prevailed. I began to reason and doubt myself, and at last plucked it off my finger and dropped it over the ship's side into the water, which it had no sooner touched than I saw a terrible fire burst out from the Alps behind the city of Venice. I perceived, too late, my folly; and my tempter with an air of insult told me that all the mercy God had in reserve for me was comprised in that ring, which I had willingly thrown away. I understood that I must go with him to the burning mountains, and that all the flames I saw were kindled on my account.

'I trembled and was in a great agony; but when I thought myself upon the point of a constrained departure, and stood self-condemned without plea or hope, suddenly either a third person, or the same who brought the ring at first, came to me and demanded the cause of my grief. I told him the plain case, confessing that I had ruined myself wilfully and deserved no pity. He blamed my rashness, and asked if I should be wiser, supposing I had my ring again. I could hardly answer to this, for I thought it was gone beyond recall. Immediately I saw this unexpected friend go down under the water, just in the spot where I had dropped the ring, and he soon returned, bringing it with him. The moment he came on board the flames in the mountains were extinguished, and my seducer left me. My fears were at an end, and with joy and gratitude I approached my kind deliverer to receive the ring again, but he refused to return it, and spoke to this effect: If you should be entrusted with this ring again you would very soon bring yourself into the same distress. You are not able to keep it; but I will preserve it for you, and, whenever it is needful, produce it on your behalf.

'Upon this I awoke in a state of mind not to be described. I could hardly eat or sleep or transact any necessary business, for two or three days, but the impression soon wore off, and I think it hardly occurred to my mind again till several years afterwards.'

In December, 1743, Mr Newton returned to England, and repeating his visit to Kent, protracted his stay in the same imprudent manner as before, and thus again disappointed his father's designs for his interest, and almost provoked him to disown his son altogether. Before anything suitable offered itself, Mr Newton's appearance as a sailor led to his being impressed, and he was taken on board the *Harwich* man-of-war. The French fleet was then hovering on our coast, and as his release could not be obtained, his father procured him a recommendation to the captain, and he was taken on the quarterdeck as a midshipman. Here he met with companions who completed the ruin of his principles, and he unhappily became particularly intimate with a man of whom he speaks 'as the greatest master of the Freethinking scheme he ever remembers to have met with, and who knew how to insinuate his sentiments in the most plausible way. And so,' he adds, 'I renounced the hopes and comfort of the gospel, when every other hope was about to fail me.' Nor was this all; while the vessel lay in the Downs (it was in December, 1744), he 'had leave to go on shore for a day. Regardless of all consequences, he most foolishly determined to pay another visit to Kent before sailing to the East Indies, whither the *Harwich* was bound. The captain was prevailed on to excuse his absence, but by this breach of discipline he henceforth lost his favour.

In a letter to Miss Catlett, dated *The Harwich*, Jan. 24th, 1745, he writes, ' . . . But for you, I had till this time remained heavy, sour, and unsociable. You raised me from the dull melancholy I had contracted, and pushed me into the world. It is now more than two years since, from which time till now I have been almost continually disappointed in whatever I have undertaken. My designs are now bent to one point, that is, this voyage, which I seriously think will either make or mar me. It is true I hope to succeed, but I take Love to witness it is not wholly on my own account.'

At length the ship sailed from Spithead, but, through stress of weather, was compelled to put back to Plymouth. Several vessels of the fleet were lost. In some of them Mr Newton's father had an interest, and his son, hearing that he had on that account come down to Torbay, resolved to see him. His object was to get into the African service, with which his father was connected, and so to avoid the long, uncertain voyage to the East Indies. 'It was a maxim with me,' he says, 'in those unhappy days never to deliberate. The thought no sooner occurred to me than I resolved I would leave the ship at all events. I did so, and in the wrongest manner possible. I was sent one day in the boat to take care that none of the people deserted; but I betrayed my trust and went off myself.' For a day and a half all went well; but when within two hours' distance of his father he was discovered by a party of soldiers, and brought back to his vessel as a deserter, and after being kept in irons some time was publicly flogged and degraded from his office.

He now became the victim of the most violent passions. He was so enraged with the captain that he conceived the purpose of taking his life; then, overwhelmed with despair, he was tempted to drown himself; but from all this the thought of the object of his attachment saved him. He could not bear that she should think meanly of him when he was dead.

Mr Newton, it will be remembered, was above all things anxious not to go to India, but to the coast of Africa. The *Harwich* was now at Madeira, and the fleet was to sail the following day, when his wish was thus remarkably fulfilled. That morning he was late in bed. One of the midshipmen came down, and, between jest and earnest, bade him rise. As he did not immediately comply, his hammock was cut down, and he was forced to dress himself. He was very angry, but dare not resent it. He went on deck, where he saw a man putting his clothes into a boat, saying he was going to leave the ship. Upon inquiry Newton found that two men from a Guinea ship had entered on board the *Harwich*, and that the commodore had ordered the captain to send two others in their room. The boat was detained a few minutes, and the captain was appealed to to give Newton his discharge. This he did, though he had refused to do so at Plymouth, even at the request of the admiral; and, so says the author of the *Narrative*, 'In little more than half an hour from my being asleep in bed I saw myself discharged and safe on board another ship. This,' he adds, 'was one of the many critical turns of my life, in which the Lord was pleased to display his providence and care by causing many unexpected circumstances to concur in almost an instant of time.'

Newton was now bound for Sierra Leone, and, what was very remarkable, he found that the captain of the ship in which he sailed was acquainted with his father. Here, then, he might have fared well, but for his careless and disobedient conduct. Can we wonder at this, when he tells us that one reason why he rejoiced in the exchange of vessels was that he could then be as abandoned as he pleased without any control? In six months the captain died; but Newton was on no better terms with the mate, and fearing that if he went with him to the West Indies he would put him on board a man-of-war he determined to remain in Africa.

And now we find this unhappy youth landed on a pestilential shore, to reap a terrible harvest of misery and wrong. Utterly destitute, he entered the service of a slave-dealer, who was settled on one of the Plantain Islands. Better thoughts came over him. He re-solved on a course of industry; but, unfortunately, before he was able to render his employer any service Newton was seized with severe illness, and was treated with the greatest neglect and cruelty. Thus he describes his situation: 'I had sometimes not a little difficulty to procure a draught of cold water when burning with fever. My bed was a mat, and a log of wood my pillow. When the fever left me and my appetite returned I would gladly have eaten, but none gave to me. My mistress – a black woman, who lived with my master as his wife, and who was a person of some consequence in her own country – from the first took a prejudice against me. She lived in plenty herself, but hardly allowed me sufficient to sustain life, except now and then, when in the highest good-humour, she would send me food from her own plate after she had dined; and this (so greatly was my pride humbled) I received with thanks and eagerness. Once I remember I was called to receive this bounty from her own hand, but being very weak and feeble, I dropped the plate, and she had the cruelty to laugh at my disappointment, and refused to give me any more, though the table was covered with dishes. My distress at times has been so great as to compel me to go at night, and, at the risk of being punished as a thief, to pull up roots in the plantation, and, lest I should be discovered, to eat them raw upon the spot. I have some-times been relieved by strangers, nay, even by the slaves in the chain, who have secretly brought me food. Of scorn and contempt,' he says, 'I had an abundant measure. I was subject to perpetual insult from this black woman, called opprobrious names, and, at her instigation, ridiculed and molested by her attendants.'

Through all this time of misery Newton's master had been absent. He now returned from his voyage, and upon going from home again took him with him. But here he suffered from the false accusation of unfaithfulness, so that he was treated with the utmost cruelty, being chained to the ship's deck when his master went on shore, and dur-ing his frequent long absences was compelled to eke out his scant allowance of food with the fish he was able to catch, and which he had to eat half-cooked. Sometimes he slept away his hunger. Nor did he suffer less from the weather and want of proper clothing, being, at times exposed for twenty, thirty, or forty hours to incessant rains, accompanied by strong gales of wind. Writing this account some twenty years afterwards, Mr Newton says, 'I feel to this day some faint returns of the violent pains I thus contracted.'

Going back to the Plantains, he was subjected to the same treatment as before, and his spirit was utterly broken. Pensive and solitary, he would go in the dead of the night to wash his one shirt upon the rocks, and afterwards put it on wet, that it might dry on his back while he slept. So poor a figure was he that when a ship's boat came to the island, shame often constrained him to hide himself in the woods from the sight of strangers. One thing he tells here, justly saying, 'Though strange, it is most true, the only volume I brought on shore was a copy of Barrow's *Euclid*, and with this I often beguiled my wretchedness, taking it to remote corners of the island, by the sea, and drawing my diagrams with a stick upon the sand. Thus, without any other assistance, I made myself master of the first six books of Euclid.'

'I remember,' says Mr Newton, 'that on one of these memorable days to which I have referred I was busied in planting some lime-trees. My master and mistress stopped to look at me. "Who knows," he said, "but by the time these trees grow and bear you may go home to England, obtain the command of a ship, and return to reap the fruit of your labours? We see strange things sometimes happen."' It was intended as a cutting sarcasm, yet it turned out to be a prediction. Mr Newton did return, commander of a ship, to that very spot, and plucked some of the first limes from those very trees!

Things continued in this miserable condition with him for about a twelvemonth. In the interval he wrote to his father, asking his assistance; and orders were consequently given to a captain in the employ of his Liverpool friend Mr Manesty to bring him home.

Mr Newton was now living with another trader; his circumstances were greatly improved, and he began, he says, to think himself happy.

In the meanwhile the ship that was to convey him home arrived at Sierra Leone. The captain made inquiries for him at the Bananas, but understanding he was at a great distance in the country, gave no more thought to the matter.

It happened some little time after, and in connection with a remarkable concurrence of favourable circumstances, that a companion of Newton's having sighted a vessel sailing past made a smoke in token of trade. It proved to be the very ship to which we have referred. One of the first questions the captain asked was concerning Newton; and as it was found he was so near he came on shore to deliver his message.

Newton's position being now so much altered for the better, he heard the proposal at first with indifference but some plausible and false statements of the captain's, and especially the thought of Miss Catlett, prevailed with him. He was received on board as a passenger, and no service expected from him. 'Thus,' he says, 'I was suddenly freed from a captivity of about fifteen months. I had neither thought nor desire of this change one hour before it took place.'

The vessel in which Mr Newton now sailed was on a trading voyage for gold, ivory, dyers' wood, and beeswax – a cargo which it takes a long time to collect, and to the nature of which, as we shall find, in the wonderful providence of God, he was afterwards instrumentally indebted for his 'great deliverance.' Having now no business to employ his thoughts, he sometimes amused himself with mathematics. 'Excepting this,' he says, 'my whole life, when awake, was a course of most horrid impiety and profaneness. I know not that I have since met so daring a blasphemer. Not content with common oaths and imprecations, I daily invented new ones, so that I was often reproved by the captain, though himself not at all circumspect in his expressions.'

Though never fond of drink, Newton, on one occasion, joined in a drinking bout, in which he narrowly escaped being drowned. Again, at Cape Lopez, going on shore too late, he and his companions were benighted in a wood; but they were unharmed, although it abounded with wild beasts. 'These and many other deliverances,' he says, 'were at the time entirely lost upon me. The admonitions of conscience, which, from successive repulses, had grown weaker and weaker, at length entirely ceased, and for months, if not years, I cannot recollect a single check of that sort. At times I have been visited with sickness, and believed myself near death, but without the least concern as to the consequences.'

At length, in January, 1748, they left the coast of Africa for England – a long navigation of more than seven thousand miles, including the circuits necessary to be made on account of the trade-winds. At Newfoundland they amused themselves by fishing for cod, little expecting – for then they were abundantly supplied with provisions – that soon those very fish would be all they should have to subsist upon. It was on the 1st of March that they left the Banks, with a hard gale of wind, in a vessel which, from the length of the voyage and the effects of the climate, was greatly out of repair. On the 9th, Mr Newton goes on to say, 'the day before our catastrophe, among the few books on board was a copy of Thomas à Kempis. This I carelessly took up, and looked at it with the same indifference as I had often done before; but while I was reading this time an involuntary suggestion arose in my mind – What if these things should be true? I could not bear the force of the inference, and shut the book. True or false, I thought, I must abide the consequences of my own choice. I put an end to these reflections, and joined in with some vain conversation or other that came in my way.'

And now we arrive at the turning-point in this remarkable history – the time of God's great mercy towards its subject, when those convictions he was unwilling to receive were to be so impressed as never again fully to pass away.

Mr Newton went to bed that night in his state of usual indifference, but was awakened by a violent sea breaking over the ship, followed by the cry that they were sinking. Going on deck, the captain desired him to bring a knife; while he returned for it, another person went up in his stead, and was immediately washed overboard. The sea tore away the upper timbers of the vessel, and made it a mere wreck in a few minutes. In spite of all their efforts at pumping and baling out the water, the vessel was nearly full, and with a common cargo must inevitably have sunk, but the beeswax and wood being specifically lighter than the water, saved them from this catastrophe. The shock, too, was received in the very crisis of the gale, and towards morning they were enabled to employ some means for their safety, which succeeded beyond their hopes. The wind fell, the leaks were stopped, and at last they perceived the water to abate. Nearly spent with cold and labour, Mr Newton tells us, upon going to speak to the captain, 'I said, almost without any meaning, "If this will not do, the Lord have mercy upon us!" This thought, spoken without much reflection, was the first desire I had breathed for mercy for many years. I was instantly struck with my own words. It directly occurred, "What mercy can there be for me?" I returned to the pumps, almost every wave breaking over my head, and remained till noon, expecting that every time the vessel descended into the sea she would rise no more; and though I dreaded death now, and my heart foreboded the worst, still I was but half convinced, and remained for a space of time in a sullen frame, a mixture of despair and impatience.

'On the next day (March 21st) I continued,' he says, 'at the pump from three in the morning till near noon, and then, unable to do more, I went and lay down upon my bed, almost indifferent whether I should rise again. In an hour's time I was called, and went to the helm. There I had opportunity for reflection. I thought, allowing the Scripture premises, there never was or could be such a sinner as myself; and then comparing the advantages I had broken through, I concluded at first that my sins were too great to be forgiven.'

About six in the evening the ship was freed from water, and there was a gleam of hope. 'I thought,' continues Mr Newton, 'I saw the hand of God displayed in our favour. I began to pray. I could not utter the prayer of faith. I could not draw near to a reconciled God, and call him Father – my prayer was like the cry of the ravens, which yet the Lord does not disdain to hear. I began to think of Jesus, whom I had so often derided. I recollected the particulars of his life and of his death, a death for sins not His *own*, but, as I remembered, for the sake of those who in their distress should put their trust in Him. And now I chiefly wanted evidence. The comfortless principles of infidelity were deeply riveted, and I rather wished than believed these things were real facts.' His great difficulty was to be assured of the inspiration of the Scriptures, and so to find a sufficient warrant for the exercise of trust and hope in God. He determined to examine the New Testament; and one of his first helps was found in reading Luke 9:13 – *If ye, being evil, know how to give good gifts to your children, how much more shall your Heavenly Father give the Holy Spirit to them that ask him?* From which passage he concluded that he must pray to God for His Spirit, and if that promise was really of God, He would make it good. His purpose was strengthened by the consideration of John 7:17 – *If any man do His will, he shall know of the doctrine, whether it be of God;* and he resolved for the present to take the gospel for granted, seeing that upon the gospel scheme there was a peradventure of hope, but on every other side he was surrounded with black, unfathomable despair.

To continue the narrative. As the wind was now moderate, and they were drawing near to their port, they began to recover from their consternation. After a sad disappointment as to the appearance of land, and the wind becoming again contrary, they were driven from the coast of Ireland as far as the Hebrides. The ship was so wrecked that they were obliged to keep the wind always on the broken side, unless the weather was quite moderate. Provisions grew short, and their labours at the pump were incessant. This lasted more than a fortnight. 'The captain, whose temper was quite soured by distress, was hourly reproaching me,' says Mr Newton, 'as the sole cause of all this calamity, and was confident that if I was thrown overboard (and not otherwise) they should be preserved from death.' But at last, when they were ready to give up all for lost, the wind came round to the desired point, and blew so gently that their few remaining sails could bear it; and at length, just four weeks after the terrible damage they sustained at sea on the 8th of April, they landed in Lough Swilly in Ireland. When they came into port their last food was boiling in the pot; and they had not quitted their vessel two hours, before the wind, which seemed to have been providentially restrained until they were in a place of safety, began to blow with great violence, so that had they continued at sea that night in their shattered bark, they must have gone to the bottom. 'About this time,' adds Mr Newton, 'I began to know that there is a God who hears and answers prayer.'

'I was no longer an infidel. I heartily renounced my former profaneness. I had taken up with some right notions, and was touched with a sense of God's undeserved mercy. I was sorry for the past, and purposed an immediate reformation. I was quite freed from the habit of swearing, which seemed to have been deeply rooted in me as a second nature. Thus to all appearance I was a new man.' But he goes on to say, 'Though I cannot doubt that this change, so far as it prevailed, was wrought by the Spirit and power of God, yet still I was greatly deficient in many respects. My views of the evil of sin, the spirituality and extent of the law, and the true character of the Christian life were still very defective.' He had no Christian friend with whom he could take counsel, and for some years had no opportunity of listening to evangelical preaching. The truth in its fulness was gradually unfolded to him. Nevertheless this was the beginning of his return to God, or rather, as he says, 'of God's return to him.'

While the ship was refitting, Mr Newton went to Londonderry, where he received much kindness, and where his health and strength were recruited. While there he went out with a shooting party, and he who had escaped so many and great dangers was very nearly killed by an accident with his gun. During his stay in Ireland he wrote to his father, who had despaired of hearing of him, supposing the vessel he was in was lost. The letter was received by the elder Mr Newton a few days before he left the country, as Governor of York Fort, in Hudson's Bay. He had purposed to take his son with him; but the latter was delayed in Ireland till it was too late. Before his departure from England he paid a visit to Kent, and gave his consent to the long-talked-of union.

At the latter end of May, 1748, Mr Newton arrived in Liverpool, just as his father sailed from the Nore; but he found another friend in Mr Manesty, the gentleman whose ship had brought him home, and whose name has already been referred to. He at once offered him the command of a ship; but Mr Newton, having now learned wisdom by experience, thought it better to make another voyage first, 'to learn,' as he says, 'to obey, and to acquire a further insight into business, before I ventured to undertake such a charge.'

It was natural enough that, notwithstanding his wonderful deliverance and his improved circumstances, his hope of a union with the object of his affections should be at times clouded; and so we find him, almost immediately on his return to England, writing to Mrs Eversfield, a connection of the Catletts, expressing his sad conviction that there seemed no reasonable prospect of his ever being able to support a wife. He, however, went to London, saw Miss Catlett, and afterwards, on his way to Liverpool, wrote to his friend and her brother, Mr John Catlett, in the following cheerful strain: 'I amuse myself on the road with building castles, amongst which the thought of improving your friendship is not the least entertaining, and, I hope, not the least probable,' and begging that his 'dear Jack' would remember him in the most agreeable manner possible to his sister, he adds, 'I shall drink her health tonight after the old Roman manner –

From the Birth of Mr Newton to His Marriage

Naevia sex cyathis, Justina septem bibetur.

It happens well her name is short, but were it as long as the Dutch merchant's in the *Bold Stroke for a Wife*, I would do it justice now and then, though I am no friend to much drinking.' Again, in another letter to the same friend, 'If I get no other advantage from loving, it will be of some service in pushing me forward in the world, and making me diligent in improving all opportunities that come in my power to promote myself, that I may one day be able to propose and talk with certainty.' The author of the *Narrative* adds that, before he left England, he received the comforting assurance that there was a willingness on the part of one in whom he was so deeply interested to await the event of the voyage he had undertaken.

Mr Newton sailed from Liverpool in August. For a little season, he informs us, he relapsed into religious indifference; but when he reached the Plantains, the scene of his former captivity, he was revisited with affliction, which was the means, he says, 'of bringing him back to God.'

And now, having considerable leisure, Mr Newton began to study Latin, though under great disadvantages, for he had no dictionary, and took Horace for his first book, yet he made good progress, and henceforth ever had Horace, as he says, *'ad unguem'* [literally 'to the finger nail'; i.e., to a nicety, to minute detail, exactly.]

In November he wrote to Mr Catlett, 'If you can inform me of my [lottery] ticket having turned up a great prize, the news will not be disagreeable;' and in the same letter, referring to his sister, he says, 'Thank her for the tolerably happy life I now lead, for to her only I owe it.' Again, in March, 1749, addressing the same correspondent from Rio Sesters, he says: '... Though we have been here six months, I have not been ten days in the ship, being continually cruising about in the boats to purchase souls, for which we are obliged to take as much pains as the Jesuits are said to do in making proselytes, sometimes venturing in a little canoe through seas like mountains, sometimes travelling through the woods, often in danger from the wild beasts, and much oftener from the more wild inhabitants, scorched by the sun in the day, and chilled by the dews in the night. Providence has preserved me safe through a variety of these scenes since I saw you last, and I hope will continue so to do. Notwithstanding what I have said in relation to the difficulties I meet with here, I assure you I was never so happy in my life as I have been since I left Liverpool.

'I can cheerfully submit to a great deal this voyage, because I hope it will be the last I shall make in an under station; and because I hope when it is finished a satisfactory meeting with my friends will make amends. I may be deceived, but, however, I find an advantage in persuading myself for the best.'

In the same letter he gives the following curious account of a monstrous fish he had caught: 'It was sixteen feet broad, and its liver alone weighed two hundred pounds. I have heard some people,' he observes, 'who would invalidate the story of Jonah, pretend that there is no fish capable of swallowing a man, but I believe if this had met one of them in the water, he would have convinced him to the contrary, for he had a mouth two feet three inches wide, and a proportionable swallow. The sailors call it a devil-fish, from two fins resembling two horns, which, you know, are seldom omitted by our painters when they would draw what they call a devil.'

Just before leaving the coast of Africa, Mr Newton had a very remarkable escape from death. It was his duty to bring in the necessary wood and water from the shore, and this service was almost completed. He was about putting off from the ship, when the captain called him on board again, and ordered another man to go in his stead. He was surprised at this, as the boat had never gone without him before. The boat, old and unfit for use, sank that night in the river, and the person who supplied Mr Newton's place was drowned. Mr Newton adds that the captain declared that he had no other reason for countermanding him at that time than that it came suddenly into his mind to do so. After a great variety of wind and weather they arrived at Antigua in July, and then proceeded to Charleston, South Carolina. Here, he tells us, there were many serious people; but he did not know how to find them out, nor was he even conscious of any difference, supposing all who attended public worship were alike good Christians, and that whatever came from the pulpit was right. He heard a dissenting minister there, with whose preaching he was very much struck, but he did not fully understand him. 'Indeed,' says Mr Newton, 'it pleased God that for some time I should learn no more than what He enabled me to collect from my own experience and reflection. My conduct was now very inconsistent. Almost every day, when business would permit, I used to retire into the woods and the fields (for these have always been my favourite oratories); and I trust there I began to taste the sweets of communion with God in the exercise of prayer and praise; and yet I frequently spent the evening in vain and worthless company, though, indeed, so little was my relish for worldly diversions, that I was rather a spectator than a sharer in their pleasures. This compliance being chiefly owing to want of light, the Lord was pleased to preserve me from what I knew was sinful. I had, for the most part, peace of conscience, and my strongest desires were towards the things of God. It was some years,' he adds, 'before I was quite set at liberty from occasional compliances in many things in which at this time I dare by no means allow myself.'

The voyage finished, Mr Newton arrived at Liverpool, December 6, 1749, receiving the same hearty welcome from Mr Manesty as before.

Thence, full of spirits, he writes to Mr Catlett: 'I hope you will find me something more like other folks than formerly, for I have in a great measure shaken off my dull, rusty gloominess, and have almost the vanity to apply Horace's words to myself –

> Me pinguem et nitidum, bene curatâ cute rises
> Cum ridere voles, Epicuri de grege porcum.'

['As for me, when you want a laugh, you will find me, in fine fettle, fat and sleek, a hog from Epicurus' herd' – Horace, *Epistles*, I.iv, lines 15–16.]

And again, in the same buoyant strain: 'I assure you, without a compliment, I have had a better opinion of Jack Newton than formerly, ever since you have been pleased to say so much in his favour.'

When the ship's affairs were settled he went to London, and from thence to Kent; and there is a letter dated from the latter place to Mr Catlett, in which, amongst other commissions, he requests him to obtain a prayer-book with the best cuts, bound in white vellum, gilt, and adorned in an elegant manner, *in usum gratissimae sororis* [for the use of his dearest sister]. Writing again to the same correspondent, January 18, he dates his letter from 'Elysium'.

2: FROM HIS MARRIAGE TO THE TIME HE QUITTED THE SEA
(1750–4)

Observations on his marriage – Sails to the coast of Africa – Events there – Position as Captain – Returns to England, Nov. 1751 – Diary and quotations – Second voyage to Africa, July 1752 – Manner of spending time at sea – Views on the subject of fasting – His Sabbaths – Letter – Covenant – Mutiny – Personal experience – A singular letter – An infamous charge – St Kitts – Letter – Reaches England, Oct. 1753 – Third voyage – Quotations from diary – Meets Capt. Clunie at St Kitts – Returns to Liverpool, Aug. 1754 – Sudden attack of illness – Abrupt termination of his connection with the sea – Observations on Mr Newton's engagement in the slave trade.

And now, every obstacle being removed, at the end of seven years all Mr Newton's fondest hopes were realised, and he was married to Miss Catlett at St Margaret's Church, Chatham, on the 12th February, 1750.

In reference to this important event he says, 'After I had gained my point I often trembled for my precipitation.' Mr Manesty had promised him the command of a ship to Africa in the ensuing season; and solely on this promise – for he had no other dependence – he ventured to marry. 'His spiritual light,' he says, 'was then as the first faint streaks of the early dawn; and I believe it was not yet daybreak with my dear wife;' and he continues, 'Had I remained at home, it is probable that I should have been drawn into what are considered the innocent gaieties of the world, and that we should have looked no higher for happiness than our mutual satisfaction in one another.

But God had designed better things for us: the season for sailing approached, and I was constrained to leave her. This necessity of absence, which then seemed to me bitter as death, I have now reason to acknowledge as one of the chief mercies of my life. *Nisi periissem periissem* [unless I had perished, I had perished]. The summons I received to repair to Liverpool awakened me as out of a dream.'

Now, when separated from his wife, he found leisure and occasion for much reflection. Serious thoughts, which had been almost smothered, began to revive. Anxiety respecting Mrs Newton led him to offer up many prayers for her and for himself, and he felt the need of that support which only religion can give. His correspondence with her during this and subsequent voyages was very considerable, and forms the greater portion of his *Letters to a Wife*. And here it may be observed that there is something very striking in the gradual development of Mr Newton's religious life, as it is illustrated in these letters. He says: 'As I began to write about the same time I began to see, in proportion as light increased upon me, my letters assumed a graver cast; and as I was led into further views of the principles of the gospel, I endeavoured to communicate to my dear correspondent what I had received. And in due time God was pleased to make them a means of affecting her heart, and impressing her with the same desires and aims.'

Even at this early period, however, he manifested his anxiety for the good of others. We are in possession of several very valuable letters, written in April and May of this year, in which he makes a very earnest appeal, and skilfully plies a series of arguments to reclaim a near relative from infidel sentiments, into which he had fallen.

Mr Newton sailed from Liverpool, August, 1750, as commander of the *Duke of Argyle,* a ship of about 150 tons burden, 'and as commodiously built,' he says, 'for a Guinea-man as any I ever saw.' He had under him thirty persons, whom he tells us 'he endeavoured to treat with humanity, and to whom he desired to set a good example.' Having now much leisure, he continued the study of Latin, with good success, so that by the end of the voyage he could, with few exceptions, read Livy from end to end almost as readily as an English author. And so in two or three voyages he became tolerably acquainted with the best classics. He also made some attempts in Latin composition.

In a letter to Mrs Newton, dated from the Bananas, November, 1750, he says: 'I have lately had a visit from my quondam black mistress, with whom I lived at the Plantains. I treated her with the greatest complaisance and kindness; and if she has any shame in her, I believe I made her sorry for her former ill-treatment of me. I have had several such occasions of taking the noblest kind of revenge upon persons who once despised and used me ill. Indeed I have no reason to be angry with them. They were, what they little intended to be, instrumental to my good.' A more particular account of this circumstance is recorded in *The Conversations of the Rev. John Campbell* — 'Upon being asked whether he ever met again with the black woman who had treated him so harshly when he was in Africa, "Oh, yes," replied Mr Newton. "When I went there as a captain of a ship, I sent my long-boat ashore for her. This soon brought her on board. I desired the men to fire guns over her head in honour of her, because she had formerly done me so much good, though she did not mean it. She seemed to feel it like heaping coals of fire on her head. I made her some presents, and sent her ashore. She was evidently most comfortable when she had her back to my ship." And he added, "I just recollect a circumstance that happened to me when I first stepped ashore on the beach at that time. Two black females were passing; the first who noticed me observed to her companion, that 'there was Newton, and, what do you think? — he has got shoes!' 'Ay,' said the other, 'and stockings too!' They had never seen me before with either."'

Writing from Shebar, he speaks of the raillery he encountered amongst the sea captains he met with. 'They *think* I have not a right notion of life; and I *am sure* they have not. They say I am melancholy;

I tell them they are mad. They say I am a slave to one woman; which I deny, but can prove that some of them are mere slaves to a hundred. They can form no idea of my happiness; I answer, I think the better of it on that account.

At length Mr Newton sailed from the African coast and crossed the sea to Antigua. Here he heard of his father's death; and he says to his wife, 'Had not that news been accompanied by the confirmation of your health and affection, I should have felt it more heavily, for I loved and revered him. But enough of this: my tears drop upon the paper.'

In a subsequent letter he gives Mrs Newton the following amusing account of his position and authority as captain: 'My condition when abroad, and even in Guinea, might be envied by multitudes who stay at home. I am as absolute in my small dominions (life and death excepted) as any potentate in Europe. If I say to one, come, he comes; if to another, go, he flies. If I order one person to do something, perhaps three or four will be ambitious of a share in the service. Not a man in the ship will eat his dinner till I please to give him leave — nay, nobody dares to say it is twelve or eight o'clock, in my hearing, till I think it proper to say so first. There is a mighty bustle of attendance when I leave the ship, and a strict watch kept while I am absent, lest I should return unawares and not be received in due form. And should I stay out till midnight (which for that reason I never do without necessity) nobody must presume to shut their eyes till they have had the honour of seeing me again. I would have you judge from my manner of relating these ceremonies, that I do not value them highly for their own sake; but they are old-fashioned customs, and necessary to be kept up, for without a strict discipline the common sailors would be unmanageable. But in the midst of my parade I do not forget (I hope I never shall) what my situation was on board the *Harwich* and at the Plantains.'

This first voyage occupied fifteen months, and Mr Newton returned in perfect safety in November, 1751, 'preserved,' as he says, 'from every harm, and having seen many fall on my right hand and on my left. I was brought home in peace, and restored to where my thoughts had been often directed.' We find him soon after writing a pleasant letter to his brother-in-law, Mr Catlett, again dated 'Elysium.'

In the month of December, 1751, while still on shore, Mr Newton commenced the life-long practice of keeping a diary, a practice which, he says, 'I have since found of great use.'

And here, before we proceed farther, we may quote the appropriate words with which the diary [a folio of 977 pp., then blank] opens, under date December 22, 1751: 'I dedicate unto thee, most blessed God, this clean, unsullied book; and at the same time renew my tender of a foul, blotted, corrupt heart. Be pleased, O Lord, to assist me with the influences of Thy Spirit to fill the one in a manner agreeable to Thy will, and by Thy all-sufficient grace to overpower and erase the ill impressions sin and the world have from time to time made in the other, so that both my public converse and retired meditation may testify that I am indeed thy servant, redeemed, renewed, and accepted in the sufferings, merit, and mediation of my Lord and Saviour Jesus Christ, to whom, with the Father and the Holy Spirit, be glory, honour, dominion, world without end. Amen.'

After referring to the signal mercy of God to him in the past, Mr Newton proceeds to form certain resolutions:

'1st. As to the disposal of my time. To begin and end every day with God. At other seasons to find opportunity for private retirement. To peruse the Scriptures with a diligence and attention suited to the dignity of the subject, being firmly persuaded that there are many excellencies in that Divine book which can never be discovered by a superficial eye, or an unprepared heart. To spend the hours of the sabbath entirely to the Lord, bearing in mind that the positive commands of God and the weight of many voluntary vows on my own part ought to have much more influence with me than any point of custom or fashion, however generally established.

'2nd. As to the ordering of my conversation. I determine to choose for my companions only good people, from whom I may derive some improvement, or, if otherwise, such as I may hope to benefit by my influence. When necessarily engaged in business with others, to stand well on my guard, that I may not be seduced by their opinions or practices, and, frequently looking up to Heaven for assistance, to endeavour often to give discourse a serious turn. Whenever I hear my Maker's name blasphemed to speak boldly for His honour, yet being careful to do so without personal ill-will or comparative contempt. Not to affect a disagreeable singularity in indifferent matters, but, as far as is consistent with the foregoing resolutions, to become all things to all men that I may save some.

'3rd. When I have done everything in my power, to subscribe myself an unprofitable servant, and esteem it the greatest fault to presume that the best services I can perform would be, strictly speaking, entitled to pardon, much less acceptance, unless offered wholly in obedience to the commands and through the faith in the mediation of my blessed Redeemer, in which trust alone I have ventured to make these resolutions, which I am well assured I have in myself no ability to perform; but that since He has promised His Holy Spirit to such as sincerely ask it, I therefore humbly put in my claim.'

A few days afterwards he quotes with much approval Sir Matthew Hale's scheme of daily behaviour, as contained in his life, by Dr Burnet. Again we find him resolving to set apart the Saturday evening, as far as circumstances will permit, as a time of solemn preparation for the Sabbath, 'when,' as he says, 'if I may use such an expression, I may post my accounts with my Maker.'

On the eve of his next voyage we have this record. 'I resolve to set apart some day (next week, if convenient) in a particular and solemn manner to recommend myself and my concerns, my journey and my voyage, to the blessing and protection of my Almighty Father.'

Upon the launching of the vessel in which he was to sail, he expresses the thought that it was an occasion rather for a serious frame than for the usual custom of festivity and extravagance. And though he says he had the prospect of setting out with all the outward advantages he could wish, yet all his comfort and assurance in business is derived from distrusting himself, his own strength, foresight, or ingenuity, and casting himself into the sure hands of Almighty providence.

In July, 1752, Mr Newton sailed from Liverpool. And he is no sooner at sea than we find in his diary the expression of his earnest desire to live wholly to the Lord.

Speaking generally of this and of a subsequent period, he says in his *Narrative*, 'I never knew sweeter or more frequent hours of Divine communion than in my two last voyages to Guinea, when I was almost secluded from society on shipboard, or when on shore amongst the natives. I have wandered through the woods reflecting on the singular goodness of the Lord to me in a place where, perhaps, there was not a person that knew Him for some thousands of miles round me.'

Writing to Mrs Newton about this time, her husband says: 'I am now settled in a regular course, for so far as circumstances will permit, I do everything by rule and at a fixed hour. My time is divided into seasons for devotion, study, exercise, and rest, and thus diversified no part is tedious.' And speaking of his devotions, he says, 'In these exercises, oh, how I remember you!'

The diary contains a full account of this 'scheme of rules'. As it is but a fuller statement of what is found on a preceding page, we need only quote the following passages: 'I will be very careful of too much indulgence in sleep, for I have observed the too common ingratitude and insensibility of converting this cordial into a poison, and instead of using it to restore life and quickness to our spirits, abusing it by excess to sink ourselves still deeper in sloth and dullness. Being exempt from labour, I think seven hours is as much as I have occasion for, perhaps six might do; however, I should look upon it as in a manner criminal to exceed eight at any ordinary time.'

Then follow rules for reading the Word of God, his secular business, his studies, his recreations, and his intercourse with others. Of this last subject he beautifully says: 'Taking care that my conversation has at no time anything in it contrary to truth, to purity, or to the peace and good name of my neighbour, and ever endeavouring to introduce some useful remark or admonition, yet habituating myself to a constant cheerfulness of behaviour, that I may not bring an evil report upon religion, or discourage those around me from the pursuit of piety, but rather let them see that a good conscience is a continual feast, and the ways of wisdom are ways of pleasantness.

'Should necessary business cause any deviation from these rules, at all events I will strive to preserve a devotional frame, and that upon no occasion shall my morning or evening exercises be wholly pretermitted; for', he adds, 'it were safer to attempt living without food or sleep than by starving my soul by passing a whole day without presenting myself before the mercy-seat of my Heavenly Father.'

After stating that he will, to the utmost of his power, dedicate the Lord's day wholly to spiritual purposes, he determines also to give everybody under his charge an opportunity of rest from their labours. A few days afterwards he set apart a day for fasting and prayer on behalf of his crew.

Such were the high and holy purposes of this good man, made in simple and childlike dependence upon the help of the Almighty; and so was laid the foundation of that piety, religious decision, and habitual strength of purpose by which his after life was characterised.

In a subsequent page we have his views on fasting. After speaking generally of its reasonableness and Scriptural authority, he concludes with these remarks: 'Upon the whole I would not confine myself to a fast absolutely of such a determined number of hours, or confine myself too strictly to forms, which often degenerate into superstition; I would rather habituate myself to a constant and orderly abstemiousness and moderation in the enjoyment of all

God's temporal blessings. Yet at some times, when most agreeable to my temper, frame and opportunities, in order to perfecting myself in this mastery over the fleshly appetites, and to keep a sense of dependence upon God's bounty and the free grace of the Saviour, and the just forfeiture I have often made of the commonest of his favours, I would look upon fasting as amongst the means of grace and improvement which I enjoy, and in some measure or manner as a duty to be frequently observed. And for the most part I dare say I should find a profit in setting apart one day in every week for this purpose.'

Soon after we find Mr Newton praying for grace to entertain a proper veneration and awe of the great and tremendous name of God, and alluding to the well-known practice of Mr Boyle in this matter.

On the 15th August he arrived in safety at Sierra Leone, for which, according to his wont, he desires to return his hearty thanks to his gracious Preserver.

On the following Sunday he complains of the distractions of business during the previous two days; and he prays God to help him to consider how poor a bargain he should make if all his wishes were effected, even were he to gain the whole world, but in the end his success were to endanger his immortal soul.

His sabbaths, though divested of the usual privileges of those holy days, were often enjoyed by Mr Newton on board ship as times of exceeding refreshment from the presence of the Lord; and on the next sabbath to the one just referred to, he expresses himself in a strain of sweet and grateful praise to God for the special manifestations of his mercy to one so unworthy as himself.

'Lord,' he prays, 'Thou hast heaped many benefits upon me, be pleased to add one more — the blessing of an ingenuous and thankful heart. Without this all the rest is but lost . . . Could my whole life be passed in a continual act of praise, it would at best be a very poor return for what great things Thou hast done for me. But, alas! a day or an hour is more than I can employ as I ought in this glorious service.'

Happy as his sabbaths at sea often were, he still speaks of it as his greatest regret, that in a seafaring life he was so much deprived of the communion of the saints, and of the enjoyment of a share in public worship. 'I am encouraged to hope,' he observes, 'that my mind is truly renewed, for I begin to find a real pleasure in spiritual things. I am glad when the Lord's day returns upon me, and I should be vastly more so were I able to keep it in the manner I could wish.'

Elsewhere he thus describes 'a Sea-Sunday' in a letter to Mrs Newton: 'The Saturday evening is a time of devotion, when,' he says, 'I especially beg a blessing on your Sunday, as I know where you are you are unavoidably exposed to trifling company. I usually rise at four o'clock in the morning, and after seeking a blessing on the day, take a serious walk on the deck. Then I read two or three select chapters. At breakfast I eat and drink more than I talk, for I have no one here to join in such conversations as I then choose. At the hour of your going to church I attend you in my mind with another prayer; and at eleven o'clock the ship's bell rings my own little congregation about me. To them I read the morning service according to the Liturgy. Then I walk the deck and attend my observation (i.e. take the latitude of the ship). After dinner a brief rest, or I write in my diary. I think again upon you at the time of afternoon service, and once more assemble the crew for worship. I take tea at four, then follows a Scripture lesson, and a walk and private devotion at six.'

October 8, he writes: 'Having for three weeks been prevented writing by business, company, or want of a suitable frame, I now again resume it, for I have reason to hope I find a real benefit in the custom of recording my resolutions, failures, and experiences, and that what I have occasionally written has, upon a re-perusal, a greater weight with me than the same thoughts much better expressed or explained by another person.' Again: 'If the same disposition of my hours which I formerly made should be now impracticable, I would still be anxious profitably to employ every interval of time in something useful, or at least innocent, yet deeming nothing innocent which is not in some degree useful to myself or others. I desire that even my recreations should be so conducted as to be in some sort the service of a rational and social creature.'

Thus everywhere do we see Mr Newton's great conscientiousness, and his anxiety to live to the glory of God.

A few days before, he writes to his brother-in-law, Mr John Catlett, thus:

'DEAR BROTHER, Morton and Manby [pseudonyms used in their former correspondence: in a previous letter he had said, 'Polly says she does not like Morton and Manby'] are no more. I was ordered to lay aside these factitious sounds some months ago. So, dear *Mr Catlett*, I do by these presents formally reinstate you in your pristine name.' He then apologises to him for his bad usage of him in the way of letter-writing while in Liverpool, giving, amongst other reasons, that he had so little of his sister's company, that time was precious to him; 'and I must acknowledge,' he goes on to say, 'that when I am with her, I am a little negligent of everybody else. Just as (if you will allow such a blazing comparison) the presence of the sun makes us bear the loss of the stars without regret; but I shall affront you again if I do not take care, though I believe you yourself would judge the expression "fort galant" if applied to a mistress; and why it should require an apology for being meant of a wife I cannot tell. But I am determined to stick to my unfashionable humour as long as I find my account in it, that is, in other words, as long as I live; for the rest, you may be assured that nothing but your sister will stand in competition for the regard I bear you ...

'The vast satisfaction of mind I possess makes me generally desirous to impart the same to every one, but chiefly to my best friends, and for this reason I have enjoined it as a rule to myself never to write a letter where I have any knowledge or intimacy without inserting a few lines that may either tend to the benefit of my correspondent, or to the honour of the Divine goodness and mercy that has been pleased to make a vile apostate an example of His patience and an instrument of His praise. As there is no one whose interest I have more at heart than yours, I make it the subject of frequent prayer that you also may be joined with me in this glorious employment, and may be completely rescued from the power of those who take pains to deceive.' Dated Sierra Leone, October 4, 1752.

About this time Mr Newton determined, 'pursuant to the advice of many godly persons, as proved in their lives,' to draw up 'a written instrument,' as he says, 'with my best care and circumspection, and in the strongest words I can choose to devote myself once more Thy servant absolutely and for ever, without any reserve or competition; and having first prepared to set a day very shortly (Thy favourable providence permitting) to consider it seriously in my heart, to sign and seal it in Thy presence, and to bespeak the blessing and assistance of Thy Holy Spirit to act agreeably thereto.'

This covenant was accordingly drawn up, signed, sealed, and dated, 'New Shebar, on the windward coast of Africa, on Sunday, the 15th of October, A.S.M., 1752.' A copy of it lies before us.

In November a mutiny of the crew was on the point of breaking out, when it was discovered by what, says Mr Newton, 'by an ill-accustomed way of speech, we call accident.' And he adds that he could not charge himself with anything harsh or unworthy in his conduct towards those under his command, and that he had resolved to entertain no personal hatred or ill will against the offenders. So again, in the following month, a plot was discovered amongst the slaves on board. They had found means to provide themselves with knives and other dangerous weapons, and were just ripe for mischief, when their purpose was found out.

About the same time Mr Newton thus writes of his own personal experience: 'I bless the wonderful grace of God that I have reason to hope that, though I am very weak, I am not insincere in my profession; and this coldness and imperfection, which clog and taint my best-intended services, are not my choice, but my greatest trouble, and what I sincerely petition to be delivered from in all my prayers. ... 'I think I have reason to charge some of my deficiencies and my neglects to the want of self-denial. I therefore purpose to be more heedful in that article, and not only to refrain from what I know to be positively unlawful, but to cut myself short from anything, however innocent in itself, that I find to have an ill tendency with regard to my own temper and circumstances. I have had, likewise, some reasons of late to set a stricter guard upon my temper. I have been surprised two or three times into indecent heats in argument, and upon very trifling occasions. I will endeavour to hold no more arguments of that kind, but whenever my opinion is disputed in things of no importance, give up the point at once for peace sake. More than once, too, I have suffered myself to speak ill of other people by publishing and repeating their faults and follies; and though I cannot say I have wilfully added to the truth, yet even that I have no business to say to another's prejudice in common.'

On the 31st December there is an entry full of grateful expressions for the goodness of the past year. So on the first day of 1753, he mourns over his defects, and resolves to stand by his covenant.

After speaking of the indifferent prospect as to the successful issue of his voyage, and complaining of his weakness and distrust, he adds: 'I ought, indeed, in justice to my employers, to use my best efforts to promote their concerns; but then, having done that, to acquiesce in whatever event Providence appoints. If the affair I have in hand should totally miscarry, and I should have nothing but my life given me for a prey, yet I should have no colour or ground for repining, but strong reasons to urge me to all possible thankfulness to the Power that preserves me.'

There is still in existence a curious document, which about this time was sent to Mr Newton from one of the traders on the coast. The note is addressed, 'For Capt. John Newton, these,' and is as follows:

'Sir — I have sent you one boy-slave on board, and I am going up to my town. I shall be down again in three days. I would not have you go from here till you hear further from me, for I intend to do what I can for you. I have no further commands at present, but I remain your friend and well-wisher,

THOMAS BRYAN

'Sir — Mr Corker gives his service to you, and has sent you one girl-slave on board, and says he will do what he can for you.'

While Mr Newton continued on the coast of Africa, a scandalous and groundless charge was brought against him. He tells us that about three nights previously he had had a dream which made an unusually deep impression on his mind, and that he should not have recorded it, but that an event soon fell out so strongly resembling it that he could not but look upon the whole affair as extraordinary. He thought he was violently stung on the finger by a scorpion; but while he was much agitated by the pain and danger, an unknown person applied oil to the wound and gave him ease. He then dreamed a kind of interpretation of it. 'It seemed', he says, 'that the same or some other person told me that what I then felt was only a dream, but that it was predictive of something that was shortly to happen to me, which would be as disagreeable and unexpected as the sting of the scorpion, but that I need not be afraid, for as I dreamt there was oil ready to cure me, so I should find it, and have no reason to be uneasy about the event, for no real harm should come of it.'

He goes on to say: 'Soon after, business required my attendance on shore, but the sea ran high, and feeling also some inward hindrance I could not account for, I returned to the ship — a thing which I do not remember to have done in all the time I used that trade. It was well I did not land, for had I done so I suppose my life would have been forfeited.'

It seems that a person with whom Mr Newton had dealings on the coast, the Mr Bryan referred to above, that very evening sent him, in a huff, the balance of his account, about a hundred pounds, charging him at the same time with an intrigue with one of his women, and refusing henceforth to have anything more to do with him.

'I do not remember,' says Mr Newton, 'that I ever in my life was struck with equal astonishment as at this imputation, which, I bless God, I was so far from deserving, so far from attempting, or even thinking on, that I hope (I speak in humble dependence upon his grace) that nothing could have induced me so to sin against God, and the mutual, conscious, happy love he has sufficiently and abundantly blessed me with at home.'

He never could discover from what quarter or from what motive this charge came; but he adds in his *Narrative*, 'that he heard no more of it till his next voyage, and then it was publicly acknowledged to have been a malicious calumny, without the least shadow of a ground.'

This accusation chiefly affected him because he feared it might bring a reproach upon the gospel. 'Lord,' he says, 'let this teach me the humiliation which consists not only in having low thoughts of ourselves, but in resting contented under aspersions, till Thou seest fit to set everything in the true light. I confess before Thee that I took fire too readily when this was first mentioned, and expressed my resentment in a manner unbecoming a guarded and resigned temper.'

Once more leaving the coast of Africa, we find Mr Newton rejoicing in the leisure the sea afforded him for more regular and prolonged attention to religious exercises. He resolves, so long as this respite is afforded him, to set apart one day in every week for devotional purposes. He speaks on one occasion of enjoying in a most happy and unusual manner an abiding sense of the Divine presence and goodness. These feelings were especially awakened by some passages in the life of Colonel Gardiner. So affected was he that he says, 'I burst two or three times into tears, which I hope proceeded from sincere repentance and shame, and was from thence brought upon my knees (as I trust) by the impression of the Holy Spirit, to humble myself for my unworthiness before the Lord with an earnestness and warmth that has in some measure continued hitherto.'

Mr Newton arrived at St Kitts on June 24th, and he says: 'One circumstance I cannot but set down here, and which I hope I shall always take pleasure in ascribing to the blessing of the God of peace, I mean the remarkable disposition of the men-slaves I have on board, who seem for some time past to have entirely changed their tempers. I was at first continually alarmed by their almost desperate attempts to make insurrections. One of these affairs has been mentioned, but we had more afterwards; and when most quiet they were always watching for an opportunity. However, from the end of February they have behaved more like children in one family than slaves in chains and irons, and are really upon all occasions more observing, obliging, and considerate than our white people. Yet in this space they would often in all likelihood have been able to do much more mischief than in former parts of the voyage.'

To Mr Newton's great disappointment, there were no letters from Mrs Newton awaiting him at St Kitts. While at sea the previous month he had written to his wife: 'My mind runs so much upon the wished-for pleasure of letters from you when I arrive at St Kitts, that I often dream I have them in my hand, and when awake am often dictating for you.' He was hardly able to exercise his usual trust in God on this occasion, and gave way to all manner of evil forebodings. His anxiety, however, was relieved by sending a boat to Antigua, where the missing letters were found.

Writing again, June 30th, and speaking of St Kitts, he says: 'I was never made so much of in my life. I cannot mention anything I like but the whole country is ransacked for it; and when I was uneasy for want of letters, you can hardly think how much concern was shown me. Good news for me; 'twas the constant toast after dinner and supper, and a thousand contrivances were set on foot to divert me, though I hid my fears as much as ever I could. All the people in general are hospitable. There are many houses that will not get a farthing either by me or by my voyage, who would in a manner take it as a favour if I would bed and board with them. Notwithstanding all this, it is a great pleasure to me to inform you that I hope to leave this good place in about three weeks.'

Within two days of the above date Mr Newton wrote a letter to his relation before referred to, from which we give the following extracts. After observing that it was formerly his unhappy folly to busy himself in perverting others to as great a degree of infidelity as his own, and being now desirous to repair the mischief he had done as far as he was able, and especially when duty and friendship united to engage him, he continues, 'I must use plain terms with you. I look upon your opinions as dangerous to profess, and destructive to persist in. My own experiences are as good as mathematical demonstrations to me. I beg you would reflect on my case: I was one of the loudest in the Free-thinking strain. Do you think I changed in a whim or a frolic? You are pleased to express a good opinion of my understanding; why then will you suppose that a change was effected in my whole conduct and behaviour, so that in one day I became diametrically opposite to what I was the day before, and have continued so without an hour's alteration to this instant (I mean as to principle, though I continually fall short in my practice)? why, I say, must this proceed from caprice? and without a cause suitable to the effect? which is not a jot less surprising than for a man born blind to obtain his sight.

'As to what you say of the impossibility of forcing ourselves to believe, I must call it downright sophistry. I acknowledge that belief is not immediately in our power, but the means are. If I should undertake to move a body of a thousand weight, you ought not thence to infer that I pretended to lift it. It is sufficient if I can contrive a purchase upon mechanical principles that shall enable me to do it, without requiring any person to help me. The allusion will hold in our argument. Faith is the gift of God; but then He is always ready to bestow it. When I was first brought to consider the evil of my life, and to endeavour at amendment, the same difficulty lay in my way. I could not pretend to say in my prayers that I believed the gospel. Alas! I did not at that time believe a word of it. I was confounded, but not convinced. However, it pleased God (as I am firmly persuaded) to lead me to the following resolution: Though I am not assured of the truth of the New Testament, yet I cannot be certain it is false; I will endeavour, therefore, that if I mistake, it shall be on the safe side. I will take its truth for granted; I will study the promises, and comply with the commands I find there; and if it did indeed proceed from God, He who revealed it, and sees my sincerity in trying to quit my prejudices, may — nay, if that is His Word indeed, He undoubtedly will assist me, and enable me to understand it by degrees, till at length I believe it from the bottom of my heart.

'This way of reasoning I dare recommend to any one; and in this view I will not come behind you in extolling the Divine mercy and goodness. It is not reasoning, but neglecting to reason, and to extend conclusions to their just consequences that I condemn as the vice of the age. What you call liberty of conscience is nothing but carelessness and inconsideration in matters of the highest importance, which the all-just Being (a term you seem fond of) will never allow in rational creatures, whom He has endowed with a capacity of distinguishing right from wrong. I would wish you to consider that the fitness of things is fixed invariably. Our debates will make no alteration in them; and notwithstanding you suppose we agree in the essentials, I fear, shall I say? — or I hope? — that we differ extremely. I would not subscribe to the best system I can pick out of your letters for a thousand such toys as made the great Alexander weep.'

On the 11th July Mr Newton sailed from St Kitts on his homeward voyage; and, impressed with the goodness of God as he once more approaches the shores of England, he gives utterance to his feelings of lively gratitude for all the mercy of which he had been the subject, notwithstanding the many and special dangers to which he had been exposed.

Then mourning over his many shortcomings, he adds: 'How seldom have I had respect, O Lord, to all thy commands! A partial, mutilated obedience is all I can pretend to, whereas my conscience tells me that my duty is an entire consistent piece, and that there is no day or hour, no company or place or employment, in which something is not required of me as a mark of my profession. A Christian should in the commonest acts of this life give some traces and marks that his conversation is in heaven, and that he walks by faith and not by sight. A zeal for God's glory, a concern for virtue, an indignation and grief at instances of vice and profaneness, should be as natural to me as it is to others to breathe or speak; for hereunto am I called, and for this cause I obtained mercy. Lord, may Thy wonderful love and long-suffering constrain me. Oh, give me to labour to do more than others, for my offences and thy forgiveness have been extraordinary.'

August 30th Mr Newton reached home, but he remained only six weeks in England, sailing in the middle of October on his third and last voyage.

On the 4th of November, on a Sunday, 'past the island Palma, and fourteen days from home,' he writes, 'A short passage, and equally safe and pleasant. The fine climate and agreeable weather free me for a time from every outward hindrance and disturbance in my duty, and invite me in the most engaging manner to improve the golden opportunity of leisure and peace to spiritual purposes. The day, too, being a sacramental opportunity at home, furnishes me with another motive to serious reflection. The last season of this kind I was myself one of those peculiarly happy ones who can from their own experience affirm that one day in God's courts is better than a thousand.'

He sets Wednesday, November 21st, apart for the special purpose of seeking a blessing upon his voyage, and for protection through its various difficulties and dangers. Then subsequently, speaking of his indebtedness to God for his mercies, and especially for the enjoyment of a competency, he says: 'As it has pleased God already to raise me above dependence, and to give me more than I could have presumed to ask, not only food and raiment, but a great variety of conveniences and comforts, insomuch that I number myself amongst the most happy on earth, I cannot but think it incumbent upon me to bestow a part of my superfluities towards relieving those who are struggling under a want of necessaries. I have not come to a full determination of the quota I intend to set apart for this purpose. I will guard against being too sparing, leaving myself, however, at liberty to suspend or leave it on such an unavoidable emergency as my conscience shall allow, and, on the other hand, looking upon it to be my duty to enlarge it, if Providence sees fit to bless me beyond my present expectations; for I cannot think I have a right to gratify myself in mere indulgences any further than as I shall purchase it by charitable actions and imparting occasionally to those who have need.'

He arrived at the Plantains December 2nd, and a few days afterwards writes thus to Mrs Newton: 'I thank you for your punctual observance of our stated hour of retirement, which has been seldom omitted on my part, though sometimes hurry of business or want of opportunity have prevented me. But if I slip the appointed minute no business or company can prevent me from putting up, at least, frequent heartfelt ejaculations on your behalf.'

As usual with him, the first day of the year 1754 was a time of serious reflection, and these are some of his thoughts on that occasion. Mourning over his little spiritual progress, he exclaims: 'Alas! most gracious Lord, what shall I say? I have nothing to offer for all Thy goodness but new confessions of guilt. That Thou art kind to the unthankful and evil I am one of the most remarkable instances. Forgive me, I beseech Thee, this year of misspent life, and charge me not with the long abuse of Thy bounty. I owe Thee ten thousand talents, and have nothing to pay, yet I entreat Thee to have patience with me; not for that it will be ever in my power to make any amends by the best I can do, but because my Saviour Jesus Christ, Thy beloved Son, has done and suffered more than sufficient to atone for all my offences, and to supply all my defects. Let me plead His merits on behalf of myself and ———. Forgive us all that is amiss, and bless the beginning year to us in turning us from all our iniquities, and give us grace to confirm our former resolutions of serving Thee, and order all our concerns to the advancing Thy glory and our spiritual interests.'

In the same month, referring to his temporal affairs as at that time under some disadvantage, he writes to Mrs Newton: 'If a sigh should escape you on this account, I beg you to recollect yourself, and not indulge a second. Remember that this failure in dirty money matters is the only abatement we have hitherto met with, and that in other respects we have as much the advantage of those who are envied by the world as we fall short of them in riches. We have blessings which riches cannot purchase nor compensate for the want of. We have need of nothing at present, and for the future we may safely rely on the good Providence that has done so much for us already.'

On the anniversary of his wedding-day, he speaks of the inexpressible benefit of his engagement to Miss C., when influenced by no other tie, and destitute of every good principle: 'I remember with horror, when quite oppressed with the various evils and sufferings into which my follies had plunged me, that I had more than once formed dark designs against myself; and I think nothing withheld my arm but the distant hopes my love inspired, though in these circumstances they were little more solid than a dream.' And he adds an earnest prayer that they may be mutually and spiritually blessed to each other.

Ever anxious that his religious life should suffer no decline, and conscious of some degree of spiritual deadness, we find Mr Newton engaged on February 8th in an exercise of diligent self-examination, confession, and prayer before God. We can only give his concluding petitions:

'O most gracious Saviour, hear my prayers, which I am only emboldened to make in dependence on Thy gracious promise. I am weary and heavy laden with the sense of my corruption; and to such Thou hast promised rest. Fulfil Thy own work in me. Thy mercy prevented my ruin when I was Thy utter and avowed enemy. Suffer me no longer to lie helpless, now I would willingly be Thy servant. Oh, let Thy wonderful love constrain me to close with Thee in the manner I ought to do. Increase my faith. Inspire me with humility, and enable me to fulfil the engagements by which I have so often and so solemnly bound myself to Thy service.

'Lord, I repent and abhor myself in dust and ashes for my frequent backslidings. Restore unto me the influences of Thy Holy Spirit, whom I have by my carelessness provoked to withdraw from me, and assist me from this day to labour with redoubled earnestness in the way of my duty, that I may at length begin to live to Thy honour and glory, and my own comfort. Amen.'

In his *Narrative*, Mr Newton speaks of a young man he took with him in this voyage. He was one of his old companions on board the *Harwich*, and was unhappily led by him to entertain infidel opinions. This person had been disappointed in a ship in which he was to have gone as master to Guinea; and Mr Newton, in the hope of repairing the mischief he had done, took him as a companion. He, however, proved a source of great trouble, nor was he at all benefited by the intercourse of his friend. Mr Newton bought a vessel for him on the African coast; but in less than three weeks the young man was cut off by fever, and died without hope.

Mr Newton had not quitted the coast of Africa a week when he was attacked with fever, and his life was for a day or two in jeopardy. But God mercifully spared him. There is reference in his *Narrative* to a somewhat singular fancy that disturbed him in this illness. 'I seemed,' he says, 'not so much afraid of wrath and punishment as of being lost and overlooked amidst the myriads that are continually entering the unseen world. What is my soul, thought I, amongst such an innumerable multitude of beings? And this troubled me greatly. Perhaps the Lord will take no notice of me. I was perplexed thus for some time, but at last a text of Scripture, very apposite to the case, occurred to my mind, and put an end to the doubt – *The Lord* knoweth them that are His. I hope,' he adds, 'this visitation was made useful to me.'

In prospect of his return to the active world, Mr Newton expresses his hope that he might carry a sense of his duty and obligations to God into the whole course of his business and his converse with men. He arrived at St Kitts on the 22nd of May. It was here that he formed the acquaintance of Captain Clunie (a member of the church of the Rev. Samuel Brewer of Stepney), whose intercourse proved of great and lasting value to him. In the *Narrative* we have the following account of his circumstance:

'For the space of about six years the Lord was pleased to lead me in a secret way. I had learnt something of the evil of my heart. I had read the Bible over and over, with several good books, and had a general view of gospel truth. But my conceptions were in many respects confused, not having in all this time met with one acquaintance who could assist my inquires. But upon my arrival at St Cristopher's this voyage, I found a captain of a ship from London, whose conversation was greatly helpful to me—a man of experience in the things of God, and of a lively, communicative turn. We discovered each other by some casual expressions in mixed company, and soon became (so far as business would permit) inseparable. He not only improved my understanding, but inflamed my heart. He encouraged me to open my mouth in social prayer. He taught me the advantage of Christian converse. He put me upon an attempt to make my profession more public, and to venture to speak for God. From him, or, rather, from the Lord, by his means, I received an increase in knowledge, my conceptions became clearer and more evangelical, and I was delivered from a fear which had long troubled me—the fear of relapsing into my former apostasy. But now I began to understand the security of the covenant of grace, and to expect to be preserved, not by my own power and holiness, but by the mighty power and promise of God through faith in an unchangeable Saviour. He likewise gave me a general view of the state of religion, with the errors and controversies of the times (things to which I had been entirely a stranger), and finally directed me where to apply in London for further instruction. With these newly-acquired advantages I left him, and my passage homewards gave me leisure to digest what I had received. I had much comfort and freedom during those seven weeks, and my sun was seldom clouded.'

Mr Newton arrived at Liverpool, completing his second voyage in the *African*, on the 9th of August, having had,' he says, 'a favourable passage, and in general a comfortable sense of the presence of God through the whole, and towards the end some remarkable deliverances and answers to prayer. I had the pleasure to return thanks in the churches (at Liverpool) for an African voyage performed without any accident, or the loss of a single man; and it was much noticed and acknowledged in the town. I question if it is not the only instance of the kind. When I made my first appearance upon 'Change a stranger would have thought me a person of great importance by the various congratulations I received from almost every gentleman present.'

Mr Newton began immediately to fit out another vessel, called the *Bee*; but early in November an event occurred which altered the entire course of his life. He was apparently in his usual health, and was sitting at tea with Mrs Newton, when he was suddenly attacked with a fit, which for a time deprived him of sense and motion. He speedily recovered, but the effects of the seizure did not so soon pass away; and indeed it was judged not prudent for him to proceed on his voyage. 'It was thought advisable,' he says, 'that I should quit the vessel, which, having humbly sought direction by prayer, I consented to do, only two days before she sailed.'

To this his 'best friend', Mr Manesty, readily gave his consent; he was, in fact, the first proposer of it, though, it appears, he had bought the ship purposely on Mr Newton's account. Thus abruptly terminated Mr Newton's connection with the sea, for he never resumed the occupation.

It would be an important omission not to say something at this particular point of the narrative in reference to the peculiar traffic in which Newton was so long engaged, and which to modern and more enlightened views seems so strangely at variance with the very first principles of the Christian religion. And here we shall let Mr Newton speak for himself. Writing in 1763, he says, 'The reader may perhaps wonder, as I now do myself, that, knowing the state of this vile traffic to be as I have described' (the reference is to a letter in which he has been speaking of the state and circumstances of slaves), 'and abounding with enormities which I have not mentioned, I did not at the time start with horror at my own employment as an agent promoting it. Custom, example, and interest, had blinded my eyes. I did it ignorantly, for I am sure had I thought of the slave trade then as I have thought of it since, no considerations would have induced me to continue in it. Though my religious views were not very clear, my conscience was very tender, and I durst not have displeased God by acting against the light of my mind. Indeed a slave ship, while on the coast, is exposed to such innumerable and continual dangers, that I was often then, and still am, astonished that any one, much more that so many, should leave the coast in safety. I was then favoured with an uncommon degree of dependence upon the providence of God, which supported me; but this confidence must have failed in a moment, and I should have been overwhelmed with distress and terror, if I had known, or even suspected, that I was acting wrongly. I felt greatly the disagreeableness of the business. The office of a gaoler [jailer], and the restraints under which I was obliged to keep my prisoners, were not suitable to my feelings; but I considered it as the line of life which God in His providence had allotted me, and as a cross which I ought to bear with patience and thankfulness till He should be pleased to deliver me from it. Till then I only thought myself bound to treat the slaves under my care with gentleness, and to consult their ease and convenience so far as was consistent with the safety of the whole family of whites and blacks on board my ship.'*

In the year 1792, when Mr Wilberforce had renewed his motion in the House of Commons for the abolition of the slave trade, Mr Newton preached upon the subject, as he had done on a like occasion in the previous year. 'I regarded it,' he says in a letter to his friend, the Rev. W. Bull, 'not in a political, but moral view. I consider myself bound in conscience to bear my testimony at least, and to wash my hands from the guilt which, if persisted in now that things have been so thoroughly investigated and brought to light, will, I think, constitute a national sin of a scarlet and crimson dye.' He then states that a motion made in the Common Council of London for a petition to Parliament on the subject had been negatived.

Nor was this all. Mr Newton, about the same time, published his *Thoughts upon the African Slave Trade*, in which he points out its fearful political and moral evils—its injury alike to the slaves and those who traffic in them. 'If,' he says, 'my testimony should not be necessary or serviceable, yet, perhaps, I am bound in conscience to take shame to myself by a public confession, which, however sincere, comes too late to prevent or repair the misery and mischief to which I have formerly been accessory. I hope it will always be a subject of humiliating reflection to me that I was once an active instrument in a business at which my heart now shudders.' And he adds—and every reasonable person will allow the justice of the observation: 'Perhaps what I have said of myself may be applicable to the nation at large. The slave trade was always unjustifiable; but inattention and interest prevented for a time the evil from being perceived. It is otherwise at present. The mischiefs and evils connected with it have been of late years represented with such undeniable evidence, and are now so generally known, that hardly an objection can be made to the almost universal wish for the suppression of this trade, save on the ground of political expedience.'

*See *Letters to a Wife*, vol. i. p. 158, note.

We cannot help thinking that this whole matter is unfairly and inconclusively put in Sir James Stephen's eloquent essay on *The Evangelical Succession*. He certainly misapprehends Mr Newton's real character. Shall his religion at this time be branded as hypocrisy, when the apostolic Whitefield and the devout Countess of Huntingdon were virtually involved in the same evil? They held and purchased slaves.* The judicious Andrew Fuller, writing on this subject to Mr Newton in 1802, well observes, 'It is amazing to think how much we are influenced, even in our judgment of right and wrong, by general opinion, especially by the opinion and example of religious men.'

Though we have here a little anticipated the order of events, it seemed desirable to present the whole subject just referred to in one view. It sufficiently proves one thing—that, whatever evils may have attached to the slave trade, and however injurious it may have proved to those engaged in it, there were few such masters of slave ships as John Newton.

---

*See *Life and Times of the Countess of Huntingdon*, vol. 1, p. 264, etc.

3: FROM HIS QUITTING THE SEA TO THE TIME OF HIS FIRST THOUGHTS OF THE MINISTRY

(1750–4)

Chatham and London – Religious intercourse – Acquaintance with Whitefield – Sacrament at the Tabernacle – Reflections on Whitefield's character and preaching – Appointment
as Tide Surveyor at Liverpool – Singular circumstances in connection with his appointment – Attends Mr Johnson's ministry – Mr Whitefield at Liverpool – Mr Oulton – Mrs Newton
joins him – Letter to a relative – Reflections on the New Year
– Religious state of Liverpool – Jedediah Buxton – Commences
housekeeping – Prints *Thoughts on Religious Associations* – Lottery
ticket – Baptism – His candour – Studies and religious exercises –
Diary thoughts – Letters to an old correspondent – Mr Wesley
– Diary – Refusal to take fees.

I t was thought desirable that Mr Newton should remain in England
for the winter; and for the present it was arranged that he, with his
wife, should reside amongst their friends at London and Chatham.
There was one sad result of Mr Newton's attack. It seemed to give a
shock to Mrs Newton's constitution which she did not recover for
many months. Indeed, her restoration was remarkable; for all the ordinary symptoms of consumption [pulmonary tuberculosis] had shown
themselves, and the means of cure for the time seemed of no avail.

Thus, at the commencement of the year 1755, we find Mr Newton
in London, without any business, but certainly not idle, unless the
diligent use of every means for the culture of a religious life is to be
accounted idleness.

Mr Newton had now the opportunity, thus most unexpectedly afforded him, of seeking out those Christian friends to whom he had been recommended by Captain Clunie. With Mr Brewer of Stepney he was soon on very intimate terms; and it was quickly evident how much he profited by his ministry and by intercourse with him and with other experienced Christians. Not least amongst Mr Newton's spiritual privileges at this time was his introduction to Mr Whitefield.

In the *Narrative* its author says: 'I chiefly attended upon the ministry of Mr Brewer when in town. From him I received many helps both in public and in private, for he was pleased to favour me with his friendship from the first. His kindness and the intimacy between us has continued to this day' (1763), 'and of all my friends I am most deeply indebted to him.'

Early in January we find Mr Newton reading with deep interest a journal and defence of Mr Wesley, and letters of Mr Whitefield and others. Without approving of all he meets with, he expresses his sympathy with the loving and earnest spirit of these productions.

Ere long he was to be better acquainted with both Whitefield and Wesley.

It was the frequent practice of the subject of our memoir to walk in the fields for meditation and prayer; and even in the month of January we find him indulging in it. He says, at a subsequent period: 'It has been my custom for many years' (and we shall see that it remained such so long as circumstances permitted) 'to perform my devotional exercises *sub dio* [under the open sky], when I have opportunity; and I always find these rural scenes have some tendency both to refresh and compose my spirits.' He then goes on to say, that the country between Rochester and Maidstone (where he was chiefly residing at the time of which we now write) 'was well suited to the turn of my mind; and were I to go over it now, I could point to many a place where I remember to have earnestly sought, or happily found the Lord's comfortable presence with my soul.'

On a Sunday, February 2nd, he rises early, and after renewing his covenant, he seeks a blessing on his expected participation in the sacrament of the Lord's Supper, assisting his meditation with Matthew Henry (the *Communicant's Companion*). The sermon, he tells us, was little to his satisfaction — 'a random harangue, without one gospel application. Oh, grant,' he says, 'that I may be duly sensible of the great blessing of an experienced gospel ministry. This one thing, might I choose, I would desire of the Lord — that I might be placed under such as understand and teach the truth as it is in Jesus. Lord, revive Thy work in the midst of the years! Pity the people who are destroyed for lack of knowledge!'

Monday, 10th February, he hears Mr Webb* at Chatham, and in remarking upon his sermon, says, 'that he took occasion fully to clear himself and the Tabernacle people and preachers from holding the grace of God in wantonness, as if believing in Christ as the only terms of salvation gave encouragement to neglect keeping His commands; but, on the other hand, that all real believers were naturally actuated by a Divine principle of love to God and the Redeemer, to abound continually in good works, though they dare not rest in them.'

Referring again to a sermon of Mr Webb, in which he had dwelt on the benefit of Christian conference, Mr Newton takes occasion to make the following observations: 'I desire to praise the Lord that of late I have had my mouth something opened, and been willing to declare what God has done for my soul. I am ashamed to think how long I hid my talent in a napkin, and neglected to give God the glory of His free grace. My acquaintance with Clunie was greatly blessed to me in this point; and since, by his means, I have been brought to converse with many more excellent Christians, who have been, I hope, of great use to me, and from a knowledge of my circumstances have been led to glorify God on my behalf. It is my judgment that

---

* The Rev. James Webb, many years pastor of the Independent Church meeting at Fetter Lane, London, and founded by Dr Goodwin in 1660.

societies formed on this view will, by the Divine blessing, be abundantly useful in promoting spiritual and vital godliness. I pray that I may always see it my duty to attempt the forming of such, and frequenting them when I have opportunity to do so . . . Before sermon had some discourse in the vestry with three or four members of the meeting — all poor people, and illiterate in the eyes of the world, but I have reason to believe they are rich in faith, learned in the gospel, and heirs of the promise.'

The next Sunday he rode to Maidstone, 'for the sake of gospel preaching.' From the middle of March, Mr Newton spent several weeks in succession in London, for the purpose of hearing the Word, and of enjoying occasions of religious conference. The following abbreviated extracts from his diary, which he now kept with great regularity, will give some idea of these engagements:

'Monday, March 17th. At the society at Mr M——'s. After prayer, etc. spent the evening in discourse chiefly upon doctrinal points. 18th. At Pinner's Hall.* Mr Rawlins on the everlasting covenant. Afterwards at the A. Coffeehouse. Heard some very remarkable cases of cures performed by unction with oil, in compliance with James 5:14, which I propose to inquire further into.

'Wednesday, 19th. This evening heard Mr Hayward, at the Lecture for Cases of Conscience.† Thursday, 20th. Heard Mr Romaine on Ephesians 6:14. May God increase the number of faithful labourers where they are so much wanted, and give success to their ministry.

'Sunday, 23rd. Rose at five. Went to the Tabernacle, and heard Mr Adams‡ on Matthew 5:6; a very comfortable sermon. The forenoon at Mr Brewer's. In the afternoon heard Dr Jennings.

* In Old Broad Street. A week-day lecture was established there in 1672, conducted by the leading dissenting ministers in and about London; and which, though the lease of that building expired in 1797, is still continued.

† These casuistical lectures were conducted at Little St Helen's, Bishopsgate St., for some years, by Messrs Pike and Hayward, and were afterwards published.

‡ The Rev. Thomas Adams, one of Whitefield's earliest fellow labourers and minister of the Tabernacle at Rodborough.

'Tuesday, 25th. Heard Dr Guyse at Pinner's Hall. Dr Guyse has for some time been deprived of the use of his eyes; but it was remarked by many how wonderfully he was carried beyond the want of them.' He preached on John 10:10; and Mr Newton gives a sketch of the sermon, saying of it; 'that it was one of the most excellent doctrinal discourses' he ever heard.

'Wednesday, 26th. Visited Dr Jennings, and was afterwards at the Cases of Conscience Lecture.

'Friday, 28th. Heard Dr Guyse at St. Helen's. In the afternoon I paid a visit to Mr Hayward. Conversation various, but chiefly religious and experimental. Obtained from him some account of the extraordinary work of grace which is carrying on in the Establishment in Cornwall, by Mr Walker, of Truro, and others. Saw two of his letters, written in a charming spirit indeed; so much zeal, and so much charity and humility, as can never reside in the same heart unless they are inspired from above. It is my duty to pray that the Lord may own him more and more; and especially as a member of the Established Church I ought to pray that the number of such faithful labourers may be increased.'

On Easter Sunday Mr Newton received the sacrament at Barking Church, and heard Mr Murden — 'one of the few whom it has pleased God to stir up to preach free grace on that side. Afternoon at Mr Brewer's; evening at Shakespeare's Walk. Mr Hayward preached.

'Tuesday, April 8th. At Pinner's Hall. Heard Mr Bradbury. He seems well nigh worn out in his Master's service; and my proud, dainty heart prevented that improvement I ought to have made, because truly his discourse was not so connected as some others I hear there, or as his were before he was weakened with an extreme old age, he having been a preacher almost sixty years.'

And thus, to the close of his visit, Mr Newton gives a full account of the various religious services he attended, and of the intercourse he enjoyed with his friends. In some of the meetings for prayer and conference Mr Newton himself took part. He says of this whole period: 'Methinks I never found time slide away so insensibly fast as since my coming to London. I have been in the constant enjoyment of the most invaluable privileges and means of grace;' and yet he expresses disappointment that he did not derive from them all the benefit he hoped for; and he wisely adds, 'Perhaps, had I the choosing of my own frames, I might value them — and myself for them — too much, and be ready to put them in Christ's stead.'

On the 8th of May Mr Newton returned to Chatham. He appears to have been little satisfied with any opportunities of public worship he could enjoy there; but he spent some of his happiest hours at this time in what he calls 'the great temple which the Lord hath built for His own honour.'

Early in June Mr Newton is in London again, chiefly that he might hear, and if possible gain the acquaintance of Mr Whitefield. The account of this visit is, in substance, as follows:

'Reached London on Thursday, June 5. On Friday morning visited Mr Brewer, and, by his advice, and in his name, waited on Mr Whitefield; but he being much engaged, I could not see him. The afternoon at Mr Hayward's. He gave me a letter to Mr Whitefield, as a testimonial for the sacrament. Heard Mr Whitefield preach in the evening on the new birth, from Revelation 21:5. I shall not here insert the heads of his discourses, which is no suitable way of judging Mr Whitefield's preaching, though I propose to commit to writing the most striking of his thoughts in the different times I hear him. However, this I say, that he described the reality and necessity of a change of heart in a very powerful manner indeed. After sermon delivered the letter; but he was so engaged in company he could neither read that nor several others given to him, but desired I should call in the morning.

'Saturday. Went to get the answer from the letter, and received in consequence a ticket for admission to the communion. I had about five minutes converse with Mr Whitefield then, and he excused himself in a very friendly, obliging manner from anything further, upon the account of his throng of business. In the evening returned to the Tabernacle; heard the prepared sermon, from Leviticus 10:3. How awful and how comfortable a discourse! When he spoke of the different ways of coming near to God, and what was meant by sanctifying Him, with the danger of neglecting it, I hope it was laid to my heart. I went home and prayed with more than usual fervency for a blessing on the ordinance in which I had undertaken to draw near to God, then went to bed without engaging in any conversation that might interrupt my views.

'Sunday. Rose at 4 o'clock. After private prayer, etc., went to the Tabernacle, was admitted upon producing the ticket, and here indeed I had a blessing. There were about a thousand people or more, of different persuasions, but all agreed in the great essentials of the gospel, and in mutual charity worshipping the Lord with one heart and soul. Never before had I such an idea and foretaste of the business of heaven. Mr Whitefield made use of the office of the Church of England, interposing exhortations, encouragement, etc., occasionally all along. And it seemed as though that composure, that elevation, and that assurance of faith which shone in his frame and discourses were in some measure diffused over the whole assembly. He made many little intervals for singing hymns — I believe nearly twenty times in all. I hope I shall have lasting reason to bless God for favouring me with such an opportunity. We were about three hours in the ordinance. At the end I went away rejoicing.'

The forenoon and afternoon were spent at Mr Brewer's; and in the evening Mr Newton was at the Tabernacle again.

'A prodigious multitude of people, so that, besides those who stood in the yard, many hundreds were forced to go away, though the place is supposed to contain five thousand. His discourse was suited to the audience — an offer and pressing invitation to the gospel, from Revelation 21:6, and with great life and power he was carried out. Though some are offended with his observing too little method in his discourses at these times, which I am well assured he does on purpose, and that this incoherent way (as it is called) of preaching has been owned in calling in many souls to the gospel. For, in speaking more particularly to the cases and experience of believers he is methodical enough. After this general sermon he prayed, and discoursed again to the society; and here he was most excellent in giving them charges with respect to moral and relative duties. I think, had any of his enemies been present, they must have acquitted him of many calumnies they have (some of them, I hope) been deceived into.'

Mr Newton rose on Tuesday at four o'clock, and at five went again to hear Mr Whitefield. He preached from Psalm 142:7. 'It is hard or impossible for me', he says, 'to give a specimen of his discourse. His subject was concerning the various prisons a believer is liable to in passing through life. He is naturally in prison in sin and in the body, and these bring him into various other straits, such as afflictions, temptations, desertions, and the grave; all which, from the confinement they lay us under, may be termed prisons. He afterwards spoke of the duty incumbent upon us when it pleases God to deliver us out of our temporary prisons; and for His promise of freeing us from the power of the grave we are to praise His name.

'Something like this was his plan. But the power, the experience, the warmth with which he treated it I can by no means express, though I hope I feel the influence of it. Still, my heart was greatly impressed, and I had little relish either for company or food all day.'

After breakfast he heard Mr Rawlins at Pinner's Hall. The discourse, he says, was excellent, both for sound doctrine and comfortable application, and he approved and admired it all; yet his heart was absent, for want of that lively address to the affections which he had found a few hours before. Mr Newton, however expresses himself with great judgment as follows: 'Here I perceive an inconvenience which would perhaps ensue were I constantly to hear Mr Whitefield preach. There might be a disposition to place a personal dependence on his ministry, as though the Lord spoke only through him. And as I find something of this a complaint with others, methinks I see a beauty in the dispensations of providence which have adapted his gifts so suitably to his calling; for were he constantly resident in one place, those who sat under him would run the risk of resting in ordinances, and despising the gifts of others. Yet, on the other hand, it is a great blessing that God has raised up a man so adapted to water, to revive, to stir up, to call in; and then sends him from place to place for the general good.'

Mr Newton, on his return home, made these concluding remarks in reference to this interesting visit: 'My principal business to town this time was to see and to hear Mr Whitefield, that I might judge and speak of him from my own knowledge. From what I have seen in different places of the great work of revival which God has owned under his hand, as well as from the character given of him by several on whose judgment I could well depend, I have long entertained a respect for him, and prayed for a blessing on his endeavours for God's glory. But now I must say, Behold, the one half was not told me. I desire to praise God for the opportunities I have had of hearing, and that in hearing I trust the Lord opened my heart to attend and profit by him. I bless God I am kept from a party spirit, and that I am neither fearful nor desirous of being called after the names of men. But if acknowledging and admiring the manifestation of His grace and providence in the person of Mr Whitefield should bring me under any kind of reproach, I hope I shall be enabled cheerfully to suffer it for the testimony of a good conscience; to stand up in a spirit of meekness for his vindication, and to remember frequently to pray for a blessing on his public labours and private concernments, that he may stand against all opposition, and always, as hitherto, find his strength proportioned to his day.'

June 15th, he writes: 'I have some hope that God will favour this place (Chatham) with a gospel minister, and in some measure perhaps honour me as an instrument in bringing it about.' He speaks of having read Mr Hervey's books again, and of the value he attaches to the doctrine of imputed righteousness, and of his wish to qualify himself to vindicate his belief. It must not be supposed that Mr Newton was all this time unconcerned about his worldly prospects. His constant friend Mr Manesty was using every means to promote his interests; and in the month of June he succeeded in obtaining for him the situation of tide-surveyor at Liverpool. Mr Newton expresses his thankfulness that he was thus freed from the African trade, and that he had the prospect of a suitable provision on shore, thereby avoiding those long separations which had been so great a trial since his marriage.

Meanwhile he tells us that on Sunday 29th he heard a Methodist preacher with great pleasure: he 'never listened to anything more sweet and impressive;' and he adores the grace and providence of God that calls out and supports such men; and he blesses God that the term of a Methodist preacher does not frighten him from attending on them.

Saturday, July 5th, he speaks of a happy, golden opportunity in the fields; and Sunday, 6th, he tells us he started at half-past five o'clock for Maidstone with Mr Duncan. They prayed, and sang, and talked together by the way, went to Mr Jenkins' meeting morning and afternoon, and returned in the evening about eight o'clock. 'Upon the whole,' says Mr Newton, 'I trust the day was not in vain to me. I was desirous to be found in the way of duty, and I know not how I could have disposed of myself to more advantage.'

The time was now come when Mr Newton must direct his steps northward. He took leave of his London friends, and he bade farewell to the scenes where he had experienced so much spiritual enjoyment. 'Walked,' he says, 'in the morning (July 31st), and found some sweet enlargement. I took a kind of solemn leave of those happy retirements, where I trust I have often found the presence of the Lord. I could hardly refrain from expressly addressing the woods and fields, that have so often been silent witnesses of my spiritual joys and alternate mournings. I found comfort in reflecting that the Lord would be with me wherever I went, and thought I could sincerely use the words of Moses, *If Thy presence go not with me, carry me not up hence.*'

On the 11th of August, he started for Liverpool, and though truly thankful for the appointment he had received, it was a sore grief to him that Mrs Newton was unable to accompany him, but was worse than she had been for some time past, and her removal from London was therefore impossible. 'Thus,' says her affectionate husband, 'I am going to leave her when I would most earnestly choose to be with her, to leave her at the uncertainty of ever seeing her again, to take possession of an office which without her will be a burden. This is the language of Sense, but Faith talks in a different strain, only my ears are deaf to hear, and my heart heavy to understand.' In his *Narrative* he adds: 'The day before I set out, and not till then, the burden was entirely taken from my mind. I was strengthened to resign both her and myself to the Lord's disposal, and departed from her in a cheerful frame.'

Thus we are brought to another important era in Mr Newton's history. Not yet, however, does the ultimate purpose of God respecting him manifest itself. For nearly nine years more was he to be disciplined and prepared for the great work of his life.

In a letter to Mrs Newton his work as tide-surveyor is thus described: 'My duty is one week to attend the tides, and visit the ships that arrive, and such as are in the river, and the other week to inspect the vessels in the docks, and these alternately the year round. The latter is little more than a sinecure, but the former requires pretty constant attendance both by day and night. I have a good office, with fire and candle, fifty or sixty people under my direction, with a handsome six-oared boat and coxswain to row me about in form.' He adds the following particulars, in a letter to his brother-in-law, Mr Catlett: 'Last week I acted as boarding surveyor, that is, going on board ships on their first arrival, some at the rock, some nearer hand. The weather was bad, and there were a great many fresh arrivals, so that I entered upon my new office under its worst appearance; but I went through it cheerfully and with pleasure, got no cold, and received no damage. But being obliged to attend tides by night as well as by day, I found myself a little fatigued at the week's end. I have now entered upon my quiet week, which is only to visit and clear the ships in the docks, without going into a boat at all, and have time enough upon my hands. This too is my week of harvest, as the former was my seed-time. When it is finished I may probably let you know the quantity of corn one crop produces, for as yet I have only had an earnest sheaf. However, I am richer and easier than if I had been a land-waiter, as at first proposed.'

And how it came about that Mr Newton got this better situation is but another of the many singular illustrations of providential intervention of which his life is so full. It was supposed, though without any sufficient ground, that Mr Newton's immediate predecessor in office intended to resign his situation. This led Mr Manesty to apply to the member for the town for it on his friend's behalf. The request was at once granted under this false impression. But now is the remarkable part of the story; no sooner was the appointment thus given, than the place did really become vacant, for the person who then held it was found dead in his bed. Nor was this all; about an hour after this painful event became known, the Mayor of Liverpool applied for the office for a nephew of his; but though thus early in his request, he was of course too late. 'These circumstances,' Mr Newton well observes, 'appear to me extraordinary, though of a piece with many other parts of my singular history. And the more so as by another mistake I missed the land-waiter's place, which was my first object.'

A few days later, he writes: 'I still find my mind unsettled; but I hope that trust in God, and a desire to seek His face, is in the bottom of my heart, though my duty engages me this week early and late, and leaves little time that I can call my own; yet it gives me great comfort to consider it as God's appointment, and while I act in it as in his view, I am in a remoter manner serving Him. How wonderful is His condescension, that is pleased to esteem my taking care of my own interest in the world as His service! I esteem it my privilege and my mercy that nothing here is capable of satisfying me; and yet I hope I can say I am contented, and see reason to be thankful for my present lot, which though it has its inconveniences (and where is the state of life without them?), yet frees me from greater which are incident to the sea.'

When Mr Newton came to Liverpool, he seems at once to have attended the ministry of Mr Johnson, who was connected with the Baptist denomination. And he says upon first hearing him, 'It was with regret I reflected that, through inattention or prejudice, I had deprived myself of his preaching for so many years as I have been in the town.' 'I hope,' says Mr Newton, 'I shall number his ministry and acquaintance amongst my many mercies;' and again, at a later date, 'He has acquitted himself in all I have heard of him like an able minister of Christ.' Evangelical religion in Liverpool was evidently at this period in a very unsatisfactory state.

So far as he was able, he united himself with the society under the charge of Mr Johnson, not only attending on the Sunday, but joining in their Wednesday evening conferences; and of these last he says, 'most charming opportunities I found them.'

Mr Newton would gladly have entered into closer communion with Mr Johnson's church; but he found that this could not be done except upon 'full terms' (namely baptism by immersion), of which he says, 'as I do not see the necessity myself, I cannot at present submit. However, I desire thankfully to receive so much of the ordinances under him as I can obtain. Oh, that the happy time was come when all the sincere worshippers of God were of one heart and mind!'

About the middle of September, Mr Whitefield visited Liverpool; and Mr Newton at this time had the opportunity of much personal intercourse with him, greatly to his comfort and satisfaction. 'Who am I,' he says, 'to be admitted into such company, and yet what is this to the hope of admission into full communion with the saints in light?' Having heard him in the early morning of Sunday, 14th, he says, 'In the forenoon I waited on him to St Thomas's Church, and had, I believe, the honour of being pointed at this day on several occasions as one of his followers, especially as he was so obliging as to go home and dine with me. He heard a preacher the very reverse of himself. No life in his delivery, no gospel in his discourse.

'At five o'clock Mr Whitefield preached in St Thomas's Square to an audience of perhaps four thousand.'

In writing to Mrs Newton in reference to this visit, he says, 'Mr Whitefield is, as he was formerly, very helpful to me. He warms up my heart, makes me more indifferent to cares and crosses, and strengthens my faith. I have had more of his company here than would have come to my share at London in a twelvemonth. Though some of the wags of my acquaintance have given me the name of young Whitefield, from my constant attendance upon him when he was here, it does not grieve me; and perhaps if they would speak the truth, they do not think the worse of me in their hearts. I find I cannot be consistent and conscientious in my profession without incurring the charge of singularity. I shall endeavour to act with prudence, and not give needless offence; but I hope I shall never more be ashamed of the gospel.'

Mr Whitefield had never visited Liverpool before, except for a single night, and therefore did not attract the crowds which usually followed him. Mr Newton, however, mentions one striking instance of usefulness which came under his immediate observation. It was the case of a lady of his acquaintance, who reluctantly consented to hear this celebrated preacher. 'At once all her prejudices were overcome, and she received the truth in her heart; and now,' says Mr Newton, 'she bears the reproach and laugh of her neighbours very well. They call her a Methodist, and she seems as easy under the charge as I am.'

On Sunday, the 21st, Mr Newton heard another Baptist minister, Mr Oulton, who was recommended to him by Mr Whitefield as an excellent, humble man. So he says, 'I have the privilege of two gospel ministers where I expected there were none. The Lord grant they may be blessings to me.' On the following day he visited Mr Oulton, and had much satisfaction in converse with him. Thus, too, he became introduced to other Christians, with whom he was much pleased, as persons of catholic spirit. So he says: 'I hope the Lord will make Liverpool a happy place to me, for opportunities of communion with Him in worship, and with His people in converse.'

'Saturday, October 4th. In the afternoon retired into the field, to beg a blessing on tomorrow's ordinances. But, oh! what heavy work is this when I am left to myself. I toiled and toiled, but my prayers were heartless and without meaning. Surely scarcely any person can be more different from another than I at times am from myself, though unworthy at the best of times. However, by the grace of God, I resolved that no defect in my frames or preparations shall keep me from waiting upon the Lord in the ways of His appointment. The more dead I am, the more cause I have to come to Christ, who is my life.'

On Saturday, 18th, Mrs Newton arrived in Liverpool, 'recovered and strengthened,' says her husband, 'far beyond my expectation.' Did our space allow, we might quote some very valuable sentiments from the letters written to Mrs Newton during the time of their separation. This one brief paragraph may be introduced, because it still more fully develops Mr Newton's prevailing tone of mind at this time, and his anxiety to act consistently with his profession: 'I much more fear our being cowardly than imprudent. But if we are of the number of those whom the Lord will not be ashamed to own in the great day, He will give us a measure of grace, and we shall not be ashamed to own His cause and people in the midst of this crooked and perverse generation. But, as you say, there is a way of doing things. I shall try to carry it handsomely to others. It is not necessary to affront or quarrel with any who treat us civilly; but experience will teach you that the less we are connected with worldly people the better. And as the Lord by His providence has placed us in a state of entire independence, and there is no consideration of trade or customers to prevent us living in all points just as we please, I hope we shall judge better than to sacrifice our happiness and true interest to an empty sound.'*

Thus settled in his new occupation, and his wife with him, and having all that his heart desires, Mr Newton complains that he is now ready to take up his rest, though he is well aware it cannot be here. 'I know,' he says, 'the reason of this want of spiritual life. *Perimus licitis* [We perish by what is lawful]. The devil attacks some by storm, with violent temptations within or without, but he lays against me, as it were, by sap, in a more secret way, but not less dangerous, by beguiling my affections. But why do I say the devil? Alas! my own heart is weak and wicked enough to ruin me. This it is that sets up idols against the Lord, and brings me under the power of lawful things.'

Before bringing the events of this year to a close, we may quote a few sentences from a letter, written December 31st, to his brother-in-law, Mr Catlett, whose spiritual state was still a subject of deep anxiety to Mr Newton.

'I protest I know not how to write without bringing in my uppermost subject, or sending you a soliloquy upon the late earthquake,† or something in some degree in my own taste; but I must try. Your dear sister is quite recovered. We have many blessings, but health, love, peace, and plenty will comprise the chief of them. I jog on very comfortably in my new proconsulship, and have struck some bold strokes in my way, one of which will perhaps put from £100 to £150 into my pocket. I am very glad I cleared myself in

---

* *Letters to a Wife*, vol. ii, p. 35.
† In reference to the great earthquake in Lisbon, intelligence of which had just reached England.

your good opinion by my last letter;* and though I find I must no more preach to you, yet depend upon it I will often pray for you, in spite of your teeth. Had you and I lived in Lisbon, one single moment had perhaps decided the long controversy between us; and, though we live in England, some future moment will inevitably decide it — but I find I am breaking out.'

We quote the following passages from Mr Newton's reflections on the first day of the year 1756:

'The last year has been the most remarkable and the most favoured of any in my life, and that in many respects. 1. In the singular advantages I have enjoyed of being clearly established in the truth and glory of the gospel. 2. For the happy administration of ordinances at times I have been admitted to. 3. For many hours of sweet, comfortable communion with God in retirement, though now my harp is hung upon the willows. 4. For an acquaintance with many valuable Christian friends both in the ministry and out of it, by whom my heart has often been warmed, my faith strengthened, and in whose prayers I hope I have a daily share and benefit. 5. For grace enabling me to improve some opportunities of usefulness, but alas, how few!'

On the day following this entry Mr Newton wrote to Mr Whitefield, and the letter is interesting in several points, and especially as giving a view of the religious condition of Liverpool at that time.

After speaking of some results of Mr Whitefield's late visit, he proceeds thus: 'The low estate of the gospel in this very populous town has, I doubt not, excited your wonder and compassion. Here are more than forty thousand people, who in matters of religion hardly know their right hand from their left, people that are destroyed for lack of knowledge, or by unskilful, corrupt teachers. Here the tenets of the Arians and Socinians are not only held, but propagated with the most pernicious address, the satisfaction and divinity of the blessed Jesus slighted and degraded, even by those

* In which Mr Newton was charged with losing his interest in his own relations, and expanding all his regard on his religious connections.

who call themselves His ministers. Here is such a departure from God as is indeed grievous to behold. Profaneness and insensibility seem to divide all between them, and a flow of outward prosperity has blinded all ranks, orders and degrees. Are these not strong motives to engage such ministers as have the cause of God and the good of souls at heart (and who would take a peculiar pleasure to own their Master's name where it is least held in esteem) to Liverpool?

'It is with pleasure I hear of a work of revival going on in so many different parts of the kingdom; and, as an inhabitant of this town, I am grieved to think that we should be as yet excluded from a share in it. It is true, we have the truth preached in the Baptist Meetings; but I believe you know the particular disadvantages they are both under, so that, though they are useful to their own people (I trust, through grace, to me also), yet they seem not calculated for general usefulness. The unhappy bigotry of Mr Wesley's people here is another great disadvantage to the cause. They have the best house in the place, yet they will neither suffer any but their own people to preach in it, nor will they keep it supplied themselves . . .'

After pressing Mr Whitefield to visit them again, he proceeds, 'I think I have heard you say you were cautious of introducing a division amongst the Methodists; but I beg you to consider that they who bear that name amongst us are very few and inconsiderable, and shall they keep out an opportunity of declaring the grace of God to thousands? However, till something can be done, I wish you would represent some part of what I have written to Mr Wesley, to set before him the importance of this great town, and urge him to send such preachers here (if none may be admitted but of his sending) as have skill to divide the word of truth in a lively, affecting manner, and may dwell upon the great essentials of the gospel in the first place, to inform the people of the truths in which all renewed Christians agree, before they puzzle them with the points in which we differ.

'To close with a word about myself. The time you were down was a harvest season with me. The Lord enlarged my heart to hear His Word from your mouth, but, for the most part, I have been since then in the valley, dull, contracted, and unuseful; but, as through Divine grace I have been led to live above and beyond my frames upon the everlasting righteousness of my dear Redeemer, to which my best obedience can add no value, and from which all my infirmities can take nothing away, so these things, though they take from my pleasure, have no considerable effect upon my peace. Therefore, though I have not yet attained, I am pressing on.'

'Wednesday, January 7th. This evening spent some hours in conversation with the noted Jedediah Buxton, greatly surprised at the force of his memory in calculations and retaining numbers, and to find that this faculty, in which I suppose the greatest mathematicians of the age must admire him at a distance, should be unaccompanied with any other, for his capacity in all other respects is very mean. He can neither read nor write, is greedy of liquor, and has not even sufficient knowledge and foresight to apply his talent to any sort of usefulness.'

Mr Newton justly observes, in reference to this case, on the little value of any power of the human mind not made subservient to some high and useful end, and how God sometimes pours contempt on the wise by bestowing such a gift upon one who in other respects is little better than a fool.

At the end of this month Mr Newton took a house; and he speaks with pleasure of having set apart a little room for the purpose of study and prayer. 'I desire,' he says, 'so far as my business will allow, to devote myself to the service of the sanctuary. And though the Lord has not called and furnished me for the ministry, which is an honour and privilege I should prefer to the possession of all the kingdoms upon earth, yet by the leisure, opportunity, and influence He gives me, He certainly puts me in the way of being an instrument of service to His church. That I may be so, I pray that He would make me very careful in the disposition of my time, and help me to aim after a large attainment in self-denial.' The same day (it was sacrament Sunday), he adds: 'This is a day of high privileges, if He please to smile upon the means. Today I am to wait upon His table; today I am to commemorate His passion. There is a little discouragement in some of the circumstances of the administration, but I pray to look above and beyond the instruments. O Lord, increase my faith to do this, and then I need not doubt finding a child's portion.'

At the close of the Sabbath, speaking of the sermon, he says: 'It was a mere declamation; nothing relating either to the place or the ordinance — Ciceronian divinity, consequently nothing to enliven a barren frame or fix a wandering heart on the Lord Jesus. At the communion my spirit was willing, but my flesh was weak. I bound myself anew to be the Lord's willing servant, though a worthless one.'

How simple, and yet how true, the following observation: 'Could not pray in the morning in secret, nor read, nor meditate; was impatient to read a new book I got yesterday and this took possession of my first thoughts, and incapacitated me for everything else.'

'March 2nd. Began to copy for the press some thoughts I had drawn up with regard to *Religious Associations*.' This subject had occupied his attention for many months.

'Too often,' he says on one occasion, 'my mind is little better than the wayside, a highway for carnal, evil thoughts of every kind.' Again, on the following Sunday: 'A dull, barren day this proved to me. Crowds of vain thoughts within me prevented my hearing with improvement.'

'March 18th. At Mr Oulton's at tea. Met a minister from the country, who informed us that there are not less than twenty gospel ministers of the Church of England in and about Bristol. Went in the evening to hear Mr Seafield at the Methodist Meeting. There seems a great deal of earnest piety amongst these poor despised people; and though I think them wrong in some things, I believe their foundation is good.'

He speaks about this time of giving attention to the study of Greek.

'Sunday, March 28th. In my morning devotions was led to pray earnestly for the numerous congregations in this land of gospel light who are left to ignorant, negligent shepherds and blind guides. I particularly prayed for the town of Liverpool, in which I reside, that, if it please the Lord, we may partake of that great enlightening which is breaking forth in different places on the Church of England side.'

'Friday, 30th. [*sic*; 30th March 1756 was a Tuesday]. Very remarkable that we have still accounts of repeated earthquakes every post, and that in distant places. Today's mentioned Lorraine and the lower part of Germany, Naples and Corfu, and even at Lisbon, so lately as the 20th ult. Yet Britain is unvisited, and, alas! for us, unaffected too.'

'Thursday, April 1st. Rose at five, and passed three hours in prayer, meditation, and reading.' 'Saturday 3rd. Essayed in the evening to recollect my thoughts for the approaching sabbath and sacrament. Oh, how fast do months and weeks flee away! and, alas! how unimproved! This is the thing that grieves me—not that my day of rest is coming onward, but that I have so little skill and diligence in my Master's business.'

The 9th and 10th he speaks of as days of much spiritual enjoyment. Just at this time he printed his *Thoughts on Religious Associations*. He sent copies to every minister in Liverpool. Then follows this memorandum: 'Make it a part of my daily prayers that the Lord would be pleased to own this my poor desire, or find some other hand to work by, and in His own way revive His work in this place.'

'Sunday, April 18th. Went to tea at Mr Oulton's, and was drawn into an unprofitable dispute about baptism. I wish I was able to decline this controversy, for of late I have not been able to hear or to say anything new upon the subject, and I find risings of pride and passion often tempting me to sin. I fear I usually forget the main thing, and have my thoughts chiefly taken up with vindicating proud, corrupt, deceitful self. It is not sufficient to be acquitted by my own conscience, but I must aim to appear right in the judgment of others. It were a valuable piece of self-denial to be content to be thought mistaken in some things, without wasting time and words to clear myself, when the opinion can have no bad consequence, and especially amongst people who, I must confess, do more overrate me in some things than mistake me in others.'

'Friday, 23rd. received a letter from Dr Jennings; and one from Miss Thorpe, mentioning comfort she had received from mine of the 17th ult. How wonderful is the Lord's kindness to me! though I am broken and cast down in myself, and have many causes of complaint, yet He does not take away my little usefulness!'

'Tuesday, May 4th. Determined this day to have a ticket in the ensuing lottery; not, I hope, with a desire of amassing money merely, but, if it should be so, of increasing my capacity for usefulness.'

In the month of December following, Mr Newton writes: 'Informed by post that my lottery-ticket is a blank. I am content. I should hardly have engaged that way if I had not supposed that my vow, and my design of usefulness therein, gave a kind of sanction thereto. And I think if the Lord had given me a prize, it would have been chiefly acceptable as a means of helping the poor, and forwarding the cause of the gospel in these parts.' We fear that the good man was in this matter hardly consistent with himself, and forgot to apply the principle that the end does not justify means (Romans 3:8) that are in themselves at least questionable.

On concluding this first volume of his diary, on the 30th of May, four years and six months from its commencement, he thus writes: 'And now, O gracious Lord, my Saviour and my God, accept my praise that Thou, who didst, I trust, put it into my heart to begin, hast spared my hand to finish. If there are any traces of a desire after holiness; any — the lowest — evidences of a work of grace in the foregoing pages, not unto me, O Lord! not unto me, but unto Thy name be the glory and the praise (Psalm 115:1). Lord, the work is

Thine. Perfect that which concerns me, for much yet remains to be done. And oh, that it may please Thee that this imperfect testimony to Thy goodness may be blessed to the use and advantage of any who by Thy providence shall be brought to peruse any part of it. May the experienced Christian be stirred up to adore the freedom of Divine grace on my behalf, that has been pleased to make such a vile, abandoned wretch a monument of Thy mercy; and may sinners be invited, from my happy experience, to taste and see how gracious Thou art (Psalm 34:8), and how desirable is the state of those whom Thou pleasest to choose to bring near to Thyself.'

Mr Newton commences the second volume of his diary with strong expressions of the benefit he found in this practice. He makes the following remarks upon a baptism by immersion which he witnessed at Mr Oulton's: 'Though I still think my infant sprinkling to be a really valid baptism, so far as to render any repetition unnecessary, I dare not pronounce absolutely upon a point wherein so many great and good men have been and are divided. With respect to persons, I look upon neither circumcision nor uncircumcision to be anything, but a new creature (Galatians 6:15). And if my heart does not greatly deceive me, those believers who differ from me in circumstantials are as dear to me as those who agree with me, provided they will join me in this one thing, that they are but circumstantials, and consequently not pretend to enforce them with the same warmth as if they were absolutely essentials. . . . I find great cause to cry to the Lord for a candid spirit. Though I am apt sometimes to think highly of my Catholicism, I cannot but confess to much bigotry and spiritual pride remaining in me. Oh that my censures might be more directed to my own faults!'

Sunday, November 14th, he writes 'Being confined at home, attempted in the afternoon, for the first time, to expound in the family. The subject, (Matt. v. 1–20).'

In the course of this year we find it had been Mr Newton's habit generally to rise at five o'clock, and to engage for two or three hours in devotional exercises. Often, too, when compelled to be early and late at the watch-house, he spent much time in reading and meditation. He also commenced, towards the end of the year, the study of Hebrew and Greek Scriptures, making use of Poole's *Annotations* and similar works to aid him in his Biblical pursuits. His attendance at the weekly conference was very regular; his evenings were not unfrequently spent at home reading to Mrs Newton, while he sought by converse with religious friends to promote a mutual benefit.

The year 1757 opens with these appropriate remarks. After speaking of the importance of the first day of the year as a season to review, and observing that the past had not been a year of much variety, he continues: 'If deliverance out of trouble or danger is a mercy of great value, it is something more extraordinary and indulgent to be kept from the very appearance of evil; to be preserved weeks, months, and years successively unhurt either in my person or best enjoyments in such a world as this, where there are so many arrows continually flying, and so many persons continually suffering,—to observe them falling before, behind, and on every hand, and yet I and mine (though daily provoking the Lord and leaning to idols) escaping without a wound, nay without an alarm,—this is surprising and distinguishing mercy indeed. How loudly does this call me to do more than others; yet, alas! on the contrary, what sloth, insensibility, unbelief, worldliness, pride, and self-indulgence must I charge myself with! . . . I know there are some particular actions or duties best befitting every moment of my life, according to the place or circumstances or company in which I am; but, alas! I must often charge myself with speaking when I should be silent, and being silent when I ought to speak; being last in an affair when I should have been first, and first when I have no cause to be concerned at all. Rashness and diffidence, partiality and credulity, betray me by turns.'

On the 8th of January we find Mr Newton addressing an old correspondent. It is an admirable plea for the wisdom of a religious life. Two or three sentences will show the spirit in which it is written: 'I should have been glad to have been with you at Chatham, to have had the pleasure of your company, and to have seen my dear friends there. In other respects I envy you not, nor would willingly exchange a happy Christmas for a merry one. I know you pity my taste, and you know I pity yours, so neither of us has cause to be disobliged.' He then goes on to show the infinite advantage of the Christian, if religion be true, and the fearful peril of the unbeliever: 'You will perhaps laugh at my needless solicitude for you, as you think it, yet I know not how to offer a more solid proof of the cordiality of my friendship. And because I know that God usually works by means, and very often by the most unworthy and unlikely, therefore I cannot avoid putting you in mind of these things, however I may suffer in your good opinion by so doing, though I do it with a trembling hand; for if my admonitions do not bring you to reflection, I well know they will one day increase and aggravate your confusion.'

'January 15th. My heart hard as stone. Prayer without life or faith. I have a name to live in the world, but am in a manner dead (Revelation 3:1). It is strange that any who has ever known the sweetness and importance of communion with God should be induced to part with it for a trifle; but such has been my folly. Lord, teach me my own nothingness. What am I when thou withdrawest? Strange that I should ever be proud, or even presume, that I should ever think lightly or carelessly of that Divine righteousness in which all my hopes of acceptance are centred.'

On the 15th March we have an account of a remarkable providential deliverance. 'I rose early,' says Mr Newton, 'and went to the watch-house till eight o'clock. At ten a most violent storm came on, doing considerable damage while it lasted. In the afternoon when I returned to the watch-house I found the roof beaten in by the fall of the chimney, and the chair in which I usually sit broken to pieces. Had the storm happened two hours sooner, or at many other times, I should have been crushed in a place where I should have thought myself in safety.'

On the 21st of March—a never-to-be-forgotten day—we have a very striking meditation on his great deliverance. Subsequently we find these observations: 'There is a great grace with which some have been favoured—an abstracted mind in the midst of a crowd, so as to converse with God while surrounded and seemingly engaged with the busy world. Such an attainment methinks I should prize beyond thousands of gold and silver.'

On another occasion: 'Prayer is the great engine to overthrow and rout my spiritual enemies, the great means to procure the graces of which I stand in hourly need. . . . I generally find all my other tempers and experiences to be proportioned to the spirit of my prayers. When prayer is a burden, nothing does me good; but as long as the door of access is kept open and duly attended I find the joy of the Lord to be my strength, and nothing is suffered to harm me.'

Again he mourns over unbelief and coldness, pride and positiveness, and resolves to speak less and less hastily: 'I acknowledge that I am an ignorant and feeble creature, and yet the next minute act and speak *ex cathedrâ.*' [that is, over-dogmatically]

Towards the end of April Mr Wesley visited Liverpool. Some prejudices which Mr Newton at first felt against him were entirely removed. He heard him several times while he remained, had frequent intercourse with him, and at the close blesses God for all he had witnessed. Mr Newton adds:

'The remaining power of bigotry in me has received a blow which (I would hope) will keep me low hereafter. I would hope that, since the Lord has taken so gracious and favourable a way to correct my ignorance and presumption, I shall no more venture to censure and judge without hearing, or dare confine the Spirit of the Lord to those only who tally in all things with my sentiments.'

The following remarks have reference to that feeling of dissatisfaction which is sometimes experienced with the allotments of Providence: 'I have lately begun to notice in myself a secret displeasure and dissatisfaction with my proper and lawful business when it has interfered with some particular engagement and design I have had in hand, and this often veiled under a view of faithfulness to myself and others. But I begin to see it proceeds from self-will and an unmortified spirit; for to be in the way in which the Lord calls me is the main point, whether the circumstances of that way are great or small according to my view.'

The next quotation will show Mr Newton's continued anxiety to have a conscience void of offence. 'I am led,' he says, 'to question my conformity to the oath I took on entering into office, by which I renounced all taking of fees or gratuities, which, however, according to custom, I have done.' He consulted his friend Mr Brewer, who laid the matter before Dr Guyse; and in consequence of their advice he resolved to leave off the practice, and henceforth refused all proffered gratuities. It is added in Campbell's *Conversations*, that Mr Newton's scruples were awakened by accidentally meeting with a book of Mr Wesley's which treated on different kinds of oaths and their violation, and this opened his eyes.

4: FROM HIS FIRST THOUGHTS OF THE MINISTRY TO HIS SETTLEMENT AT OLNEY (1757–64)

First thoughts of the ministry – Dr Taylor of Norwich – Journey to Yorkshire – Special season of prayer and meditation in reference to the ministry – Preaches at Leeds – Seeks Ordination in the Church of England, and is refused – Mr Okeley – Public events – Publishes sermons – Supplies the Independent Church at Warwick – Speaks in the house of Mr Grimshaw at Haworth – Letters – Observations on the Reformers – Begins to expound the Scriptures in his family – Visits Yorkshire – Death of the Rev. Mr Jones of St Saviour's, London – Views of the Ministry – Preaches at Bolton – Letter to the Rev. J. Warhurst – First sketch of his *Narrative* – Mr Haweis – Proposal to take orders in the Church – In Yorkshire – Providential escape – *Ecclesiastical History* – Accepts the Curacy of Olney – Receives Deacon's Orders – Preaches at Liverpool – Ordained Priest – Olney – Mr Whitefield's letter.

In October of this year (1757) we find Mr Newton entertaining his first definite thoughts of the ministry. Some happy results had followed his efforts to do good, and he had received several hints from friends upon the subject. Henceforth this important question is constantly upon his mind, and he is almost morbidly anxious lest unworthy motives should influence him. So in the beginning of the following year he expresses himself as 'in doubt, not knowing whether the views I have of late aspired to are the motions of His gracious Spirit, or the fruits of self-will and sufficiency. I commit myself to the Lord, who will perhaps in one way or other determine for me in the course of the year.'

In February Mr Newton wrote an address for the approaching fast in connection with a society he had formed for religious converse, of which three thousand copies were printed.

About this time we learn that Mr Newton fell into the company of the famous Dr Taylor of Norwich, was greatly pleased with his conversation, and was led at first to look favourably upon his views. Subsequent intercourse, however, induced Mr Newton to think differently; and in after years, speaking with Mr Cecil of the opinions of Dr Taylor, he made use of the following homely but striking illustration. 'He told me,' says Mr Newton, 'that he had collated every word in the Hebrew Scriptures [the Old Testament] seventeen times. "And it is strange," he added, "if the doctrine of atonement which you hold should not have been found by me." I am not surprised,' observes Mr Newton, 'at this. I once went to light my candle with the extinguisher on it. Now prejudices from education, learning, and so on, often form an extinguisher. It is not enough that you bring the candle: you must remove the extinguisher.'

So at another time, referring to the same subject in talking with Mr Campbell, he said: 'Criticisms in words, or rather ability to make them, are not so valuable as some may imagine. A man may be able to call a broom by twenty names, in Latin, Spanish, Dutch, Greek, etc., but my maid, who knows the way to use it, but knows it only by one name, is not far behind him.'

Desirous to see the progress and flourishing state of the gospel in some parts of Yorkshire, of which he had heard very much, in the month of June, accompanied by Mrs Newton and a young friend, he took a journey thither. His first call was on Mr Scott,* an

* The Rev. James Scott, who, after labouring at two or three other places, settled in 1754 at Heckmondwike (Milbridge was in its immediate neighbourhood). In the year 1756, at the suggestion, and through the influence of some friends of the gospel truth in London, who were anxious to stay the progress of Socinian and Arian opinions then prevailing in Yorkshire, Mr Scott was led to superintend the studies of pious and orthodox young men, who might thus be prepared for the work of the ministry in that part of the country. Labouring in this good work till the year 1783,

Independent minister at Milbridge. He was at Leeds on the sabbath; and the following words will show how happy a season that was, as also his subsequent visit to Haworth: 'What a friendly reception we met with, what a people we found ourselves among, I shall not attempt to say. I hope I shall never forget it; yet I cannot but say, happy Leeds! Blessed indeed are the people that are in such a case. Heard Mr Edwards three times; was pleased and edified likewise by Mr Crook, on the side of the Establishment [that is, the Church of England], whom I heard expound twice. In conversation, etc., I had many sweet hours, and it was with much reluctance I forced myself away on Monday. Our short acquaintance was watered with tears. Some of our dear friends accompanied us ten miles homeward.

'We dined with a young clergyman at Cleckheaton, who seems a useful, zealous labourer. He accompanied us to Haworth. We had an indifferent journey, the weather being rough; but we made good amends by finding Mr Grimshaw at home, lodged with him, and had a truly Christian welcome and entertainment. Had it been the will of God, methought I could have renounced the world to have lived in these mountains with such a minister, and such a people, but from hence likewise I was constrained to move.'

In the same month Mr Newton resolved to give himself to deliberate and prayerful consideration on the subject of the ministry. We are in possession of a little book containing the whole history of his procedure in this matter, exhibiting in a most striking way the spirit of deep humility, and the earnestness of desire to know the Divine will, in which this important subject was entertained by him. He determined, in addition to his own serious deliberation, to seek the advice of his most judicious friends, and to enter upon a course of prayer and waiting upon God. He purposed to devote as much time

---

when he died, Mr Scott was the means of introducing more than sixty ministers into the church of Christ. The institution thus originated still continues, and flourishes at the Rotherham College.

as he could command for the next six weeks, until the return of his birthday, to seek the Lord, to examine his own heart, and to consider at large the great work of the ministry. He then gives in detail the course he intended to follow. Upon the last day of these exercises, he thus writes:

'The day is now arrived when I proposed to close all my deliberations upon this subject with a solemn, unreserved, unconditional surrender of my whole self to the Lord. I now enter upon and give myself up to a new view of life. From this time I only wait for light and direction, when and where to move and to begin. And for this I pray that I may be enabled to wait patiently, till I clearly see the Lord going before me, and making me a plain path. But in my own mind I already consider myself as torn off from the world and worldly concerns, and devoted and appointed for sanctuary service . . . It is drawing near five in the evening, and I have been waiting upon the Lord in retirement, with fasting and prayer since six in the morning. When I go from hence I shall take my refreshment with a thankful heart, humbly trusting that the Lord has accepted my desire, and that in His good time He will both appoint the work and furnish me with great wisdom and strength to perform it.'

This remarkable document then concludes with a brief and earnest expression of thanksgiving.

With such depth of feeling as to its nature and importance did Mr Newton entertain the thought of the ministry. It was, however, not till after five years of patient waiting that he actually entered upon the work.

In September he says: 'Since I wrote last I have had a winnowing time of temptation, a conflict of several days, in which I was often cast down and wounded; but the Lord, the restorer of my soul, at length gave me peace. It is not easy to say what experience I have at times of the deceitfulness of sin, how I am foiled and fooled by mere nonentities.' On another occasion he speaks of temptations overcome, of a comforting sense of the Divine presence, and of the benefit he derived from reading Thomas à Kempis, Howe on *Delighting in God*, and the lives of Philip and Matthew Henry. Of Philip Henry's *Life* he remarks, 'So far as it is lawful or proper to make a mere man a pattern, methinks I would as soon have chosen him for my model as any one.'

At the end of the month Mr Newton was at Leeds. 'Mr Edwards engaged me,' he says, 'contrary to my inclination, and indeed to my judgment likewise, to make my first essay amongst his people. I had severe exercises of mind all that day; however, at the appointed time, I adventured.' He began with comfort, but lost the thread of his discourse, and was obliged to desist. 'It is not easy or possible to describe the storm of temptation and distress I went through the next day.* On Thursday, two days afterwards, visited Mr Crook, had long converse with him, which revived my desire towards ordination in the Church of England, and likewise softened many of my objections, which I deemed insurmountable. I began to see I had been too hasty in making that essay on Tuesday, and too adventurous in refusing the aid of notes.'

'November 8th. Began to read Hooker's *Ecclesiastical Polity*, where I hope I may find my scruples more fully resolved. I greatly fear my own spirit leading me to choose that which seems easiest, though perhaps it only seems.' He resolves to prepare drafts of meditation against his appearance in public. On the 18th he received a letter from Mr Crook, pressing him to apply for ordination, and again he hears, telling him that his title to his curacy is ready. Mr Newton goes to three clergymen for testimonials, but they are all afraid to own a suspected Methodist.

Having received his title, he at once proceeded to London and on 22nd of December he wrote to Mrs Newton: 'Well! it is over for the present, and I have only cheated you out of a journey to London. Last night I waited on the Bishop of Chester; he received me with

---

* A more particular account of this circumstance may be seen in the *Life and Times of the Countess of Huntingdon*, i. 271.

great civility, but he said, as the title was out of his diocese, he could do me no effectual service, and that the notice was much too short. However, he countersigned my testimonials, and directed me to Dr N——, the Archbishop's chaplain. On him I waited this morning. He referred me to the secretary, and from him I received the softest refusal imaginable. He had represented my affair to the Archbishop; but his grace was inflexible in supporting the rules and canons of the Church. I am quite satisfied and easy. The Lord will make all these things subservient to our good.'

In another letter, a few days later, he says: 'Though the Lord permits difficulties and hindrances to arise for the trial of our faith and patience, I cannot believe that he either disapproves, or will finally disappoint my desire to serve Him. I cannot express the satisfaction your dear letter gave me in finding you so easy and resigned upon the event of my late attempt. Nothing disquieted me from the first of my design, but the fear of involving you in difficulties, or causing you uneasiness.'

In a letter written by Mr Newton during the course of this year, there are the following words: 'I thank you for Mr Romaine's book. I have endeavoured to observe his appointment, as likewise the Dissenters' hour on Wednesday mornings. Blessed be God for a prevailing Intercessor, a great High Priest, who bears all our prayers and all our concerns before His throne. The times are indeed dark.'

The publication here referred to is entitled, 'An earnest invitation to the friends of the Established Church, to join with several of their brethren, clergy and laity, in London, in setting apart an hour every week for prayer and supplication, during the present troublesome times.' 'One of the most useful publications,' says the Rev. J. C. Ryle, 'that Mr Romaine ever sent forth.'

(1759.) After Mr Newton's return home in January, he says: 'Had I been properly informed, I might have been spared the journey, for I was quite too late.' He saw Mr Romaine and Mr Jones in London, and called on Dr Young at Welwyn, by whom he was received very courteously, and who encouraged his design of entering the ministry. The Sunday was spent at Everton, the residence of Mr Berridge, 'an eminent instrument whom God has raised up, and by whom He is carrying on a memorable work.'

'Since my design of episcopal ordination,' says Mr Newton, 'has taken place, I have thought it proper to attend steadily at the Established Church. I meet with little or nothing in preaching that has a tendency to quicken my faith and graces.'

In February he wrote to the Archbishop of York, enclosing the necessary papers; but he received an answer containing a flat refusal of ordination, 'with no further reason assigned,' Mr Newton adds, than that 'his grace thought it best for me to remain in my present situation. O Lord, Thou art my hope, and the object of my views and vows. Do Thou order all my concerns according to Thy wisdom and goodness. When Thou wilt, where, and how Thou wilt. Only comfort me with Thy presence, and enable me to wait on Thee alone.'

'February 21st. The refusal of my ordination makes much noise. I have not yet determined how to proceed. It seems incumbent on me to require a further explanation; but I am afraid of espousing my own cause, lest pride and self-will take advantage. Perhaps it may not be the will of the Lord that I should appear on that side, but I think to pursue my application during this year.'

March 21st was as usual observed as a special day; and on the next Mr Newton speaks of beginning to study Syriac.

In April a further application was made to the Bishop of Chester.

When Mr Wesley visited Liverpool in the preceding year, he was accompanied by a Mr Okeley, a Moravian minister. Mr Newton was very much impressed by his singularly amiable and Christian spirit. Soon after, he addressed a letter to him,* and we quote from it more especially now as showing Mr Newton's views upon letter-writing, and some other topics. 'I know not,' he says, 'if my heart was ever more united to any person in so short a space of time than to you,

* See *Cardiphonia*, i. 279.

and what engaged me so much was the spirit of meekness and of love (that peculiar and inimitable mark of true Christianity) which I observed in you. I mean it not to your praise. May all the praise be to Him from whom every good and perfect gift cometh . . . I hope to hear soon and often from you. I number my Christian correspondents among my principal blessings, a few judicious, pious friends, to whom, when I can get leisure to write, I send my heart by turns. I can trust them with my inmost sentiments, and can write with no more disguise than I think. I shall rejoice to add you to the number, if you can agree to take me as I am (as I think you will), and suffer me to commit my whole self to paper, without respect to names, parties, and sentiments. I endeavour to observe my Lord's command, to call no man master upon earth; yet I desire to own and honour the image of God wherever I find it. I dare not say I have no bigotry, for I know not myself, and remember to my shame that formerly, when I ignorantly professed myself free from it, I was indeed overrun with it; but I can say I allow it not; I strive and pray against it.'

April 30th, he writes: 'I might inscribe vanity of vanity on the history of every day. My life seems as much a blank as my book — worse than this, each page filled with folly and impertinence. I have sinned, and the Lord is withdrawn. How I lost Him I cannot particularly say, but I know by sad experience He is gone, and now I only weep away my time. Yesterday was a cold, unfruitful sabbath indeed. Made some faint essays at prayer. When shall these heavy, tedious intervals be over? Oh, when shall I be all eye, all ear, all heart, in serving and waiting upon God?'

In May Mr Wesley again visited Liverpool; and now Mr Newton is in doubt whether he can consistently go to hear him. He, however, decided in the affirmative, and observes, 'I thought if it might be prudent to forbear going on the whole, it might be proper to go once, to show that I was neither afraid nor ashamed to attend him.'

Later in May Mr Newton goes into Yorkshire, and finds Mr Crook has written to Mr Venn to engage Lord Dartmouth's interest in his favour. 'I was invited,' he says, 'to accept an Independent charge when at Mr Scott's. Had this come some months sooner, I would willingly have complied; but since I am embarked so far on the other side I shall not stop till I have tried the *dernier ressort* [last resort].' At this moment Mr Newton received a letter from the Bishop of Chester to the effect that his hands were tied up by the Archbishop's prior refusal. In consequence of this communication Mr Newton was led to write to Lord Dartmouth.

In August Mr Newton wrote a full account of his situation to Dr Young, but he was unable to help him. 'I have only now,' he says, 'to appeal to my Lord of Canterbury, and to leave the issue with the Lord; for I think upon a refusal there — which I am prepared to expect — that I will retract the pursuit, and take up the conclusion Mr Romaine has already made for me, that it is not the will of the Lord I should appear on that side.'

Returning in September from his summer retreat at Vernon's Hall, 'I hope now,' he says, 'to renew my diary and my studies, which have been discontinued of late.' He especially gives himself to study and composition, with a view to the future.

'October 20th. News came to-day of the surrender of Quebec to our arms. The interposition of Divine providence in our favour of late has been extraordinary. A very surprising change within this two years has taken place in our affairs; and the victory gained in Germany last August* gives a reality to our naval advantages. Nothing is wanting but a true, thankful spirit; and I trust there are many whose hearts and knees are bowed before the Eternal. But in general a presumptuous, boasting tone is apparent.'

'November 4th. A great alarm in town that the French are on their passage to attack this place. Lord, I commit myself and my all to Thee!'

'December 5th. The Divine goodness which has appeared in our behalf in all quarters of the world has just now favoured us with

* The Battle of Minden, 1 August 1759, during the Seven Years' War.

an important victory near home, over the French fleet, which, after waiting two years for an opportunity to sail, ventured out three weeks since, to escort a large body of troops to invade our happy and favoured land; but they were intercepted, defeated, and dispersed by Sir E. Hawke (off Quiberon), on the 20th ult., before they had reached the place of rendezvous, under a variety of disadvantages — a storm of wind, a lee shore, a winter night, and a foul, unknown coast.'

We now come to the year 1760. Mr Newton was hindered by business from devoting New Year's day, as was his custom, to meditation and retirement.

At the close of the past year he had received an invitation to become pastor of an Independent church at Warwick. This subject now occupied much of his thoughts. 'Mr Romaine,' he says, 'advises me to accept it.'

'Now a call seems to await me, flesh and blood are alarmed at the undertaking, and seem to say, Keep back; but I cannot, I dare not. My own inclinations, the dispensations of Divine providence, the advice of my friends, join in with the secret and repeated engagements by which I have bound myself, and urge me forward. Yes, I must go. But why? or with what? Oh, for faith! This can move mountains, and raise the dead. This can impart eyes and ears and tongues. This is the channel of every gift and grace. Oh for a spirit of prayer, of humility, of purity.'

It may be proper to observe here, that about twelve months before the present time, when Mr Newton hoped for a speedy admission into the Church, he wrote several sermons in anticipation of that event. These he now thought fit to publish. 'Not,' as he says in the preface, 'for his own vindication, but because of the importance of the subjects treated of, and the probability that, thus presented, these subjects might awaken the attention of his friends and others.'

In a communication to the Rev. Mr Whitford, on January 10th,*

* *Cardiphonia*, ii. 92.

he alludes to Cennick's Sermons, saying of them: 'They are in my judgment sound and sweet. Oh that you and I may have a double portion of that spirit and unction which is in them.' Addressing the same correspondent again in November,* he says: 'If your visit should be delayed, let me have a letter. I want either good news or good advice — to hear that *your* soul prospers, or to receive something that may quicken my *own*.'

About this time he speaks of having lately committed to memory some of the most expressive and comprehensive passages of the Greek Testament, and reads Cicero *De Officiis* and Rollin's *Ancient History*.

Thus conscientiously and sedulously did Mr Newton prepare himself for that work to which, in spite of all the discouragements he met with, he evidently felt assured that God had called him. To preach the gospel of Christ, to honour to his utmost ability Him whom he had so dishonoured, was the height of his ambition; and though it is evident his preferences were, on the whole, for the Establishment, whether it was here or there was after all a matter of inferior consideration, so long as this, his heart's desire, was accomplished.

Upon Mr Wesley's coming to Liverpool again during this month, Mr Newton availed himself of every opportunity of hearing and holding intercourse with him. 'This,' he says, 'is a golden harvest season. I hope I feel the good effects of his company amongst us, and that as the Lord has always sent me a blessing by him hitherto, so I am not wholly disappointed now.'

In April, Mr Newton visited Yorkshire. Here he was again induced to preach, and after his former embarrassment resolved to use notes. But in this he had no better success, for he says: 'The moment I began my eyes were riveted to the book, from a fear that if I looked off I should not readily find the line again. Thus with my head hanging down (for I was near-sighted), and fixed like a statue, I conned over my lesson like a boy learning to read, and did not stop till I came

* Ibid., ii. 94.

to the end. I am convinced,' he says, 'that unless I can speak warm from my heart, God helping me, it will be in vain.'

At length in May — why this long delay, does not appear — after a day of fasting and prayer, Mr Newton went to Warwick, and remained there nearly three months. 'The visit,' he says, 'I enjoyed very much; and the people are desirous, with a degree of impatience, that I should settle amongst them.'

Writing to a friend at Warwick, in the year 1782, Mr Newton thus refers to this event: 'How many mercies has the Lord bestowed upon me since my first visit to Warwick, which is now more than twenty-two years! I often think of that time with pleasure. Then the Lord opened my mouth. Many retired places in your neighbourhood were endeared to me by seasons which I can still remember, when I was enabled to seek the Lord, and to pour out before Him prayers which He has since abundantly answered.'

There is a letter in existence from Lady Huntingdon, in which she speaks of Mr Newton as having won the affections of the people, and of his ministerial usefulness at Warwick.

Some of his friends advised him to accept the invitation, others that he should reapply in connection with the Church; but he says, 'That point I think is already determined by what has passed.'

August 6th, he went into Yorkshire, to take counsel of his friends. He spent the sabbath with Mr Grimshaw at Haworth, and spoke in his house with comfort, visited the Moravian settlement at Yeadon, and before his return he saw Mr Venn at Huddersfield. In November he received another pressing invitation from Warwick, of which he says, 'I cannot but think it amounts to a clear call.' But again, and only a few days after, unexpected circumstances arose which threw the whole matter into doubt, and that too when Mr Newton was just on the point of giving up his situation. So he writes to his brother-in-law Mr Catlett, 'Polly and I are *in statu quo*, not yet removed to Warwick, nor preparing for it. I rather believe that view will not take place; but in this life you know there is nothing certain but uncertainty!'

We find in the last volume of Mr Newton's works, published in 1808, a letter written in September of this year to Miss Medhurst, in which he says: 'I still reflect with pleasure on the opportunities I was favoured with among you; and if, as I hope, my latter visits were not unacceptable to each or any of you, let us not lose a moment in apologies or compliments to each other, and refer the whole praise where it is wholly due.'

In November also, there is a letter to Mr Wesley, referring to his Yorkshire visit, in which Mr Newton tells him that he had had the honour to appear as a Methodist preacher. 'I was at Haworth; Mr Grimshaw was pressing and prevailed. I spoke in his house to about one hundred and fifty persons... It was a comfortable opportunity. Methinks you are ready to say, very well; why not go on in the same way? What more encouragement can you ask than to be assisted and accepted?' Then giving his reasons why he could not become an itinerant preacher, he concludes: 'So that though I love the people called Methodists, and vindicate them from unjust aspersions on all occasions, and suffer the reproach of the world for being one myself, yet it seems not practicable for me to join them further than I do. For the present I must remain as I am, and endeavour to be as useful as I can in private life, till I can see further. I shall always be obliged to you for your free sentiments on my case.'

1761. The intention of Mr Newton to throw up his situation and to enter the ministry, especially amongst the dissenters, seems to have been very distasteful to some of his worldly friends. He thus replies to a letter of remonstrance on the subject: 'But, my dear sententious brother, from whence arose this new and sudden warmth? Do you not remember that we settled the point in London; and you were not only reconciled to let me go on my own way, but promised to come to Warwick to let me preach at you? I thank you for your letter, and accept it (as you meant it), a proof of your friendship and regard. As to your reasonings, though I do not think them unanswerable they require no answer from me at present, as the point to which they refer is already determined according to your wish. All that I think needful to say may be included in a few words. I am not mad. I was not mad when I intended to settle at Warwick. No circumstance of my life was ever conducted upon so much deliberation and advice as this business. I love my friends, and I would serve each and every one of you to the utmost, nor can I grieve you in any point without grieving myself. If this is not a sufficient security for my behaviour, consider further that I love your sister. Have you known me so long, and do you consider me capable of staking her peace and happiness for a trifle? As you would hardly allow me the claim of an infallible spirit, I suppose you do not pretend to one yourself; and without such a spirit you have no right to be sure that I judged wrongly in the part I was about to act. Remember *my thinking differently from you is no proof that I was mistaken.* I had as sure ground as any demonst-ration in *Euclid*, to be sure of one of these two things — either that my removal to Warwick would be happy and comfortable to me and all concerned, or else that something would happen to prevent it. Now you cannot justly condemn my conclusion, unless you understand the force of the premises I went upon — which you do not — especially as I am justified by the event.

'However, though I love myself, my friends, and my wife, I confess a deference to conscience, and wherever I judge the duty I owe to my God and Saviour is evidently concerned, I hope no friendship or regard will influence me to act against the light of my own mind, or refuse to encounter a few seeming difficulties which may be laid in the way to prove my sincerity. I do not like disgrace or poverty, but I fear God more than either. Is this absurd? I would do much to please my friends, but I would do more to please Him who died for me. Only take this with you, that I believe the Scriptures and the God therein described, and you will not think it strange that I love Him and serve Him and trust Him!'

Anxious to make himself as conversant as possible with the precise meaning and force of the phraseology of the Scriptures, Mr Newton commenced about this time an exposition or explanation of the principal words in the Greek Testament. He calls it his *Critica*, and it was a long-continued and favourite work. How far it proceeded we know not, but the letter *a* occupies about six hundred and twenty-four pages.

Having read Foxe's *Book of Martyrs*, we find the following remarks: 'I observe, in reading the account of the disputations at Oxford, etc., how much our reformers were embarrassed in their defence by admitting the authority of the Fathers for four hundred years conjointly with the Scriptures. Had they gone a little lower, and cleared quite to the foundation before they began to build, they might have supported their doctrines with more clearness. The Scriptures would have borne them out, when I think now the Fathers do sometimes leave them to the mercy of their adversaries. Yet under all disadvantages they did great things. The Lord was with them in life and in death, suffering all their own schemes, not undertaken in faith, to fail. Such seems the attempt to set aside the succession of Mary and force the crown upon Lady Jane.'

In April, Mr Wesley was once more in Liverpool. On one occasion Mr Newton heard him preach on the doctrine of perfection. He objects to his views, but beautifully says: 'Yet I would rather pray for and press to nearer advances towards it than fight and dispute against it. I am sure that to keep the commandments, to redeem time, to abstain from all appearance of evil, is the best way to maintain light and joy and communion with the Lord; yet after all I expect to be saved as a sinner, and not as a saint!'

Writing to the relative before referred to, just after Mr Wesley's visit, he says: 'Mr Wesley has been a week in Liverpool. He breakfasted with me yesterday morning, and then set out for Scotland. I wish you liked him, and could benefit by him as I do. But it seems you and I must still converse *usque ad aras* ['even to the altar', that is, 'for ever'], and there we part. What a pity that our intimacy must break off in the very pleasantest part! You will not be angry if I tell you that I frequently pray on your behalf.'

Anxious in every way to do good, Mr Newton procured an electrical machine. He says: 'I have set up for a doctor, and hope to cure many diseases and pains by a touch. I have seen surprising things performed by this wonderful instrument, and know not how to do so much good at so little expense in any other way as by employing an hour or two of my time every day in relieving the poor and ailing.'

We find an important entry, Saturday, April 18th: 'I am about attempting to be regular in expounding the Scriptures in my own family on Sunday evenings, and to invite a few friends to join me. To-morrow I make the first essay.' Accordingly he began with the first Psalm, 'found much liberty and enlargement,' and thenceforth continued the practice.

Once more the Warwick business comes up. Mr Newton, it appears, had written some things in the way of explanation to one of his friends at Warwick. 'This brought a reply,' says Mr Newton, 'full of resentment and provocation.' We refer to the subject for the sake of the following wise remark: 'I am more confirmed in what I have often observed and have expressed in print, that self-justification usually does harm, and seldom answers the end proposed. I hope to decline it for the future; for though I hope I said nothing but the truth, yet I find it more than he could bear, and his answer is more than I can bear. Thus in the multiplicity of words there wanteth not sin. The Lord pardon us both.'

About two months afterwards he received 'two comfortable letters' from Warwick, which more than made amends for Mr V—'s unkindness.

In June he visited Yorkshire, and stayed three days at Mr Venn's; and he writes thus to an old correspondent from Preston: 'We are upon a tour to visit our friends in Yorkshire. The principal point in view is the establishment and strengthening [of] Polly's health, by exercise and change of air. We propose a circle of about two hundred miles round . . . Farewell. Remember that you are a frail mortal, and that life and all in it is uncertainty. Set not your heart too closely upon that which is not, but pray God to give you true wisdom and enduring riches. This is good advice, whether you can take it or no, and I shall not cease to offer it. Though I have little to hope of you as yet, I shall never despair about you, for I well know that He who changed my heart is able to change yours. He who is so little thought of and often so hardly spoken of, He who once suffered without the gates of Jerusalem as a malefactor, is now possessed of all power in heaven and earth; and I am sure a word from Him (He can speak to the heart) would bring you, like St Paul, to the ground in a moment. For the rest I refer you to Mr Romaine. I wish you dare hear him often.'

About this time he observes: 'My season of evening worship in the family at home is now settled. I have preached extempore several times. Several friends join me in these services.'

'Thursday, August 6th. Mr Venn surprised me with a call. It pleased God to give me influence to get him St George's pulpit; and I had the pleasure to hear him there proclaim the truth in a bold, lively, engaging, and powerful discourse on 2 Corinthians 5:14, 15. Some stared, some mocked, some were pleased, and some, I hope, affected.'

'September 2nd. This afternoon Mr Venn called again, and I spent two or three agreeable hours in his company. I breakfasted with him at the inn next morning, and was introduced to the acquaintance of Mr Hill, the son of a baronet in Shropshire, whom the Lord has been graciously pleased to call to the knowledge of the truth.'

At the beginning of the year 1762 a proposal was made to Mr Newton to write notes and a preface to a new edition of the *Homilies*, to be published in weekly numbers. He observes: 'I think it would be a useful attempt. I long to see that valuable system of practical and experimental divinity in many hands; and I have little doubt that a few short and spirited notes to explain and illustrate some passages, with application to the present times, might do well.'

In the month of June, Mr Jones, minister of St. Saviour's, Southwark, died. He was a man of great gifts, and great trials, and was eminently useful. The removal of this 'dear and honoured friend' of Mr Newton greatly affected him, and quickened his desire to enter upon the ministry. He felt he could no longer be silent, and thought that he might make an effort in Liverpool. From this, however, Mrs Newton dissuaded him; and in referring to the subject long afterwards he says: 'I believe no arguments but hers could have restrained me, for almost two years, from taking a rash step; of which I should have perhaps soon repented, and which would have led me far wide of the honour and comfort I have since been favoured with.'

In August, Mr Newton went to supply a destitute congregation at Bolton — as he says, 'to assist the poor forsaken flock at Bolton.' 'I spent the sabbath comfortably amongst them, through the Lord's tender mercy. Though unbelief pressed me sore at times, I was favoured with freedom, and found acceptance.'

On the week preceding this Sabbath we find Mr Newton writing as follows to the Rev. Caleb Warhurst, an Independent minister at Manchester: 'I should be glad of an opportunity to see Mr Scott (of Heckmondwike), either at Tockholes or at his own house, to let him know that I am disposed to accept a call within his connection, and under the sanction of his judgment and recommendation, if any favourable opportunity should offer, and he thinks proper to encourage me. I begin to be weary of standing all the day idle; and there seems not the least probability of beginning anything at Liverpool. The Lord hath made me willing, nay, desirous to set about it. I would prefer it to anything else. I have made all the overtures towards it that the situation of things will bear; but it will not do. There is not a person (one woman excepted) who is willing to concur in the necessary preliminaries.

'If I should not have an opportunity to meet Mr Scott, will you tell him, so far as I know my own heart, I have quite done with the Established Church, so called — not out of anger or despair, but from a conviction that the Lord has been wise and good in disappointing my views in that quarter; and I believe if the admission I once so earnestly sought was now freely offered, I could hardly, if at all, accept it.

'I hope your soul prospers, that the Lord comforts, refreshes, and strengthens you in your inner man and your outward labours. I hope the house you have built to His name is filled with His glory. Happy they that know the grace of our Lord Jesus Christ; but happy above all others are those who receive appointment and power to proclaim this grace to poor sinners, and who find the Lord confirming their word by signs following. To be thus engaged among a few faithful, lively people, to dispose all my faculties, studies, and time to this service, is the one thing that I continually desire of the Lord, and which I think I could, without hesitation, prefer to the honours and possessions of a lord or a prince.'

'Thursday, September 2nd. Began to write upon the Gospels.'

'28th. Finished to-day the brief account of the Lord's gracious dealings with me from my infancy to the time of my settlement here. I pray God this little sketch may animate those who shall peruse it to praise the exceeding riches of His goodness to an unworthy wretch.'*

November 6th, Mr Newton abandons his work on the Gospels, 'leaving that,' he says, 'in possession of Mr Adams,' and begins upon the Acts of the Apostles.

We may close this year's history with some extracts from a letter addressed to Mr Newton's brother-in-law. After referring to the long silence of the latter, he continues: 'You are, I suppose, pushing on to be a great man, and I wish you all reasonable success; but

* This work, in a somewhat extended form, constitutes the well-known *Authentic Narrative*, of which we have already given the substance.

consider what good will your money, and offices, and titles do you, if they will not suffer you to remember what you owe to yourself and to your friends? I tell you all your thousands (when you get them) will not purchase you such cordial well-wishers as two old-fashioned acquaintances (not to say a sister and a brother) who lie by neglected at Liverpool. Surely you could rise a quarter of an hour earlier once in six months to retrieve an opportunity of favouring us with a letter!

'However, I encourage you, I send you a free and absolute pardon for all that is past, and exempt you from the trouble of apologies of every kind, real or imaginary, provided that, before you go down to Chatham this Christmas, you testify your repentance by your amendment. Otherwise expect a letter upon coarse paper, in a coarse style, as tart as vinegar, as bitter as wormwood (Proverbs 5:4), as angry as my Lord Bishop of G——.

'We go on in the usual way. Polly has often slight complaints, but is seldom very ill. Her constitution is tender and feeble, but many stronger have gone before her, and at the present writing she eats and sleeps and looks as well as she did seven years ago. Our health is like our wealth — in a mediocrity. The God whom we serve does not see it good for us to be rich, but I trust He will give us what is needful and best, and I hope we do not envy those who ride in coaches. . . . As I said before, I wish you success in your business — I would propose nothing inconsistent with a due regard to it. But can I bound my desires for you within such narrow limits? Allow me to wish you everlasting riches, greater honours and better pleasures than this world can afford. Alas! what a poor acquisition to be what is usually called a thriving man for a few years, and then to drop unawares into an unknown eternity! What a contrast between living to-day in affluence and pleasure, regardless of that great God who has made us, and to-morrow, perhaps, being summoned away to appear, naked and alone, before His tribunal, to give account what use we have made of the talent so long entrusted to us! I pray God to impress this thought upon your heart before it is too late.

'I have tried both ways, and find that religion — I mean the true inward religion which is so generally scorned and opposed — does not destroy, but greatly heightens the relish of temporal things. It teaches me to live comfortably here, as well as enables me to look with comfort beyond the grave. In this way I possess peace, which in every other way I sought in vain. I heartily commend you to the protection and teaching of God.'

The publication of *Omicron's Letters* is erroneously ascribed, in Cecil's *Life of Newton* and elsewhere, to this year.

1763. January 4th, Mr Newton writes: 'I was pleased to-day with a very kind letter from Mr Haweis, late of Oxford. He informs me that he had seen my eight letters to Mr Fawcett,* when he was lately at Sandwich; that he was much affected with reading them, and desired that I would send him an account to the same purpose, but more in detail. My case is uncommon indeed, and I perhaps am the only person who considers it without being greatly affected. He inquired after my present views and engagements, particularly if I was yet willing to enter the [Established] Church, supposing an opportunity offered.'

'Friday, 7th. Engaged three days in answering Mr Haweis' letter and transcribing for his perusal what I have written by way of introduction to the Acts and the notes on the fifth chapter. . . . I have informed him under what restrictions I shall retain my desire of Episcopal ordination.'

'24th. Received a letter informing me that Lord Dartmouth desired a copy of my *Narrative*; wrote to him, and received an obliging answer.'

'March 10th. A letter from Mr Haweis, making a distinct proposal of my taking orders in the Church. He hints there is no great temptation to accept such a call from motives of filthy lucre, which indeed

* The *Narrative*, then only in manuscript.

I am glad of; but perhaps some thought of this kind might assist me in getting over two or three small scruples which I yet retain. They are comparatively small, and I hope they are but scruples. I do approve of parish order where practicable. I approve of the Liturgy, as to the sum and substance. The only difficulty is to subscribe, *ex animo* [from the heart], that there is not a line contrary to the Word of God. I think, indeed, that there are not many; but I observe a few expressions in the Burial and Baptismal offices, and in the Catechism, which I cannot fully approve. But I can assent to the whole in such a manner as is due to any writings of human authority, which are not pretended to be written by infallible inspiration. My desire is to peace, union, and usefulness. My talent and temper seem best adapted to that side; my principal friends and counsellors are there; and I think at this time the greatest measure of the Lord's power and Spirit is there likewise.

'Join where I will, my own private sentiments in nonessentials must, more or less, give place to the judgment of others. So that if, after all that has passed, the Lord should be pleased to incline the hearts of those in power to admit me into the Establishment, by means not of my own seeking, I think I can conscientiously comply. But before I give my answer I must seek for a blessing and direction, that if this proposal be from Him, if He intends it to be for the praise of His grace, to the comfort of my own soul in His service and to the good of others, it may succeed. And if otherwise, that He would be pleased (as He has heretofore done) to hedge up my way with thorns, and not suffer me to take a single step contrary to His will.

'My friend asks if I could content myself with £40 per annum for the present, and trust futurity to the Lord, and methinks I can cheerfully say I *can*, provided only I see my call clear from Him. I know that if He employs me He will take care of me. I am willing, heartily willing, to trust Him in this matter. This is the least of my solicitude; only I pray that I may not be left to act in my own spirit, nor to attempt anything in my own strength, but that I may see His hand point out my path, and find His power according to my day, and in all the rest let Him do as seemeth Him good. O Lord, enable me to wait earnestly upon Thee; and give me this day (if it please Thee), a comfortable experience in my soul that Thou art a God that hearest and answereth prayer.'

'Saturday, 26th. Favoured in some degree with a spiritual frame through the whole of this week, and have redeemed more time than usual for prayer, etc.; and I often find that prayer is the index of my present state. It is indeed the gate of heaven.'

April 25th. 'Set out on a Yorkshire circuit. A hearty reception from Mr Venn at Huddersfield. Heard him twice on Sunday, and communed, and heard him address some catechumens. In every exercise, in the whole of his converse and carriage, he seems eminent and exemplary. I stayed with him almost a week. A happy time at Leeds. Met there Mr Ingham* and Miss Medhurst. At Yeadon had a pleasant day with my dear friends. Dined with Mr Scott.'

Associated with Mr Ingham were three brothers, the Messrs Batty, all Cambridge men, and Mr Newton's name occurs in connection with them, as having at times taken part in their religious services. Mr Christopher Batty in particular says, in reference to one such occasion: 'Multitudes were melted into tears while Mr Newton dwelt on our Lord's expostulation, "Is it nothing to you, all ye that pass by?" and many received the word of reconciliation as the thirsty land doth the dew of heaven. And the next day he preached again to a very crowded audience, on "The kingdom of God is at hand: repent ye, and believe the gospel." The people were all attention, and the word did not return void, but accomplished that for which it was sent.'†

*For a very interesting account of Mr Ingham's labours in Yorkshire, and their large results, see *Life and Times of the Countess of Huntingdon*, i. 242, etc.

† The quotation from this letter has been kindly furnished to us, and there can be no doubt of its authenticity; yet it is strange that there should be no reference to these facts in Mr Newton's diary, kept through the whole of the Liverpool period with so much regularity and minuteness.

Writing to his friend Captain Clunie, Mr Newton says: 'I have lately been a journey into Yorkshire. That is a flourishing country indeed, like Eden, the garden of the Lord, watered on every side by the streams of the gospel. There the voice of the turtle is heard in all quarters, and multitudes rejoice in the light. I have a pretty large acquaintance there among various denominations, who, though they differ in some lesser things, are all agreed to exalt Jesus and His salvation. I do not mean that the truth is preached in every church and meeting through the county, but in many — perhaps in more, proportionably, than in any other part of the land, and with greater effect, both as to numbers and as to the depth of the work in particular persons. It is very refreshing to go from place to place and find the same fruits of faith, love, joy, and peace.'

July 30th, we have the following account of a remarkable providential deliverance. 'There has been,' says Mr Newton, 'an awful accident at the river. An outward-bound ship blew up, and eleven persons perished. I had a providential escape. I was going down the river, but was unexpectedly delayed about twenty minutes beyond my intended time, otherwise I should probably have been very near her, but she blew up just as I was going into the boat.'

On November 8th, Mr Newton speaks of frequent correspondence with Mr Haweis. 'He has prevailed upon me to engage in an important and difficult work — an Ecclesiastical History, to trace the gospel spirit, with its abuses and oppositions, through the several ages of the Church — a subject of my own pointing out; but I little expected to have it devolved on me, and I have desired to decline it, sensible how poorly I am furnished for the undertaking; but my friend will have it so, and the Lord can supply. I am collecting books for the purpose.' It was not, however, till the year 1769 that the first and only portion of this work appeared.

1764. In February Mr Newton received proposals from a Presbyterian congregation in Yorkshire, but clogged with some unfavourable conditions, so that he says, 'I believe I should not have pursued it, even if I had had no other engagements in view.'

'Saturday, February 4th. I believe myself to possess the privileges of a child of God, yet am I lean, uncomfortable, unfruitful. Why is this? It arises from two grand causes, which mutually produce and run into each other, a want [lack] of faith, or a want of watchfulness. I suffer much from both, much from the latter. Self-seeking, earthly cares, worldly conformity, neglect of the means of grace, or formality in their use, are the enemies to comfort and usefulness.'

'February 6th. Another letter from Mr Burgess about the Yorkshire congregation, removing objections.' Mr Newton promises to give it serious thought, and writes to Mr Haweis for his advice, resolving meanwhile to wait upon the Lord.

'26th. A letter from Mr Haweis, stating that in consequence of my last he had prevailed on Lord Dartmouth to give me the presentation of Olney, in Bucks, where Mr Moses Browne has many years preached the gospel. He desired to know whether I would accept it.* I would not hesitate upon a comparison of the two proposals, either with regard to my own comfortable settlement or, which I hope lies nearer to my heart, the probability of superior usefulness. I sent him my acceptance, with many thanks to him and Lord Dartmouth. Thus I find the Lord fulfilling His promises, and giving me light to lead me through the perplexities of my own mind. Had the proposal been deferred one week longer it would have been too late. Wonderful is the chain of Divine providences. My first acquaintance and renewed intimacy with Mr Haweis were quite unsought by me. I would not be too sanguine, but I cast myself in this matter upon Him who careth for me.'

On Sunday, March 4th, Mr Newton writes, 'On Thursday I received a kind letter from Lord Dartmouth, with the offer of the living at Olney, accompanied with a letter from Mr Haweis, directing me to break off everything, and to repair to London for ordination.' With this request Mr Newton immediately complied, after having procured the necessary testimonials, which were readily given.

*The curacy (such it was, not the living) was first offered to Dr Haweis himself, but he declined it, and proposed Mr Newton to Lord Dartmouth as a suitable person.

Several weeks were spent in London during the months of March and April. 'I met,' he says, 'with some difficulties, but all were overruled. My protracted stay gave me the opportunity of acquaintance with many whom perhaps I should otherwise never have known. I have cause for wonder, praise, and humiliation, when I think what favour the Lord gave me in the eyes of His people — some of rank and eminence. I was likewise exceedingly happy in point of ordinances, chiefly though not wholly, at the Lock.' He writes to Mrs Newton, April 12th, 'I was with the Bishop of Lincoln this morning, and he has fixed on Monday next for my examination.' And in speaking of it again on the 16th, he says that, 'It lasted about an hour, and was chiefly upon the principal heads of divinity. As I was resolved not to be charged hereafter with dissimulation, I was constrained to dissent from his Lordship upon some points, but he was not offended. He declared himself satisfied, and has promised to ordain me either next Sunday in town, or the Sunday following at Buckden. Let us praise the Lord.'

It was on Sunday, the 29th, that Mr Newton was admitted to deacon's order at Buckden. 'The Bishop,' he says, 'behaved throughout with the greatest candour and kindness. Having received my papers, I took leave of him the next day, and went to Olney to take a glance at the place and the people.'

On Mr Newton's return to Liverpool, he was asked to preach for two of the clergymen who had signed his testimonials. At St George's he addressed a crowded and various auditory. 'I hope,' he says, 'I was enabled to speak the truth. Some were pleased, but many disgusted. I was thought too long, too loud, too much extempore. I conformed to their judgment, so far as I lawfully might, on the Sunday when I preached at the other church in the morning, and at the Infirmary in the afternoon. The next and last Sunday I preached at Childwell, and was followed by many from town, both of my own friends and others.' Mr Newton says further in a letter to Captain Clunie: 'The Lord was very gracious to me at Liverpool. He enabled me to preach His truth before many thousands, I hope with some measure of faithfulness, I trust with some success, and in general with much greater acceptance than I could have expected. When we came away I think the bulk of the people, of all ranks and parties, were very sorry to part with us. How much do I owe to the restraining and preserving grace of God, that when I appeared in a public character, and delivered offensive truths in a place where I had lived so long, and there appeared a readiness and disposition in some to disparage my character, nothing could be found or brought to light on which they could frame an accusation!

'Monday, May 21st. This day we took our leave of Liverpool (where the Lord has shown us so many mercies during a residence of eight years), and of our many friends.' 'I think,' he says, writing to a friend, 'the bulk of the people of all ranks and parties were sorry to part with us. Slept this night at Warrington; dined on Tuesday at Manchester; reached Northampton without the least inconvenience, by the favour of a kind providence, on Friday evening, where we met some kind friends, who conducted us safely to Olney to breakfast the next morning.'

'Sunday, May 27th. Opened my commission at Olney, preaching in the morning from Psalm 80:1; afternoon, 2 Cor. 2:15, 16. Blessed be God for ennobling me and honouring me thus far. I find a cordial reception amongst those who know the truth, but many are far otherwise minded. I desire to be faithful and honest, and patiently to pursue the path of duty through both good and ill report.'

'Saturday, June 2nd. I went to desire a neighbouring clergyman to sign my testimonials for priest's orders, but he treated me with great contempt and indecency. This is the first time I ever had the honour to be publicly insulted for the gospel's sake. Lord, teach me to deserve it. Yet I found my heart ready to take fire. I desire to pray for the poor man, who meant no ill to me personally, but is unhappily prejudiced against the blessed gospel.

'On Monday waited on two other clergymen. The one readily consented, the other gave me a civil refusal.' A few days afterwards he writes, 'The affair of my testimonials is happily completed. Mr Barton, Vicar of Ravenstone, came here on Wednesday from his usual residence in Rutlandshire, and he readily complied.'

'Wednesday, 13th. To Buckden, to receive priest's orders. Called at Aldwinkle; met dear Mr Haweis, who came down but last week. We were mutually rejoiced to meet. I stayed all night. On Thursday Mr H. accompanied me a few miles on the road. Reached Buckden by noon, and was favourably received by the Bishop. Found eleven candidates for deacons' orders, and five for priests', besides myself. But, alas! few, if any of them seemed impressed with a serious sense of what they are about to undertake.'

'Sunday, 17th. This day ordained priest by the Bishop of Lincoln. My affairs went on very smoothly. I was slightly examined by the chaplain, and exhibited a Latin thesis. Much of my time at Buckden passed indifferently, being unavoidably connected with company which I should not have chosen. When afternoon service was over, the Bishop sent for me to drink tea with him, and dismissed me very kindly. On Monday returned to Olney. What shall I render to the Lord? He has carried me easily and quickly through this great business, which lately appeared so impracticable. Oh, for grace to remember the vows of God which are upon me. Lord, I would dedicate myself to Thee. Be Thou my sun and shield. Let Thy glory be my only aim, and Thy presence my exceeding great reward.'

Thus, after long patience and many disappointments, the desire of Mr Newton's heart was given him. That season of preparation was not in vain. Though self-taught he had laboured diligently in every way to qualify himself for his work; he had enjoyed much religious intercourse with some of the most intelligent and devout Christians of his time, and had been enabled, by the aid of the Holy Spirit, so to cultivate and discipline his spiritual life as to fit himself for the work to which he was at length called.

Soon after his settlement at Olney, Mr Newton received from many of his friends strong expressions of sympathy in this happy issue of his long-cherished hopes. Amongst these we find the following beautiful letter from Mr Whitefield, which, though not written till the following year, may be most suitably introduced in this place:

'REV. AND DEAR SIR,

'With great pleasure I this day received your kind letter. The contents gladdened my heart. Blessed be God, not only for calling you to the saving knowledge of Himself, but sending you forth also to proclaim the Redeemer's unsearchable riches amongst poor sinners. "God," says Dr Goodwin, "had but one Son, and He made a minister of Him." Gladly shall I come whenever bodily strength will allow to join my testimony with yours in Olney pulpit, that God is love. As yet I have not recovered from the fatigues of my American expedition. My shattered bark is scarce worth docking any more. But I would fain [gladly] wear [out], and not rust out. Oh! my dear Mr Newton, indeed and indeed I am ashamed that I have done and suffered so little for Him that hath done and suffered so much for ill and hell-deserving me. "Less than the least of all" must be my motto still. Cease not, I entreat you, to pray for me. I am sure my good old friend, Mr Hull, will join with you. As enabled, you shall both, with all your connections and dear flock, be constantly remembered by, my dear, dear sir,

'Yours, etc., etc., in a never-failing Emanuel,

'G. WHITEFIELD

'London: August 8, 1765.'

PART TWO

MR NEWTON CURATE
OF OLNEY

5: OLNEY
(1764–6)

First impressions of Olney – His ministerial work – Hampstead
– Quotations from diary – His housekeeper – *Narrative* printed
– Loss of his property – Mr Thornton – Death of Mr John Catlett
– Great House – Children's meetings – Mr Ryland – Delicacy
of feeling – New gallery – Mr Bowman – Visitors – Reflections
– Lord Dartmouth's proposal declined – Dunton – Messrs Brewer
and Clunie – Mr Thornton's liberality – Prayer meetings – Per-
sonal Experience – Illness of Mrs Newton – Correspondence with
Wesley – Samson Occum – Mr Bull – Pastoral Work – Mr
Maddock – Mr West – Letters – Proposal from Mr Venn.

Mr Newton commenced his ministry at a very important
period in the religious history of our country [Britain]. The
apostolic labours of Whitefield and Wesley and their coadjutors had
aroused the nation from its spiritual slumber, and all classes were led
to inquiry. There was not, as we have seen, a more interested spectator
of this work than Mr Newton, especially in Yorkshire; and though
circumstances prevented his taking any very prominent part in it,
it engaged all his sympathies. When he entered the Church these
feelings suffered no abatement; and though he did not feel himself
called upon to be so 'irregular' as Venn and Berridge and Haweis,
and some others of his friends, he yet steadily promoted the same
work; and before many years had passed he occupied a conspicuous
and most influential position in the Evangelical party.

Mr Newton's first impressions of Olney are given in the following words from a letter addressed, June 21st, to his friend Captain
Clunie: 'I have reason to be satisfied with my situation, if the Lord
should fix me here. I have some very cordial friends already, both in

town and country. There are some adversaries, but I think not many. Mr Browne* endured the main brunt of the opposition, and they were almost weary before he left them. The situation of the place is very pleasant at this time of year; but I suppose we shall find it cold and damp in winter. This will call for large fires, an expensive article,† but which seems in a manner necessary to my well-being. However, I, above most, have reason to depend on those words, "The Lord will provide".' It was probably somewhat later that he wrote to another friend, 'The Lord has at length brought me into the ministry, according to my desire, and beyond my hopes placed in a fruitful part of His vineyard, where his gospel is known, loved, professed, and possessed by many.'

Deeply impressed with the responsibility of his present engagements, Mr Newton at once betook himself to their fulfilment with a zeal that never grew weary, and with a skill in devising various means of usefulness which true devotion to a cause will always suggest.

On Thursday, June 28th, he commenced his weekly lecture, which was well attended. He says, 'I had a considerable auditory. Many dissenters present.' Soon after we have the following sentence: 'Read the funeral service for the first time, over a woman, and ventured to omit a clause in one of my prayers, as I propose to do in such cases hereafter.'

Speaking of a visit to Northampton in July, he observes: 'The few in these parts who love the truth are mostly such as attended upon dear Mr Hervey.‡ It is affecting to hear how they speak of him and of his death at this distance of time.'

---

* The Rev. Moses Browne was appointed vicar by Lord Dartmouth, but having a large and expensive family, he accepted the chaplaincy of Morden College, Blackheath, and thus Olney became vacant. Mr Browne was somewhat distinguished as a poet; but, what is of more consequence, he was a good man, an earnest preacher of the gospel, and had been the instrument of much good at Olney.
† Mr Newton's income was only £60 a year.
‡ Mr Hervey died in 1758.

Mrs Newton being in London in the month of July, he writes: 'I don't repent the earnest desires I long entertained toward the ministry. I rejoice in the honour the Lord has done me more than in much riches. I trust He will enable me for it at all times; yet I find it a serious, important, and difficult service to speak in His name ... All friends seem to vie in civility, and those who are not friends are kept very quiet. I neither see nor hear anything disagreeable. May the Lord give me prudence, not to provoke them unnecessarily. If they will be offended with me for preaching the truth, this I cannot help. Our friends believe that the collection will exceed twenty guineas. I am easy about it. I trust the Lord, who found me in Africa destitute of everything, who has given me you, and dealt so bountifully with us hitherto, will not forsake us, or suffer us to want any good thing, now He has so visibly displayed His power and providence in placing us here ... On Sunday a very great congregation.' In the same letter Mr Newton says, 'The moment the coach was out of sight, I set off for Olney. Passing through Emberton, an old woman came after me, and invited me to her cottage. I went. Five or six women soon joined us. We talked, sang a hymn, and prayed, and I thought it a good bait by the way.'

Scarcely was Mr Newton settled at Olney, before some of his friends, perhaps not very wisely, suggested to him another and better position at Hampstead. But he most judiciously declined even to entertain the thought of such a change. He writes thus on the subject to Mrs Newton, July 14th: 'I observe what you hint about Hampstead; it would indeed be a situation in many respects desirable, and was I to be governed only by my affection for you, I could not but wish to see you placed in circumstances so much more agreeable than I can expect to procure at Olney. But let us take warning by the striking example of Mr Browne, and rather prefer the place where the Lord shall fix us to an over-hasty prospect of great things. I have convincing proof that the Lord has led us thus far; and without as clear an intimation of His will, I hope I shall not indulge the remotest wish for a removal. The people love me so well, express so warm a desire of the gospel's continuance among them, our assemblies are so crowded, and the Lord's presence (as I trust) so comfortably with us, that I should be base and ungrateful, and even blind to my own comfort if I was not satisfied. On Sunday we had a larger congregation than ever, and it seems as if it would increase every week... Last night I was at Mr Walker's meeting, to hear Mr Grant, from Wellingborough. A more excellent sermon I never heard; never was my heart so melted down since the golden days when I first attended Mr Brewer and Mr Whitefield. It was a pleasing sight to see the warmth of a young convert and the solid experience of an aged Christian of seventy united. It was likewise a very suitable word to follow the intimation you had given me of Hampstead. His text was Exodus 33:15. I hope I shall never forget the advice he gave us in the ministry, for we were all there ... I am engaged to dine with Mr Grant at Mr Ashburner's. I shall take this opportunity to set the door of acquaintance wide open. If they choose to keep it so, it is well; if not, I have but done my duty.'

Mr Newton's manner of life at this period is thus described in his diary:

'July 19th. My time passes pretty evenly. In the forenoon I write and read. In the afternoon walk about an hour or two among the people, and sometimes drink tea with them.'

Again, '25th. Walked to Emberton, and spent a pleasant hour with M. Cooper and seven or eight of her companion-cottagers. What an admirable thing is the grace of God — adapted to every state of life! It makes the rich humble, and the poor happy. I have been favoured with the sight of grace in persons of distinction and splendid appointments, and it affords a pleasing view there. I bless the Lord I can visit it with as much pleasure when it dwells within mud walls, and lies buried from public observation under a roof of thatch.'

In a letter to Mrs Newton, on the 28th, after writing of graver matters, he indulges in the following strain concerning his housekeeper:

'I miss you every hour, yet am tolerably easy without you. The Lord has been pleased to bless me with a peaceful frame of mind ever since we parted; and the house is so snug and quiet, I seldom care to leave it. I talked of going to Kettering, Aldwinkle, etc., but have no inclination to stir from home. My housekeeper suits me well. In many respects she supplies your place: she calls me out of the garden when it's cold, puts me on my great coat, watches my countenance, and asks me if I am well several times a day, tells me if she is afraid this or the other will not agree with me. On the other hand, I read some of my letters to her before I send them away, read books to her, in short, in all common matters she does as well as the finest and politest lady in England would do. I want no other company till I can have yours. About ten o'clock I bolt her out, and let her in at six. I come down to breakfast at eight, find all ready, up again to the study till one. When the clock strikes I go down, to find the dinner upon the table. In the afternoon we entertain one another, as I have said — only when I take my rounds among the people or my walks in an evening. And thus we go on regularly as the chimes, or much more so, for they have been out of order several times. How I have laboured to get towards the bottom of the paper! It draws towards eleven. Good night, my dearest. My love to all friends. Pray for your affectionate and obliged husband,   JOHN NEWTON.'

'Sunday, 29th. A good deal of company at home, for I have desired those who come from far to dine with me on the Sunday. I trust the Lord will enable me to keep up this custom.' Some, it appears, came in from six or more miles' distance.

Mr Newton's *Narrative*, of which such frequent mention has been made, had been read by many, but was hitherto only in manuscript. In the month of August it was published, with a preface by Dr Haweis. It naturally awakened a good deal of attention. Mr Newton writes: 'I have reason to hope that the publication of my letters will give some additional weight to my ministry here. The people stare at me since reading them and well they may. I am indeed a wonder to many, a wonder to myself, especially I wonder that I wonder no more.'

Many friends congratulated Mr Newton on this publication. 'I rejoice exceedingly,' says his old friend Mr Edwards of Leeds, 'that your letters are gone to the press. Such a narrative of the wonders of Divine providence and grace, in favour of one poor sinner, will certainly bid fair to excite other poor prodigals to come and taste and see how gracious the Lord is. And I think they cannot fail of a favourable acceptance in the Christian world.'

At the beginning of September, Mr Newton is at Aldwinkle on a visit to Mr Haweis, and preaches in the neighbourhood. In November Mr Berridge is with him, and he says how much he enjoyed his preaching and his conversation.

November 1st, he writes: 'A young woman, who came from Sherington to attend the machine for the relief of a rheumatic disorder,* had the opportunity of attending church, and told me today that the Lord had been pleased to own my poor word to her conviction.'

In November, Mr Newton hears of the failure of his friend, Mr Manesty, and he thus beautifully remarks upon it: 'Had advice today that my friend, J.M., at Liverpool, is bankrupt, so I suppose what I had in his hands is quite lost. It was not much, but it was my all. I repine not at this. The Lord has made him an instrument of much good to me in times past; and though creatures fail, the Lord will not want means to give me what He sees necessary; but I am concerned for him and his.' He had looked to this little reserve, he says, to meet the expenses of his removal and settlement. But he can trust the Lord. 'If He send it as fast as I want it, is not this sufficient? Is not the money in the bank as good as money in the house? And are not the promises of the all-sufficient God better and surer than a whole realm of bank-bills?'

---

* Mr. Newton still practised with his electrical machine.

This unusual trust in God was soon to be rewarded in a very signal manner; and the spring that failed, dried up in one place only to break forth in a far more abundant supply in another.

Mr Newton thanks his friend Captain Clunie for Bibles and books, procured through him from the Book Society. 'Persons,' he says, 'to whom I give the Bibles value them more than gold. We have many here who esteem the Word of God as their food, and yet are very poor, and unable to buy a Bible. Several such hearts I have gladdened by what I received from you and Mr Gwyther.'

And in reference to his congregation, he says (it is in November he writes), 'Neither short days, uncertain weather, or dirty roads, make any considerable diminution in our assemblies, and their attention and seriousness gives us hope that they do not all come in vain.'

'November 6th. Walked today to Denton (six miles from Olney), and spent a few hours with a little knot of the Lord's people.'

'Saturday, 17th. My leisure chiefly taken up this week with writing letters. Indeed my correspondence is so large, that it almost engrosses my time (pulpit preparations excepted), and I know not well how to contract it.'

'Friday, December 6th. Amongst the few to whom I intended to present one of my books, I thought of Mr Thornton, and lately wrote him a letter to beg his acceptance of it. I had one from him today, which seems to promise acquaintance, and assistance of which I had no expectation. Surely it is of the Lord. He gives me favour in the eyes of others. May I be humble, and depend upon Him alone, and not trust in the best and greatest any further than as instruments. By his writing he seems truly serious and spiritual. I hope he will be a means of increasing my usefulness and acceptance.' Mr Thornton's reply was accompanied with an expression of his good-will, in the shape of substantial pecuniary assistance. And this was soon followed by presents of books, for the poor and for Mr Newton himself.

In July of this year we find the commencement of Mr Newton's correspondence with Mrs Wilberforce, aunt to the distinguished

William Wilberforce, and sister to Mr Thornton. Mrs Wilberforce was probably one of the valuable friends he speaks of having found in his visits to London. And thus he might have been already introduced to the excellent and large-hearted John Thornton. At any rate, his acquaintance with the latter soon ripened into an intimacy which was productive in many ways of the most important issues to Mr Newton, and to the great cause of evangelical piety, so dear to the hearts of both these good men.

Frequent mention has been made of Mr Newton's brother-in-law, Mr John Catlett, and of the deep interest and earnest efforts of his relation for his spiritual good. In December he was attacked by fever, and died after a few days' illness.

On the 1st January, 1765, Mr Newton writes: 'The last year filled with distinguishing mercy. My introduction to the ministry and my dear's recovery, together with the liberty, acceptance, success, and comfort I have been favoured with here, call for special acknowledgement. Preached the annual sermon to the young in the evening. The young people usually make a present on this occasion. It was much larger than at any former time.

'I propose to establish three meetings — one for the children, another for young and inquiring persons, and a third to be a meeting with the more experienced and judicious, for prayer and conference. The first I am particularly solicitous about, as a matter of indispensable duty.'

There was at this time in Olney a mansion commonly called the Great House, the property of Lord Dartmouth.* Being unoccupied, and Mr Newton thinking its spacious rooms might be available for some of his religious services, he obtained use of it, in the first instance for the meetings of the children. It became henceforth the scene of many very happy Christian gatherings. Here he began to

* This mansion stood at the south end of the town, not far from the church. It was erected by William Johnson, Esq., who settled at Olney about 1642. It subsequently became the property of the Dartmouth family. For an engraving and description see *Sunday at Home* for 1857.

meet the children on Thursday afternoon; 'not so much,' he says, 'to teach them a catechism (though I shall attend to that likewise) as to talk, preach, and reason with them, and explain the Scriptures to them in their own little way.' The number so increased that ultimately it was necessary to remove them to the chancel. Here more than two hundred would sometimes be gathered. Mr Newton also commenced in the Great House an evening meeting for prayer and exhortation, which proved a service of great interest and usefulness.

'Sunday, 27th. Congregations large and serious. Almost every week I hear of some either awakened or seriously impressed. We have now a fixed little company who come to my house on Sabbath evening after tea. We spend an hour or more in prayer and singing, and part between six and seven.'

'Friday, February 22nd. Set out this morning at ten — walked with three or four friends to Mr James', near Denton, to meet Mr Ryland* of Northampton, by appointment. Our first interview an agreeable one. After dinner we had a little congregation. I began with prayer. He preached from Matthew 4:16, and Mr Smith of Barton concluded with prayer. Returned home by seven. Had a pleasant walk both ways.'

Writing to a friend in the month of March, he says: 'All my plantations flourish. The prayer-meeting is well attended, and in general, I hope, proves a time of refreshment; so that some of the younger and more lively sort are encouraged to attempt another on Sunday mornings at six o'clock, to pray for their poor minister and for a blessing on the ordinances.' He adds a request for some accounts of the Lord's work in America: 'Such is the news I want. I am little concerned with the treaties and policies of the kings of the earth; but I long to hear of the victories and triumphs of our King Jesus, and that the trophies of His grace are multiplied.'

'April 19th. Have some thoughts of making a little excursion to London, if Mr Browne comes down as he proposes. He seems

* Rev. John Ryland, Baptist minister, father of Dr Ryland.

desirous I should; and perhaps it may be as well to avoid occasions of jealousy and partiality. If my heart does not deceive me greatly, I am so far from being afraid, that I am really desirous he may be received with the greatest respect and tenderness, and I recommend it upon all occasions; but some might perhaps grieve him by an injudicious expression in their regard for me.'

Accordingly, in May Mr Newton went to London, where he preached not less than fourteen times. Again in July he made a preaching tour in the country, declaring the truth in houses and churches, as he had opportunity.

The accommodation in the church at Olney was insufficient for the large numbers who now regularly attended Mr Newton's ministry, and, to meet this want, he was anxious to erect a gallery. This object was effected, and it was opened in July; but 'there seemed no more room in the body of the church than before.'

August 4th, he writes to Mr Clunie: 'The people are as lively and attentive as ever. All our meetings are well attended, and some new additions, which I have good hopes of ... I have been engaged about six hours in speaking at church and at home, yet find myself in good case, little or nothing fatigued; but, if there was occasion, I could readily go and preach again.'

In the previous month Mr Wilberforce, with another friend, paid a visit to Olney. 'We had,' says Mr Newton, 'many opportunities of prayer and converse, and they seemed much pleased with the people.' About the same time Mr Newton visited Northampton. 'Met Mrs West at Mr Ryland's by appointment. Had the pleasure of conversing with many of the Lord's dear children, particularly Mr Hextal, the Independent minister. Mr Ryland would have had me preach at his house, and the people had been prepared to expect that I should do so; but I thought better to decline it. The next day (it was Thursday) returned, and brought Mrs West and Mr Ryland with us.'

'Friday. The day spent mostly in conversation. In the evening Mr Ryland preached at Mr Walker's meeting (Baptist) from 1 Thessalonians 4:3; a good and seasonable discourse. May the Lord bless it to the hearers.'

In September of this year Mr Newton commenced his correspondence with Mr Bowman, vicar of Martham, Norfolk. Six letters to him will be found in the second volume of *Cardiphonia*. In the first of them, written at this time, he says that he had heard of him in the month of June when in London, and had since read a volume of his sermons. 'Though,' he writes, 'we have no acquaintance, we are already united in the strictest ties of friendship, partakers of the same hope, servants of the same Lord, and in the same part of His vineyard. I therefore hold all apologies needless.' Mr Newton then goes on to speak of 'the pleasant lot' to which the Lord had led him, where the gospel had been known many years, and was highly valued by many.

In September Mr Newton writes: 'One of my great complaints is that my time flies away and nothing done. This is much owing to my having lost the habit of early rising. This not only breaks in upon my study, but cuts me short of secret exercises. What wonder I am lean when I often miss my regular meals!

'. . . I seek, I want, I mourn all too faintly, but I trust my desire is to Jesus and holiness. I want more communion with Him, more conformity to Him. Oh, when shall it be?'

'Sunday, 13th. In the evening had a full house. I have lately sent tickets to those who I hope are serious, to exclude some who only come to look about them. Upon these occasions I have reckoned about seventy persons of both sexes, of whom I have good hope the Lord has touched their hearts. Oh that I had a greater thirst for souls.

'Monday, 14th. Have appointed a meeting for conversation at my own house on Monday evenings for the few men who belong to our little society.'

In November of this year a proposal was made to Mr Newton which, had he seen it right to accept, would have given an entirely new direction to his future life, and probably the Christian world would have known little more of him than as the author of the *Narrative* of a most remarkable conversion to God.

He went to London at the wish of Lord Dartmouth, and writes thence to Mrs Newton in the following terms: 'The secret is out. My first suspicion is right. My Lord' (Lord Dartmouth) 'is the prime manager of Georgia. Mr Whitefield's orphan-house is to be converted into a seminary, college, or university; and Mr Newton is desired to be president thereof, with the annexed living of Savanna, the chief town. My love to Olney and your hatred of the water are the chief reasons which moved me to say I would not accept it, otherwise it is a most important service.' Elsewhere he says: 'The offer is great; but unless the Lord calls and clears my way, may I be preserved from listening to the sound of honour and profit.'

'Tuesday, 26th. Omitted our prayer-meeting tonight and attended Mr Bradbury, who preached a very good sermon at Mr Drake's. I am glad of such opportunities at times, to discountenance bigotry and party spirit, and to set our dissenting brethren an example, which I think ought to be our practice towards all who love the Lord Jesus Christ and preach His gospel without respect to forms or denominations.

'Wednesday. Mr Bradbury came to me about eleven and stayed [for] dinner. I like his spirit well.'

'Wednesday, 18th. Some days since a cordial letter from Mr Moody, rector of Dunton, to inform me that, having seen my *Narrative*, he desired an interview.' This invitation was accepted by Mr Newton, who also visited Winslow, 'where,' he says, 'I found a few pilgrims. We seemed to rejoice to see each other. Left Dunton this morning, and returned in safety to my peaceful, happy home.'

'Monday, 23rd. My dear friend Mr Brewer arrived, with Mr Clunie. My heart rejoices to see him, and I hope I have prayed the Lord to make his visit a blessing.

'Tuesday. Mr Brewer spoke tonight at the prayer-meeting from 2 Corinthians 7:6, an affecting subject, and a melting season to most present. The Lord grant it may be attended with much good, and make us thankful for our peculiar privileges.

'Wednesday, December 25th. Preached this morning and administered the sacrament. Afternoon, Mr Brewer at Mr Drake's. In the evening it was my turn again. I hope it was a good day, a feast day to many.

'Thursday. Took my friend in the morning to see some of our dear people, with whom he was much comforted. He preached in the afternoon at Mr Walker's from Matthew 3:16–18. In the evening I preached the lecture. Mr Drake and Mr Walker dined with us.

'Friday. This day we had chiefly to ourselves; but in the evening we had an occasional prayer-meeting at my dear friend's desire, which was very full. He took leave of the people in an affectionate prayer and a warm, seasonable discourse from Acts 2:42. It was a solemn, refreshing time, and we mutually commended each other to God with many tears.

On the last day of the year, after referring to the many mercies of the past, Mr Newton adds: 'Oh for a thankful heart. We are highly favoured. I am especially. What times have I lived to see! and yet what returns! Lord, pardon, accept, inspire. I would be Thine only, and for ever.'

Eighteen months had now elapsed since Mr Newton commenced his ministry at Olney. It seems to us impossible to read this interesting detail of his labours, characterized by so much that was earnest and conscientious and Christian – of his happy contentment and trust in God, of his large catholic spirit, of his kindly and ever-wakeful sympathy, of the many valuable friends who seemed to be irresistibly attracted by his genial and devout temper – and not admire the man, and bless God on his behalf. One thing might awaken our surprise, and even lead to the thought of imprudence on the part of Mr Newton, were we not in possession of the key to its solution. We have seen that the vicarage at Olney was seldom without guests, that many came from far to seek his counsel, or to enjoy the benefits of his society and ministry; and it may well be asked, how could he thus keep open house upon the scanty income he was receiving? The simple explanation is this — Mr Thornton, as soon as he became acquainted with Mr Newton, evidently formed a high estimate of his character. He was fully aware of the peculiarity of his circumstances, and of the expenses his position was likely to involve; and so, in the exercise of his singular liberality, which so often flowed in unusual channels, he annually contributed a large sum to supply the wants of his friend. 'Be hospitable,' he says, 'and keep an open house for such as are worthy of entertainment — help the poor and needy: I will statedly allow you £200 a year, and readily send whenever you have occasion to draw for more.' 'Mr Newton told me,' says Mr Cecil, 'that he thought he had received of Mr Thornton upwards of £3,000 in this way during the time he resided at Olney.' This circumstance is unquestionably not one of the least remarkable in Mr Newton's singular history. He came to Olney having given up much for God, and yet with implicit reliance upon the Divine bounty, taking as his motto, 'The Lord will provide.' His trust was not in vain.

He thus speaks of Mr Thornton's kindness: 'What astonishing dispensation have I seen, and still the Lord seems to lead me in a peculiar way — a way that calls for a peculiar humility, self-abasement, watchfulness, and prayer.'

1766. Mr Newton continuing to do good after his own special manner, says: 'January 8. Set out early and walked to Yardley — breakfasted at Mr Garlick's; stayed till eleven — thence to Denton; stayed till half-past three — returned safe by dark; and I hope on the whole it was a profitable day.'

'Saturday, 11th. Walked to Ravenstone. Endeavoured to put the few people who know the Lord there (as I did at Denton) upon forming themselves into a little society to meet for prayer. I have seen good effects, I trust, from these prayer-meetings at Olney, and would therefore recommend the practice to others.'

'Friday, 17th. Another excursion today with Christian friends. Had a very pleasant walk to Turvey. Added two gracious women there to my stock of Christian acquaintances. Had much conversation there and by the way, with which I hope we were all refreshed.'

Thus did Mr Newton cultivate and promote the friendship of the saints, and thus piously endeavour to search out and to build up in their most holy faith the scattered members of Christ's flock. It mattered little to this truly good and earnest man how humble or how poor they might be, so long as they were among the number of true believers.

And now follows a reference to his own personal experience: 'Saturday . . . My inward frame I know not how to describe. In general I seem unable to get near the Lord, and yet by grace am restrained from wandering very far away. Coldness in prayer, and darkness and formality in reading the Word are almost my continual burden. I want to be more lively, feeling, and affectionate in spiritual things, but I feel the dead weight of unbelief and indwelling sin keeping me low. I think my desire is towards the Lord. My hope, my trust is in Jesus; other refuge I neither have nor desire.'

In a letter written at this time to Mr Bowman, Mr Newton speaks of his high estimate of the writings of Dr Owen. He says: 'I agree with you in assigning one of the first places as a teacher to Dr Owen. I have just finished his discourse upon the Holy Spirit,* which is an epitome, if not the master-piece of his writings.' He then speaks with great admiration of Archbishop Leighton's *Commentary and Prælections*.

And referring to another topic, he says: 'You send us good news indeed, that two more of your brethren are declaring on the gospel side. The Lord confirm and strengthen them, add yet to your numbers, and make you helps and comforts to each other. Surely He is about to spread His work.'

* This is in Owen's *Works*, vol. 3, reprinted, London: Banner of Truth, 1965.

Saturday, 8th, he writes: 'Nothing yet done, nor as I see, can yet be done, in the troublesome affair of Aldwinkle.' *

Towards the end of February Mrs Newton was dangerously ill; and in a letter to his friend Mrs West, Mr Newton says, in reference to this event: 'I can assure you, upon new and repeated experience, that the Lord is good, a stronghold in the day of trouble, and He knoweth them that put their trust in Him. The Lord hath been pleased to put us in the fire; but, blessed be His name, we are not burnt. Oh, that we may be brought out refined, and that the event may be to the praise of His grace and power! Mrs Newton was taken ill on Monday, the 24th of February, and from that till last Wednesday was a sharp season. But let me not forget to tell you that this visitation was accompanied with spiritual supports both to her and to myself. I believe the Lord gave our dear people a remarkable tenderness of spirit to sympathise with us, and to strive in prayer as one man in our behalf. Oh what a privilege is it to be interested in the prayers of those who fear the Lord!'

It may not be uninteresting to speak in this place of a correspondence between Mr Newton and the Rev. John Wesley, upon some points in which they differed. This subject, however, is not introduced with any view to the statement of the arguments on either side of the questions in dispute, which, were it desirable, could not be done, inasmuch as the correspondence is incomplete on Mr Newton's side, but just to show the spirit of each of these good men, and how Christians may differ and yet not disagree.

The occasion of Mr Wesley's first letter to Mr Newton, which is dated April of the preceding year, was the perusal of the *Narrative*. He tells him that what he there says of Particular Redemption, and the points connected therewith is spoken in so cool and dispassion-

---

* The reference is to the circumstances under which Dr.Haweis held the living of Aldwinkle, a matter about which there was a great difference of opinion amongst his friends. It is, however, only just to say that some who did not approve of his conduct in this instance still entertained a high opinion of his piety and worth.

ate a manner as cannot give offence to any reasonable man; that their acquaintance ('perhaps I may say even the friendship, between you and me') was commenced on the ground of faith in Jesus Christ and in a life suitable to such a profession. 'We both knew there was a difference in our opinions, and consequently in our expressions. But, notwithstanding this, we tasted each other's spirits, and often took sweet counsel together, and what hinders it now?' Reference is then made by Mr Wesley to the statement of Mr Hervey respecting himself and his sentiments, and to his impression that even Mr Newton was thus made afraid of him.

Mr Newton replied in a few days, and the first paragraphs of his letter are as follows:

'I thank you heartily for the opportunity of reviving a correspondence which always was, and I am persuaded will be, both pleasing and profitable to me. I can assure you the interruption was not owing to any abatement of my regard to you, neither was it simply negligence, but some things that happened after I saw you last embarrassed me. I knew not how to write without either baulking the freedom of my own spirit or assuming a part from me to you which I thought would appear unbecoming and forward. I thank you for giving our past acquaintance the tender name of friendship; so I was desirous it should be on my part; so I always found it on yours. May this friendship flourish. I hope I shall do nothing to forfeit it. I trust I still do, and shall account it both a pleasure and an honour to be considered in the number of your friends.

'As you doubtless expect an ingenuous answer, I shall make no apology for writing freely, though if you had not put the occasion in my hand I should have thought that, your years, character, and services considered, it would be (as I have hinted already) impertinent in one of my standing to address you with any other view than that of receiving your advice and instructions. And this is still (those things excepted in which we must unavoidably differ) my chief motive for wishing our correspondence may continue.'

Mr Newton then proceeds, in a very decided but most Christian temper, to advocate his views on the subjects of Particular Redemption, Final Perseverance, and the doctrine of Perfection.

Mr Wesley writes again in May, and thus commences his letter: 'Your manner of writing needs no excuse. I hope you will always write in the same manner. Love is the plainest thing in the world. I know this dictates what you write, and then what need of ceremony?'

This correspondence was closed by two letters more from Mr Wesley, controversial, but still Christian and conciliatory, to which Mr Newton no doubt replied in a like strain.

'March 12. A visit from Mr Symonds. He is supplying a vacancy at Bedford.* I shall be glad if the Lord sees fit to fix him there. I think him a sensible, spiritual, humble young man, and believe he would make an agreeable and useful neighbour. Heard him preach in the evening from John 12:21.'

'May 3rd. Engaged to preach at Bozeat, but prevented, as I understand, by the efforts of the neighbouring clergy. I desire to value the privilege of Olney.'

'Monday, 9th June. Went in a postchaise, and brought Mr Occum, the Indian,† from Northampton. He preached in the evening to a great auditory, and said many things of the Lord's work in America.'

---

* The Congregational church assembling at what is now called 'Bunyan Meeting House.'

† The Rev. Samson Occum was a Mohegan [Mohican?] Indian. This tribe was visited by Mr Whitefield, M. Tennant, and other ministers; and Occum became the subject of religious impressions. Desirous of being useful to his tribe, he went for instruction to the Indian school of Dr Wheelock; and after teaching for some years, he was ordained to the ministry, and became a zealous preacher amongst his own people. Coming to England on behalf of the Indian charity school, he was received with great kindness by Lady Huntingdon, and preached with much popularity in various parts of the kingdom .— See *Life and Times of the Countess of Huntingdon*, i. 411.

'Saturday, 14th June. The long-expected visit of my Lord Dartmouth and Mr Madan* took place. It was a good time. What do I owe the Lord for such countenance on every side! My house is now to be enlarged to my mind. I preached twice on Sunday, and Mr Madan in the evening — a great auditory, and an excellent sermon. My noble guest left us on Tuesday. Much affected with his kindness and generosity, and the Lord's goodness to us. The rest of the week had Mr Foster,† a gracious student from Oxford, and Mr Stuart, son of the Lord Provost of Edinburgh, a prodigy of grace and knowledge for his years. He went this morning, and now we have Mr Clunie and Oswald. I find some inconvenience from such an incessant round of company, and am endangered by so many favours and distinctions on all hands. I want retirement, and find my spirits too often discomposed. But O Lord, help! I desire the light of Thy countenance, and to consider everything but loss and of small account without Thee.'

'Sunday, 22nd. Instead of our usual meeting in the evening, attended at Mr Drake's, to hear Mr Ashburner of this place, who has lately finished his studies and entered the ministry. He promises to be a useful, spiritual minister. The Lord make him such.'

About this time Mr Newton was introduced to the Rev. William Bull, of Newport. This acquaintance soon ripened into a most intimate, and, as it proved, life-long friendship. The fourteen last letters in the second volume of *Cardiphonia* are addressed to this friend. There is also an entire volume of Mr Newton's letters to Mr Bull, which was published separately in the year 1847.

Again Mr Newton speaks of Mr Symonds. He was about to be settled at Bedford, and called at Olney on his way thither. 'He spoke at the Great House, much,' says Mr Newton, 'to my gratification, and I hope I was not at all pleased when some of the people told me afterwards that they would rather have heard me.'

* The Rev. Martin Madan, founder and first chaplain of the Lock Hospital.
† The Rev. Henry Foster, afterwards rector of St. James's, Clerkenwell, London.

In a letter addressed, about this time, to Captain Clunie, Mr Newton tells him of a new meeting, in which he says: 'My sheep and lambs are to be divided into small flocks of eight, or ten, or twelve at a time, for conversation, so that their turns will come round about once in six weeks. Pray for us, that we may be healthy and thriving, and that the wolf may be kept from the fold. I have about twenty lambs, every one of which is worth more than all the cattle that will be in Smithfield these seven years.' There still remains a memorandum-book containing lists of these classes.

To his brother-in-law, Mr Cunningham, Mr Newton writes: 'I hope you approve Mr Witherspoon's books. I think his *Treatise upon Regeneration* is the best I have seen upon this important subject. How few are there, in this day of dissipation, who understand what is meant by being born again! how much fewer have experience of it in themselves! and yet Jesus Christ Himself has said that without it no man can enter the kingdom of heaven.'

'July 29th. For some days past I have been able to be close and steady in retrieving my time in secret exercises, etc. The Lord help me to persevere.'

'Sunday, August 3rd. Captain Scott* and Mr Barrett, two Christian officers from Northampton, visited us. Blessed be God, His grace appears in some instruments in every station of life. Our prayer-meeting to-night greatly crowded.'

'August 6th, Wednesday. Set out for Kettering. A safe and pleasant journey; an agreeable interview with Mr Maddock.† He complains he has little success. I have reason to praise God for placing me where He has so many lively people, and where the spirit of opposition in

---

* Captain Scott, of whom we shall have occasion to speak hereafter, was a convert of Mr Romaine. The circumstances connected with that important event are related in the *Life and Times of the Countess of Huntingdon*, i. 317.

† This good man, we are told, in the *Life and Times of the Countess of Huntingdon*, after labouring faithfully at Kettering for nine years, and suffering much persecution, was driven away for no other reason than the crime of collecting large congregations, and being blessed to the conversion of many souls.

others is so much suppressed. With him it is otherwise. He has many gainsayers, and few to strengthen his hands.'

'Sunday, 7th September. A larger number of communicants than usual, several from Northampton' (twelve miles distance from Olney).

'Tuesday, 9th. At the prayer-meeting spoke from 2 Peter 1:10, chiefly on account of my maid, Molly, who is perplexed and tempted on the point of election.'

Mrs Newton was now absent in London, and very admirable are the letters her husband addresses to her on this occasion. 'I hope,' he says, 'you will take care of your heart, and your time. You have many errands at the throne of grace, both for yourself and for me. Pray that I may be kept from every evil, and that when we meet, we may meet with praise. I have had a visit from a lively and judicious Christian from Shipton, in Worcestershire. His name is Richard Rand. He had heard famous things of Olney, and came to see it.'

Again, in a subsequent letter to her, he says: 'You might find a richer people, but none, I think, who would love you better. I have the question to answer many times a day, "when does Madam come home?" They think the home looks so *unked* [lonely, dreary] without you ... I hope we shall be thinking and praying for each other some part of the day at the same minute, and that particularly our hearts will meet when you are at Mr West's and I at the Great House.'

'22nd. Captain Scott and Mr Barrett came, to avoid the races at Northampton. Thursday. Set out with my two friends to visit Mr Berridge; preached for him in the evening. I had a good number to hear me, and some from far.'

About a fortnight afterwards Mr Newton revisited his few Christian friends at Winslow.

'Thursday, October 7th. Proposed to spend this day in prayer, with fasting. I have not observed a day in this manner since I came to Olney. I am sensible of the advantage of occasional seasons of more solemn retirement. As the weather was fine, I chose to wander in the woods and fields. I hope the Lord was, in a measure, with me, and gave me some sincere desires and breathings.'

'Tuesday, October 14th. Instead of meeting at the Great House, we attended on Mr Hall,* of Arnsby. He called on me twice, and seems a man of a right spirit.'

During the month of November Mr Newton received a letter from Mr Venn, in which the latter says: '. . . I know not how your situation is at Olney; but this I am sure of, that I am bound to do the best I can in providing a good shepherd for as large a flock as at Slaughwaite. And, if Mr Newton would choose it, of all the men in the world I should prefer him. The income is certain, fifty-six pounds per annum. I have but little hope of your seeing it a call to you . . . I never long forget either of you, my dear friends. I have much communion with you, and remember you where I can do you the most good.

'In a long tour I have been taking, I have seen some very glorious instances of the power of Jesus — particularly in Wales. Mr Howell Harris has a large company of people — I think the most excellent I ever saw. There is united in them the deepest humiliation before God, as vile and abominable in themselves, and yet a most striking confidence and rejoicing in the Lord. When I left these happy exemplary followers of Jesus, I came through Shropshire to Manchester, where our friends are going on prosperously.'

Mr. Newton declined this offer of Mr. Venn; but his mind was soon to be exercised, and as we shall see, somewhat painfully, with another offer, which he felt could by no means be dismissed without serious thought.

---

* Father of the Rev. Robert Hall, and the author of *Help to Zion's Travellers*.

6: OLNEY
(1767–9)

'The Cottenham Affair' – Publishes sermons – Journey into Yorkshire – Visitors – Journey to Huntingdon – Letter to Mr Cowper
– Mr Unwin and Mr Cowper at Olney – New Vicarage – Reflections – Catholic Spirit – Correspondence of Capt. Scott and Mr
Newton – Mr Newton in Norfolk – Letters – Dr Dixon – State
of things at Olney – Letters – Great Room in the Great House
– Capt. Scott – Cards – Collingtree – Oxford – Illness – Death
of Capt. Clunie – Publishes his *Review of Ecclesiastical History* –
Remarks thereon.

The commencement of the following year gives us the story of
the proposed change and its issue.

Mr Newton, it appears, was put in nomination for the living of
Cottenham, in Cambridgeshire, but was greatly perplexed to know
how to decide the matter. He thus speaks in reference to it: 'When
I look round me upon my dear people, I am willing (as the thing is
not yet finally determined) to pray and hope that the Lord will direct
to some expedient at once, to supply the opening for Cottenham,
and to gratify our desire of continuing together. I know the great
Healer of breaches can provide Olney with a better shepherd, and
fully make up the loss of unworthy me. Oh, that it may be so if He
takes me away; but there is such a natural affection and suitableness
between us, through His blessing, that will make a separation, however circumstanced, very painful on both sides, at least for a season.'

Mr Newton went to London, saw Lord Dartmouth and Mr Thornton, and, to use his own expression, 'came home with a happy event
of my journey', and on the following Sunday he preached thanksgiving sermons.

He says: 'I told Mr Thornton my unanswerable objections to leaving Olney, and he was far from being offended with me. Mr Conyers is against him for the pressing way of his dealing; and I believe, from what I can yet judge, neither he nor I have a single friend in London but what judges my removal from Olney would be a wrong and dangerous step. I am just come from Lord Dartmouth, and he expressed much satisfaction at my resolution to stay, as I did not see it, in conscience, right to go.'

On the review of these circumstances, he says: 'The Lord wonderfully interposed, and I account it one of the greatest and most valuable deliverances in the course of my life; for it seemed to me that if it had taken place I must have sunk under the weight of a broken heart. Now it is over I can bless the Lord for having knit me and my dear people so close in mutual affection; and I hope that nothing but the express intimation of His will would be henceforth able to separate us.'

In the preceding year Mr Newton prepared a volume of sermons for the press. They were now published. 'My design in printing them', says the author, 'was twofold. First, to exhibit a specimen of the doctrines I taught, to satisfy those who desired information, and if possible to stop the mouth of slander; and second, to promote the edification of my people.'

Early in March, when the Cottenham affair was 'happily settled,' Mr Newton, having taken a farewell of his people on the Tuesday evening prayer-meeting, set out with Mrs Newton for Yorkshire. On their way to Ferrybridge the chaise broke down, but the accident did not occasion any serious hurt or inconvenience. At Aberford they called on Mr Ingham, and after a few days' travelling reached Helmsley, the residence of Mr Conyers, Mr Thornton's brother-in-law. Mr Newton preached there and in the neighbourhood, and speaks of the happy times he passed with 'dear Mr Conyers and his people.'

On the 30th March they quit Helmsley, and visit their old friends at Hunslet. There Mr Newton preached, and again at Kippax on the following Sunday. On the 6th April the day was spent in praying, conversing, and expounding. He sees his old friends, Mr Edwards at Leeds, and Mr Scott, the Independent minister at Cleckheaton, goes to Yeadon, and renews his acquaintance there, spending a pleasant day with 'his dear friends'. On the 11th, taking leave of Leeds, they proceed to Huddersfield, and on the next Sunday Mr Newton preaches twice for Mr Venn. Then two days afterwards he is at Manchester. Reaches Liverpool on Thursday, and preaches there on Friday and Sunday, and again the following week. His visit to Liverpool naturally awakened mingled feelings of pleasure and pain. 'It was,' he says, 'a scene of incessant hurry — seeing friends the whole time — my spirits depressed.' He adds, however, that he was graciously supported in public service, though under many disadvantages, and chiefly the want of seasons and opportunity for secret duties.

He is at Berwick on the 25th; preaches and visits the prisoners in the jail. The 5th of May he arrives at Wem, and preaches at the house of Mr Henshaw. On the 7th, his friend, Captain Scott, who was now settled in that neighbourhood, spends the day with him. Mr Newton has converse with many Christian friends; and having elsewhere on this wise fulfilled his ministry, arrives on the 12th of May at Warwick. 'The people,' he says, 'amongst whom my mouth was first opened, and where I met some sweet encouragement on my first entrance to the ministry, will always be dear to me.' He calls on Mr Venner, and adds: 'It gave me much pleasure to have that long breach healed.' On Saturday, 16th, Mr Newton reached home, and remarks: 'So great a journey (six hundred and fifty miles) without hurt, and to find all well at home, calls for earnest praise.'

In June of this year, the Rev. Dr Conyers spent a few days with Mr Newton at Olney. At this time, the Rev. Mr Unwin and Mrs Unwin were residing at Huntingdon, and Mr Cowper, then unknown to fame, was an inmate of their family. Dr Conyers requested Mr Newton to pay them a visit, and he did so not long after. But in the interval Mr Unwin met with a fatal accident. Under these circumstances, it was found necessary that Mrs Unwin should change her residence; this brief interview with Mr Newton, and a subsequent visit to Olney, led to a desire on all sides that they should become neighbours. The circumstances of Mr Cowper's close connection with the Unwin family are well known; and Mr Newton informs us in his unfinished sketch of Mr Cowper's history, that Mr Unwin 'had intimated to his wife his desire that if she survived him, Mr Cowper might still dwell with her'. When the matter was settled Mr Newton addressed Mr Cowper as follows:

'DEAR SIR, I congratulate myself on the pleasing prospect of our hoped-for intercourse, and the accession our Lord seems [to be] providing to our numbers and strength by Mrs Unwin's removal from Huntingdon. May He who has promised to direct the steps of those who wait upon Him guide you all to us in peace, and give you reason to say that He has cast your lot in a pleasant place. May He use us as instruments and means to animate and quicken each other in our Christian course.'

Accordingly, on the 14th of September, Mr Cowper, Mrs and Miss Unwin, came to Olney, residing with Mr Newton till the well-known house in the Market Place, often designated as Orchard Side, was ready for their reception. The gardens of this house and of the vicarage were separated by a little paddock, over which a right of way was obtained, and so the friends had easy access to one another.

Thus was established a connection that led to very important and happy results. Mr Cowper was anxious for retirement, and, indeed, the great attraction which Olney possessed for him consisted, as he tells us, in its distance from the busy world, and in his having there a friend so thoroughly devout and sympathetic as Mr Newton. In after years, Mr Newton, describing his intercourse with Cowper, speaks in high terms of his genius and scholarship, and adds: 'But these acquisitions were of small value compared with what he had learned in the school of the Great Teacher. In humility, simplicity, and devotedness to God, in the clearness of his views of evangelical truth, the strength of the comforts he obtained from them, and the uniform and beautiful example by which he adorned them, I thought he had but few equals. He was eminently a blessing both to me and my people by his advice, his conduct, and his prayers. The Lord who had brought us together so knit our hearts and affections, that for nearly twelve years' (that is, till the time Mr Newton left Olney) 'we were seldom separated for twelve hours at a time, when we were awake and at home. The first six I passed in daily admiring and trying to imitate him; during the second six I walked pensively with him in the valley of the shadow of death.'

In October, Mr Newton took up his abode at the new vicarage, and he thus appropriately refers to the circumstance: 'We removed last week into the vicarage, which Lord Dartmouth has kindly rebuilt and enlarged for us, so that from one of the most inconvenient, I have now one of the best and most commodious houses in this county. I did not solicit the favour for myself, nor should I have expected it. I should be thankful to the instrument, but I desire to look through all means and second causes to the Lord of my life, who has in every respect wrought wonderfully for me since he brought me into the ministry. I am desirous to set this apart as a day of solemn prayer — to ask the Lord to afford us His gracious presence in our new habitation; and I desire to humble myself before Him for my faint sense and poor improvement of all His mercies, and to make a new surrender of myself and my all to His service... Thou hast given an apostate a name and a place amongst Thy children — called an infidel to the ministry of the gospel. I am a poor wretch that once wandered naked and barefoot, without a home, without a friend; and now for me who once used to be on the ground, and was treated as a dog by all around me, Thou hast prepared a house suitable to the connection Thou hast put me into.'

Mr Newton's study was at the top of the house; and to this day there are found the following sentences painted in large letters on a panel over the mantelpiece: *Since thou wast precious in my sight, thou hast been honourable (Isa.* 43:4). *But thou shalt remember that thou wast a bondman in the land of Egypt, and the* LORD *thy God redeemed thee (Deut.* 15:15).

Sitting in that same room as a visitor in June, 1792, he thus writes to a correspondent in London: 'The texts over the fireplace are looking me in the face while I write. A thousand thoughts crowd upon me. What I have seen, what I have known of the Lord's goodness, and of my own evil heart, what sorrows, and what comforts in this house! All is now past; the remembrance only remains, as of a dream when we awake. Ere long we shall have done with changes.'

Wednesday, December 30th, Mr Newton went to the Baptist Meeting-House, to hear the sermon to the young people; and on Thursday, 31st, he put off his lecture, not to interfere with Mr Drake's sermon, addressed to the same class, which Mr Newton also attended. The sermon at the church was preached on the first day of the next year.

This custom of preaching to the young at each of the places of worship at Olney continues to the present time, and in the same spirit of accommodation.

We find during this year a correspondence between Mr Newton and Captain Scott on the subject of the latter entering the Church. From this Mr Newton dissuaded him. *

In August, Captain Scott writes again to his friend, telling him that his religious doings had awakened the notice and dislike of his commanding officer, who had in consequence determined to deprive him of his commission. And in the next letter to Mr Newton we have an interesting account of his interview with General Howard, the colonel of the regiment. We give the substance of what occurred on that occasion.

'After a dinner, given by the colonel to the officers,' says Captain Scott, 'he sent for me, and after many apologies told me he wanted to talk to me about my preaching. He had heard, he said, that I

See Newton's *Posthumous Letters,* vi. 116, etc.

had perverted some of the soldiers to my way of thinking, and that for his part he could not see that any one had the right to draw weak and ignorant persons into such ways; that there was no knowing to what it might lead; adding that there were teachers in our own church to instruct them. He thought every one ought to keep his religion to himself. I said it was quite true I had preached; that the Major (who was present) had heard me, and I hoped had not heard me advance anything inconsistent with the Scriptures. I also appealed to him whether I had in any way neglected my duties as an officer, or whether he found the soldiers whom the General had said I had perverted had neglected theirs. He confessed that I was more diligent than formerly, and that the men were good soldiers, only he thought them stupid. But why, the General asked, could not the men be taught in our own church? I said I had nothing to say against these teachers, but merely stated a fact when I said that they had gone to church for years without any appearance of religion amongst them, but when I had spoken to them, and got them together for religious worship, many of them were changed for the better. As to my having no right to do this, I was bound by the command of God to do all the good in my power, and I appealed to the General whether I ought not to have the same liberty to serve God without molestation, as others had to run every excess, provided they did not break the laws of their country, or the rules of the service. I said it was unfair to object to my drawing the soldiers from church, as I never met them at the times of public worship.

'I concluded by saying I hoped the General would always find me an obedient and diligent officer as long as I remained in the regiment, but as for religious matters, I would never be controlled or guided by any one in them further than they brought Bible authority. He candidly confessed he had no right over any one's conscience in such weighty matters.

'In the course of my speaking to him it came into my way to take notice of some oaths that were sworn during our being together after dinner, and some obscene talk, upon which I left the company. The General was one of the transgressors. I reminded him of it, and told him why I left. He confessed it was wrong; and so, after having on both sides hoped that there had been nothing said that had given offence, we parted very good friends, or seemingly so, he confessing he had nothing else to lay to my charge.'

In a letter to Mr Newton, two months later, Captain Scott speaks of his preaching at York, in the Wesleyan Chapel, and of the crowds which came to hear him. He also mentions a visit he had made to Helmsley, to see Dr Conyers, of whom he speaks in most ardent terms, saying he had much of the tender heart and manner of St John, the beloved disciple. Mr Newton also, in his reply, adds his testimony to the worth of Dr Conyers: 'I am glad you have been at Helmsley; I made no doubt but that you would love my dear friend; possibly I may over-rate him; I own he is but a man, but I think him an uncommon one; an eminent instance of the true Christian spirit. This is what is most taking with me. Gifts are useful; but they are mere tinsel compared with the solid gold of grace. An eminency in gifts is specious and glittering; but unless grace is proportionable, very ensnaring likewise.'

From some cause that does not appear, Mr Newton omitted to write in his diary from the beginning of the year 1768, and throughout the three following years, so that for some time we lose this clue to his more private and daily history. There are, however, letters and other sources of information which enable us to continue our narrative without any material omission.

Early in April there is a letter to Mrs Newton, then in London, a portion of which is published in *Letters to a Wife*.* It contains a detail of his doings amongst his people, an account of the ailments of some, and the recovery of others, and how he had ministered to their temporal as well as to their spiritual necessities. And at the close he says: 'My heart has been rather more lightsome this week than for some

* Vol. ii. p. 112

time past; and I believe Dr Conyers has taught me to endeavour to avoid the complaining strain in which I have perhaps abounded too much. May the Lord turn our mourning into joy, or rather teach us the apostle's experience, to be sorrowful, yet always rejoicing; delighting in Him, and loathing ourselves for all our abominations.'

Soon after this Mr Newton went to Norfolk, to visit Mr Bowman. On his way thither he writes thus to Mr Cowper: 'I send my hearty love to dear Mrs Unwin, and to Miss. Tell our dear people I bear them, jointly and severally, upon my heart from morning till night. It comforts me to think I have a place in their prayers, for I have been sadly hurried and straitened in myself since I left Olney ... Tell them my soul longs for their peace and prosperity, and that their welfare is the object and the joy of my life. Methinks I can safely use the apostle's words, "Now we live if ye stand fast in the Lord." I hope the Lord will give them a blessing by Mr Foster, and give him comfort among them.'

Again, two days later, on the 16th '... I see here fresh reason to be thankful for my situation at Olney. Poor Mr Bowman has as yet few or none to pray for him or strengthen his hands. How glad would he be to be encompassed as I am ... I shall return to them (as I always do) with great pleasure; for I never think myself so well situated as when in the midst of them. What I am to speak of or from to-morrow I know not, but hope the Lord will provide. I trust it shall be something concerning Jesus, and Him crucified. God forbid that my tongue should cease to talk of His goodness and beauty, or to set Him forth as the foundation and topstone of a sinner's salvation.'

Having returned to Olney, Mr Newton thus writes to his wife, who was still in London: 'I went this morning into the pulpit, as having only a small piece of bread and of fish to set before the multitude. But through mercy it multiplied in the distribution, and I hope there was a comfortable meal for those who were present, and some fragments left that will not be lost. It is not choice but necessity that makes me sometimes live, as we say, from hand to mouth. While my head is full of new persons and places I cannot do otherwise. And I have reason to be thankful that my hopes are seldom disappointed upon such occasions; though I know not when I have been so strait-ened and embarrassed as I was the other night at the Lock. I rather wonder that this happens so seldom, than that it happens at all. How justly might the Lord take His Word of truth out of my unworthy mouth! Perhaps He saw it good for me that Mr Self should have his comb cut rather there than in another place; I hope there is that in me which is as willing to appear to a disadvantage (if it must be so) at the Lock as at Olney; though to be sure flesh and blood is pleased to be thought somebody, when among dear friends or fine folks.'

In September of this year Mr Newton opened a correspondence with Dr Dixon, Principal of St Edmund's Hall,* Oxford. Fourteen letters thus addressed, extending over a space of nine years, are to be found in the last volume of the published works.

In one of the letters written at this time he says: 'The longer I live the more I am constrained to adopt that system which ascribes all the power and glory to the grace of God, and leaves nothing to the creature but sin, weakness, and shame.'

Writing, in September, to a friend at Liverpool, Mr Newton thus describes the peaceful and happy state of things at Olney: 'We are quiet and happy at Olney. We know nothing about disputes or divisions. If you pass a flock of sheep in a pasture towards evening, you may observe them all very busy in feeding. Perhaps here and there one may just raise his head and look at you for a moment, but down he stoops again to the grass directly. He cannot fill his belly by staring at strangers. Something in this way I hope it is with us. We care not who makes the noise, if we can get the grass. If they like talking, they may talk on; but we had rather eat.'

Later in the year he thus addresses his brother-in-law, Mr Cunningham: 'The account my sister sent of the man who died with

---

* It was from this Hall that the six students were expelled in 1768 for their 'Meth-odism', though Dr Dixon warmly espoused their cause.

the cards in his hands is very awful. I wish it may determine her and all whom I love to have nothing more to do with such wasters of time. Surely our hours are too precious to be thus squandered away. Time is short; Eternity is at hand. If our hearts are rightly affected with the love of Christ, we shall have better pleasures in His way than the world can afford . . . We join in love to you both, commending you to the care and blessing of the great Shepherd. May He guide all your steps, sweeten all your cares, sanctify all your comforts, and make you rich in that faith which works by love, and overcomes the world.'

This year Mr Newton printed a very earnest and faithful address to the inhabitants of Olney, deploring the evils that still prevailed, notwithstanding all their religious advantages. *

1769. In a letter to Mr Clunie, in April, Mr Newton speaks of a journey to Kettering, and of his preaching there, and says: 'I have been pretty full-handed in preaching lately. I trust the Lord was graciously with us in most or all of our opportunities. We are going to remove our prayer-meeting to the great room in the Great House. It is a noble place, with a parlour behind it, and holds one hundred and thirty people conveniently. Pray for us, that the Lord may be in the midst of us there, and that as He has now given us a Rehoboth, and has made room for us, so that He may be pleased to add to our numbers, and make us fruitful in the land.'

It was for this occasion that two of the hymns in the Olney Selection were composed — the 43rd and 44th of the second book. The first beginning 'O Lord, our languid frames inspire,' by Mr Newton; and the second, 'Jesus, where'er Thy people meet,' by Mr Cowper.†

---

* It will be found in his *Works*, vol. vi. p. 549, etc.

† Elsewhere the editor of this volume has erroneously stated that these hymns were written when the Great House was *first* used for religious services. This could not have been, as Mr Cowper was then unknown at Olney. The present more correct statement explains the reference in Mr Cowper's hymn to the renewal of former mercies, and to a more enlarged space.

Again we find Captain Scott in correspondence with Mr Newton. Captain Scott, perceiving that there was a determination to get rid of him from the army, sold his commission, and from that time devoted himself to the ministry among the Dissenters.

Mr Newton writes to him: 'My heart is as much with you, I trust, as it would be had you the most canonical appointment and the most regular sphere of service. And I would as willingly hear you in your usual places as if you preached in St Paul's.'

It may be added that Mr Scott gathered a congregation at Wallerton, near Wem, where he built a chapel. He was the means also of erecting several other places of worship; and after being settled for thirteen years at Matlock Bath, he died in 1807.

Mrs Newton being in London, Mr Newton writes: 'I am sorry to hear that after what has happened abroad and at home, the idle amusement of cards should be still indulged in our families. Alas! how poor and uncomfortable will the review of hours thus spent soon appear! The Lord forbid that any near and dear to us should be snatched away with the cards in their hands, as was the case of the poor gentleman last year. I should not write thus to you, but that I hope you will read it to them as from me. I know Mr C. does not love them; and if my dear sister would make a resolute stand, and refuse to play, I dare promise her it will not abridge her of one real comfort in life, and she will not repent it in a dying hour.'

In his next he speaks thus of a journey to Collingtree:* 'We went yesterday in the postchaise, as last year. I walked from Piddington with a company of more than fifty: had a church full at Collingtree, many from Northampton; amongst the rest Mr Hextal, Mr and Mrs Ryland, and Mr and Mrs Trinder, with many of the children from both schools.† Preached from Psalm 142:7, and returned safe home

---

* Mr Cowper, and sometimes Mrs Unwin, accompanied him on these visits, as we gather from other parts of the journal.

† Mr Ryland kept a boys' school, and Mrs Trinder a school for young ladies, both of which were often visited by Mr Newton.

about half-past eight. It was on the whole a very pleasant day, and the evening was crowned by your welcome letter of the 16th . . . I did not understand by your former letter that Mr West's illness had been dangerous, but I hope the Lord will fully restore him; for this I dare promise Olney prayers will not be wanting. We prayed for you as assembled on Tuesday night, but I hope our prayers found you all, wherever you were. We were walking on the Delectable Mountains,* from whence we hope to have several comfortable and instructive prospects hereafter.'

In this letter Mr Newton speaks of an invitation to himself and Mr Cowper from Dr Dixon, to visit him at Oxford. The journey was undertaken the following week. But the excessive heat, and the fatigue of riding on horseback, which always somewhat tried Mr Newton, brought on a slight fever. He says: 'It was rather a hindrance to me whilst amongst my friends, but, taking all things together, I never had a more pleasant and comfortable journey. I felt such a peace and composure in viewing myself in the Lord's hands as I can seldom obtain in health. I felt not an impatient or anxious thought, but was (if ever in my life) as a weaned child, and seemed quite willing, if the Lord had so pleased, to have died on the road. In a word, this little chastisement is from a Father's hand. It could hardly have been lighter. It was graciously sweetened; I trust it will be sanctified. I hope this account of my indisposition will not hurry you home sooner than you intended, for I am quite recovered.'

Two days afterwards he says: 'I have such a levee [morning reception] of kind visitors and inquiries every morning, that I meet with many interruptions in writing. It is pleasing to be beloved, and doubly pleasing to me to know that the favour the Lord has given me here is chiefly for the gospel's sake.'

In June, Mr Newton writes to Mr Clunie, expressing anxiety about his friend's state of health. 'You were remembered,' he says, 'at our

---

* Referring to his lectures on *Pilgrim's Progress*.

Bethel to-night. Our hearts, you may be assured, are much interested in your welfare. I hope to see the day when you will come and join with us in praise to a prayer-hearing God.'

That hope was never realised. A few months later this excellent man, whose friendship had proved so pleasant and so valuable to Mr Newton, was removed to a better world. In all Mr Newton's letters he addresses Mr Clunie as his 'dear brother'.

In November of this year Mr Newton published his *Review of Ecclesiastical History*, a work to which reference has been previously made. This undertaking was commenced by him at the suggestion of Mr Haweis, before his introduction to the ministry, but was wholly intermitted for several years, owing to the pressure of other engagements. Its design was to give the internal and spiritual history of the Church. The author speaks of it as 'The Apology of Evangelical Christianity, to obviate the sophistry and calumnies which have been published against it'. It is, however, only a fragment, and reaches but to the end of the first century. It was Mr Newton's hope that he should be enabled to carry on the work; and there is a letter from the Rev. Augustus Toplady, to whom he had applied for assistance in its prosecution, referring to this point, as well as to the part already finished. Mr Toplady writes: 'I am much indebted to your favour of the 12th inst.,* but much more for the profit and pleasure I have received from my revisal of the judicious, candid, and well-executed work of yours now in the press. The Lord breathe on what He has already enabled you to do, and give you health for the accomplishment of what remains.'

The Rev. John Campbell tells us, at a later period, that on asking Mr Newton why he did not continue his *Ecclesiastical History*, the latter replied that he had not read enough of Church History; but he added, 'I was the remote cause of Milner writing his. He got the hint from me.'

* The letter is dated 21 December 1769.

Very high praise is given to this work by Mr Cowper. He says: 'The facts are incontestable, the grand observations upon them are all irrefragable [incontrovertible], and the style, in my judgment, incomparably better than that of Robertson or Gibbon.' He refers again, in another letter, to the same subject in the following terms: 'That you may not suspect me of having said more than my real opinion will warrant, I will tell you why. In your style I see no affectation. In every line of theirs nothing else. They disgust me always; Robertson with his pomp and strut, and Gibbon with his finical [= finicky] and French manners. You are correct as they: you express yourself with as much precision; your words are arranged with as much propriety, but you do not set your periods to a tune. They discover a perpetual desire to exhibit themselves to advantage, whereas your subject engrosses you. They sing, and you say; which, as history is to be said and not sung, is, in my judgment, much to your advantage.'

From a letter to Mrs Wilberforce, it appears that she had visited Olney in the course of the present year. 'We are much obliged to you,' says Mr Newton, 'for your late visit, and I am glad to find that the Lord is pleased to give you some tokens of His presence, when you are with us, because I hope it will encourage you to come again. I ought to be very thankful that our Christian friends in general are not wholly disappointed of a blessing when they visit us.'

7: OLNEY
(1770–3)

Death of the Rev. John Cowper, and of the Rev. George Whitefield – Letters to Mr Cowper and Mr Brewer – From Messrs. Venn and Edwards – Miss Manesty – State of things at Olney – Letter to Mrs Wilberforce – Collingtree – Hymns – Reflections on the year 1772 – Return of Mr Cowper's Malady – Particulars – Observations – Defence of Mr Newton from the Reflections cast upon him in his treatment of Mr Cowper.

It was in the spring of this year that the Rev. John Cowper, the brother of the poet, was removed by death. It will be readily supposed that Mr Newton would be deeply interested in all the circumstances connected with this painful event. They were, in fact, watched by him with the greatest anxiety. This is abundantly evinced by the letters he wrote to his friend while at Cambridge. 'You are remembered by me,' he says, 'not only jointly with the people, but statedly in the family and in secret; and, indeed, there are not many hours in the day when I do not feel your absence and the occasion of it.' After referring, in another letter, to his great satisfaction at the spiritual change in Mr John Cowper, and speaking of the joy it would afford the Christian community at Olney, every member of which seems to have been interested in each other's spiritual welfare, and to have sympathized with each other's joys and sorrows, he adds: 'Remember me affectionately to your brother. I can truly say I esteemed him; I loved him before. My regard has been increased by the share I have taken in his concerns during his illness; but how much more is he dear to me since I knew that we were united in the love of the truth! With what pleasure shall I now receive him at Olney, now the restraints we were mutually under, for fear of giving each other pain, are removed.'

In the month of May, Mr Newton writes to his wife, then absent from home: 'I feel your absence, and long for your return, but I am not disconsolate. It was otherwise with me once. I can remember when the sun seemed to shine in vain, and the whole creation appeared as a blank, if you were from me. Not that I love you the less. The intercourse of many successive years has endeared you more and more to my heart. But I hope the Lord has weakened that idolatrous disposition for which I have so often deserved to lose you ... Many prayers are and will be put up for you and Mrs Unwin while you are away. To be interested in the simple, affectionate, and earnest prayers of such a people is a privilege of more value than the wealth of kings. In answer to their prayers the Lord has placed a hedge about all our corners, blessed our going out and coming in, and preserved us and ours in health when sickness and death have been in almost every house around us.'

On the last day of September of this year died at Newburyport, in the United States, that great and most successful preacher of the gospel and eminent man of God, George Whitefield. This event is mentioned here, because, on the 11th November, Mr Newton preached a funeral sermon for him in Olney Church, from the very appropriate text, John 5:35. 'He was a burning and a shining light.'

In February and March, 1771, Mr and Mrs Newton were in London, whence the former writes to Mr Cowper:

'MY VERY DEAR FRIEND, ... I *feel* myself already in London. Forced to lie in bed, and straitened for leisure and retirement when up, I steal a few minutes before breakfast to tell you, that as soon as that is finished we go into the City to hear Mr Brewer at Pinner's Hall. We are to dine with Mrs Wilberforce, at Mr West's, and in the evening I am to speak to the little company there. There I trust we shall meet you, Mr Foster, and all my dear people, in the spirit.

'Pray for me that my heart may be looking to Jesus for peace, wisdom, and strength. Without Him all is waste and desert. And every thought in which he has not a place or rule is treason. I trust, yea,

I know He will be with you. He will cover your head in the day of battle, and give you many a song of triumph before the great day of decision, when all enemies shall be finally bruised under your feet.' Again on the 27th: 'On Tuesday evening I spoke (*vice* [in place of] Mr Brewer) to the society at Mr West's. On Wednesday preached at the Lock; Friday at St Antholin's. Sunday morning at Blackfriars; afternoon in Bishopsgate Street. In these several public services the Lord was pleased to give me liberty. He can touch the rock and make the waters flow forth. I thank you for yours of the 21st. I pity your conflicts, and I try not to envy your comforts. You are in safe hands. All your combats and all your victories are already marked out for you. I hope Molly Coles is recovering apace, and that the quarantine between the two houses will soon be taken off. Please to give my love to her, as likewise to Molly Mole (who I hope will be a very good girl), and to all the Marys, Mollys, Sallys, Sarahs, &c.; that come in your way — particularly Sally Johnson and Judith. I trust we live in the daily remembrance of you and dear Mrs Unwin, and we doubt not we are the better for your prayers. I think we shall be both glad to see Olney again. Yet, as I am abroad, I hope to make myself tolerably easy till the time comes. Please to give our love to Miss Unwin, Mr Foster, Mr Palmer, &c. To Mrs Unwin and Sir Cowper we join in more than a common salutation. We are bound to you both by the fourfold cord of Esteem, Friendship, Communion, and Obligation. Judge, then, how warmly and sincerely we can assure you that we are most affectionately yours,

JOHN and M. NEWTON.'

On the 2nd of March Mr Newton replies to a letter of Mr Cowper, not extant, from which, however, it appears that one of the servants at Orchard Side had smallpox, and that Mr Cowper and Mrs Unwin had been obliged to leave their house. Mr Newton, after telling his friends of his various preaching engagements, thus refers to this incident: 'How is it I have written so much about myself before I expressed my great grief to think of the inconveniences to which Mrs Unwin and yourself must be exposed at the Bull? I think, had we been at Olney, we could not have suffered you to have gone there. I long for Tuesday, that I may again think of you as living snugly at Orchard Side. What can you both do at the Bull, surrounded with noise and nonsense, day and night? Well, we cannot help it now. You have had a great cross, and I hope the Lord has sweetened it, and enabled you to bear it. I know His presence can comfort you in the midst of bulls and bears. That Molly should stay a day or two after the time appointed for her departure, on purpose that she might die in the house, was a very serious dispensation; but it was not by chance. Some voice, some end, there certainly was in this providence, though I am at present unable to guess it. The Lord can easily make up to you and Mrs Unwin the trouble it has occasioned.'

About this time was commenced a correspondence with the Rev. Joseph Milner, of Hull. In a letter written in July, Mr Milner says: 'I desire to remember you at the throne of grace, and should be glad of a letter from you now and then. I trust the Lord will make your correspondence useful. Your letter shows you are deep read in the wiles of Satan, and able to give good counsel to the afflicted.'

Writing to Mr Brewer in July, Mr Newton observes: 'We should have been glad if it had suited you to have made Olney your retreat during the month of your recess from preaching. But, as you did not, hope some other time you will be able to visit us. You know we love your company and your ministry. If you can do Mr Parish, whom I sent you, any service, I doubt not of your willingness; and I believe him to be a deserving man, and one who has suffered a good deal from sickness and a strait income. I cannot but pity ministers who, besides the proper care of their calling, are exercised with anxious thoughts about food and raiment, and to provide things necessary for their families. It would probably have been my own case if I had settled at Warwick, but the Lord was pleased to prevent it. The remembrance of what I then escaped has made me compassionate to others in the like circumstances. If it was not that there is a liberal spirit in London, I know not what many worthy ministers in the country could do, those who are most willing having little ability, and those who are most able having little heart to provide for them.'

It may not be irrelevant to introduce in this place an extract from a letter of Mr Venn. He had been compelled through enfeebled health to remove from Huddersfield to Knightsbridge. He says: 'The people gather to hear, and I have in the church three times the number which were wont to come. To this number I can speak without straining. The same effects as at Huddersfield begin to appear. Amazement, attention, conviction, and tears in some follow the sound of the truth. I would rejoice with you in your success. It was in a sweet manner, yet with increase to the last, that sinners were added to the church at Huddersfield; and both the numbers of hearers and our comfort in the people called was more and more.'

The last communication of this year to which we refer is from Mr Newton's old friend Mr Edwards, of Leeds. It seems he had not written to Mr Newton for some little time past: 'I am determined to remind you,' he says, 'that though you have been neglected you are not forgotten, that your name is still mentioned with pleasure at Leeds, and that you and yours are remembered at the throne of grace, especially on our Wednesday evening meetings. I confess I found it somewhat grievous on my last visit to London to come within twenty miles of highly-favoured Olney, cast a wishful look that way, and be obliged to pass on the other side. Well, my dear friend, the delightful business assigned me here is pretty nearly finished, and the time of my departure approaches fast. You, likewise, brother, before very long will receive your letters of recall, and return with shouts of everlasting joy unto your Father's house. O happy day! and it draws nearer while I write this line. Then shall we no more complain of sin, sorrow, disappointments, or distance from each other, or any of us from the centre of our Union, from our precious Jesus, for evermore. Amen. Hallelujah! With great pleasure I have heard from one and another of your affairs — that your plantation is enlarged, and that those who are planted in the house of the Lord are lively and flourishing in the courts of our God. May the Lord bless your soul, and bless your labours yet more abundantly.

'We, too, have much to be thankful for at Leeds. The lines are fallen to us likewise in a pleasant place, and we have a goodly heritage. Our chapel is enlarged. We have at least three hundred stated hearers more than we had in the times when we were favoured with your visits. And I trust most of them have been brought under the power of the Word. About fifty, within the compass of the last two years, have made a good confession before many witnesses, and have received the right hand of fellowship. The Lord's people are in general judicious, lively and steady. Very few who have set their hand to the plough are suffered to look back, and we have been preserved for many years from any material offences. Thus, my dear friend, all is as well as can reasonably be expected; and I, wretched, hell-deserving *I*, am surrounded with honours and blessings on every side — yet not without a needful mixture of well-deserved trials. My Divine Master judges better than to send so crank a vessel [a nautical term for a ship with a tendency to roll easily] to sea without a just proportion of ballast. Yet I must acknowledge that the sharpest trials that I am exercised with either arise *from*, or are greatly increased *by*, my pride, impatience, and unbelief. O wretched man that I am! I trust, however, I can say at the worst of times, "I thank God through Jesus Christ my Lord."

'Have you seen Dr Priestley's penny appeal? He has been answered by Walter Cellon, by Cornelius Cayley, and one Morgan, and he has replied to them all by queries in our public papers — calls them all very justly Arminians, and says they mean no less than he asserts, only that they are a set of inconsistent bunglers. He wonders where all the staunch Calvinists are fled. You have a good pen, my friend. I will send you, any time, the whole of this controversy to Newport Pagnell, and I will take upon me to publish anything you will favour me with in any manner you shall direct. I really think it may be of good service.

I have exchanged two letters very lately with Captain Scott, who gives a glorious account of the work in Shropshire. From my heart I salute dear Mrs Newton, Mr Cowper, Mrs Unwin, and all amongst you who love our Lord Jesus in sincerity. Beg all the dear souls to pray hard for, my very dear brother, Yours in indissoluble bonds,

JOHN EDWARDS.'

It will be remembered that it was in Mr Edwards' chapel in Leeds that Mr Newton first opened his lips in public in the year 1758. Mr Newton in speaking of Mr Edwards on one occasion described him as one of our first preachers.

We now reach the year 1772, and are able once more to take advantage of the information contained in the diary.

January the 1st, Mr Newton writes: 'Since the date of the preceding page (October 30, 1767), I have kept a brief account of the principal events that have occurred, in several pocket-books. I now return to my former method.' Then follow some general remarks about God's goodness to him in his person and his ministry. And once more he makes a solemn surrender of himself to God for another year.

He speaks with much pleasure of his children's meetings. 'Several of these young people,' he hopes, 'are awakened and seeking the Lord.'

On Tuesday, 13th, he checks his complaint of daily interruptions, saying: 'Why should I call them so when they are providences, and bring each of them a call of duty with them?'

In the preceding year Mr Newton's early Liverpool friend, Mr Manesty, died, and now his widow and daughter came on a visit to Olney. In expectation of it, Mr Newton says: 'I hope the Lord has inclined them to come that they may receive His gospel. I would be thankful for an opportunity of showing my gratitude where the Lord had laid me under early and great obligations.'

During this month Mr Newton writes again to his friend Mr Brewer: '. . . It has been, and I hope still is, a time of grace and revival. I know not but we have had as many awakened within about three months past as for two or three years before, and they all seem in a hopeful way. Many of the Lord's people have had refreshing seasons in the public ordinances. Our Great House assembly on the Lord's-day evening is thronged exceedingly. The Lord enables those who lead in prayer to plead earnestly for a blessing. I think on the whole things were never better with us than at present . . . Though I think there never was a people less disposed to think themselves qualified to teach their ministers, yet they have often taught me without intending it, and sent me away from them with tears in my eyes.'

The above letter refers to those who offered prayer in these meetings held at the Great House. There is in possession of the editor a paper, which has been singularly preserved, containing a list of those who engaged on these occasions. It gives weekly dates for nearly twelve months, with a single name attached to each; and Mr Cowper's appears about eight times. We have it on record, as said by one who often heard Mr Cowper at such times, 'that of all men he ever heard pray, no one equalled Mr Cowper'.

'The sharp trial concerning Cottenham was not forgotten, and it was agreed to keep the day in yearly remembrance;' so, says Mr Newton, 'I have appointed a meeting at the Great House tonight.' It was Saturday, February 1.

'Sunday, February 9. A visit from Mr Margate, of Northampton, and Mr Bailey, an Oxonian, who stayed with us all night.'

'Friday, 14th. Went to meet the little society at M. Mole's. The Lord has been pleased to awaken several young persons of late, and to incline their hearts to meet together.'

'Saturday, 15th. Being one of our anniversary days,* I dined and drank tea at Orchard Side.'

'March 31st. I go on in my usual round abroad and at home. Have had my two young ladies in my study. Miss Manesty I trust has been truly awakened and brought to the feet of Jesus since she came down. What a mercy to her, what an honour to me! Miss Moody, likewise,

* The day on which Mrs Unwin and Mr Cowper entered upon their home.

who was seeking the Lord when she was here five years ago, seems in a growing way.'

Miss Manesty, having left Olney, writes expressing her great gratitude to Mr Newton as the instrument of spiritual good to her, telling him that if she had not herself experienced the change the Lord can make in the heart she could not have conceived it possible — the things she once delighted in having become altogether insipid.

'April 27th. Attended the Archdeacon's visitation at Stratford — a poor, uncomfortable service. Heard a sermon in the usual strain from Romans 1:22. Met Mr Simpson,* who is likely to be forced from Buckingham. The poor people who have willingly received the gospel are much to be pitied.'

Not long after this Mr Simpson left, as Mr Newton feared.

'Thursday, May 14th. We are now free from company for the first time since January 20th. But the Lord has done great things under our roof. Oh that every one whom He sends in His providence to us may receive a blessing amongst us.'

'Sunday, 31st. Text this afternoon Isaiah 58:13, 14 — to countenance and strengthen the endeavours of the constables, etc., who are at length trying to put a stop to the profanation of the Lord's-day.'

Two days afterwards, writing to his friend Mr West, he speaks thus of Olney:

'When will you come and see the flock at Olney? By the blessing of the Good Shepherd we have had a good number added to the fold of late, who are in a very promising way. You would like to hear their bleatings. Pray for us: for notwithstanding what I have said, wickedness still abounds amongst us in the town. And many, having long resisted the convictions of the Word and Spirit, are hardened and bold in sinning to a great degree; so that Olney is like the two baskets of Jeremiah's figs, the good are very good, and the bad are exceedingly bad.'

'Wednesday, 10th. Preached at Collingtree. Had a large congreg-

* Rev. David Simpson, author of the *Plea for Religion*.

ation. The church crowded, the chancel and belfry nearly full. My dear and Mr Cowper went with me.

'Friday. Went to the Mole Hill.' This seems to have become the familiar designation of the prayer-meetings at Molly Mole's even after its removal elsewhere.

In June mention is made of a visit to Oxford, Reading (where Mr Newton found a hearty welcome from the Rev. Mr Talbot, vicar of St Giles's), and London.

'Tuesday, July 7th. Time fully taken up in visiting and receiving visits. Finished Omicron's letter for the month. Drank tea at Mr Drake's. Preached at the Great House from Hebrews 2:18, to which I was led by Mr Cowper's prayer. In a letter to Mrs Newton (then in London) two days afterwards, he says: 'Dear Sir Cowper is in the depths as much as ever. The manner of his prayer last night led me to speak from Hebrews 2:18. I do not think he was much the better for it, but perhaps it might suit others.'

The following is quoted from a letter written about this time to Mrs Wilberforce: 'It is now Saturday evening, and growing late. I am just returned from a serious walk, which is my usual manner of closing the week when the weather is fine. I endeavour to join in heart with the Lord's ministers and people, who are seeking a blessing on tomorrow's ordinances. At such times I especially remember those friends with whom I have gone to the house of the Lord in company, consequently you are not forgotten. I can venture to assure you that if you have a value for our prayers you have a frequent share in them.'

'Friday, 21st August. Mr Hurly, curate of Harrold, has attended at church these three Thursdays past.'

'Saturday, September 10th. [*sic*. September 10, 1772 was a Thursday.] Today busy in preparing a new paragraph for another edition of Bogatzky's *Golden Treasury*.' Mr Thornton published this edition, to which he induced several of his friends to contribute new papers.

'Wed., 16th. Went to Collingtree to preach, as usual, to a crowded congregation ... accompanied by Mrs Unwin and Mr Cowper.'

'Friday. Went to open the new Mole Hill at Goody Bear's. The pleasantest hour I have had for some time.'

'Wednesday, 7th October. To Everton with Mr Perry.* Found Mr and Mrs Venn; had some pleasure in the interview.'

'Tuesday, 20th Oct. With Mrs Newton visited Mr and Mrs Trinder at Northampton. Could have no admission into a church, but spoke several times in my friend's house. Twice to the children in the school. Again on Wednesday and Friday evenings. On the latter occasion the house quite filled. Seven or eight ministers or preachers were present. A pleasant visit, may it prove profitable to me and others.'

'Tuesday, 19th. [*sic.* Presumably a date in November, but there was no Tuesday 19 in this month.] Mr Cowper has been ailing these two or three days, but I hope he is better.'

'Tuesday, December 1st. At the Great House began the *Pilgrim's Progress* again.'

'Sunday, 6th. Expounded my new hymn at the Great House on the subject of a burdened sinner.' Here is the first allusion we have to one of the series of pieces, afterwards constituting the larger portion of the *Olney Hymns*, of which we shall have more to say hereafter.

December 31st, Mr Newton writes: 'The comforts, the trials of another year finished, and can be repeated no more. It has been to me a year of great mercy and great sinfulness. Many proofs of the Lord's goodness, and of the evil of my own heart has it afforded.' And then, in reference to the fact that he had come to the end of the second volume of his diary, he adds: 'It is now more than sixteen years since I began to write in this book. How many scenes have I passed through in that time — by what a way has the Lord led me! — what wonders has He shown me! My book is now nearly full, and I shall provide another for the next year. O Lord, accept my praise for all that is past. Enable me to trust Thee for all that is to come, and give a blessing to all who may read these records of Thy goodness and my own vileness. Amen and Amen.'

* One of Mr Newton's most devoted people, a miller at Lavendon.

1773. Appropriate reflections are made on the 1st of January; and this sentence in particular we may quote: 'The afternoon I devote to retirement, and to beg a blessing upon the important service of the evening — an annual sermon to the young people — which is usually laid upon my heart with more weight than any other opportunity in the course of the year. Afterwards, was favoured in preaching with remarkable liberty.'

And now we have to refer to a most melancholy event that beclouded the commencement of this year — the recurrence of Mr Cowper's most painful and mysterious affliction. Some premonitions of this evil will have been already noticed.

Mr Newton thus writes on the 2nd of January: 'My time and thoughts much engrossed today by an afflicting and critical dispensation at Orchard Side. I was sent for early this morning, and returned astonished and grieved. How mysterious are the ways of the Lord! How much seems now at stake! But while all is in His hands all is safe. Could hardly attend to anything else.'

'Sunday, 3rd. Sent for again in the morning — an affecting scene. I was told appearances were worse afterwards; but before noon the Lord interposed in mercy.'

'Tuesday. I have devoted myself and time as much as possible to attend on Mr Cowper. We walked today, and probably shall daily. I shall now have little leisure but for such things as indispensably require attention. At the Great House I mentioned the case in general terms, and made it the subject of my evening discourse. It was a solemn and affecting time, and I hope earnest prayer was, and will be poured out to the Lord.'

'Wednesday. Much as yesterday. I have now to perform family worship morning and evening in two houses. The storm is heavy, but I perceive the Lord is present in it, preserving from all sallies of passion, and maintaining a gracious meekness of spirit. I find the Lord has laid the case much upon the hearts of the people. Surely this is a token for good.'

'Tuesday, 12th. My post of observation was very painful last week, but now it is pleasing. The shade grows lighter every day. Yesterday and this morning the conversation was very instructive to me. I trust I may be enabled daily to improve what I see and hear.'

'Saturday, 16th. Our hopes of a speedy deliverance damped today by a return of the temptation.'

A week later: 'My dear friend still walks in darkness. I can hardly conceive that any one in a state of grace and favour with God can be in greater distress; and yet no one walked more closely to Him, or was more simply devoted to Him in all things.'

'Sunday, 24th. A very alarming turn roused us from our beds, and called us to Orchard Side at four in the morning. I stayed there till eight, before which time the threatening appearance went entirely off, and now things remain much as they were.'

And thus hope and fear alternated, depression of spirit and temptation continued; yet on Monday, February 15th, Mr and Mrs Newton dined at Orchard Side, 'as usual on the anniversary of the settlement there. But the late dispensation has brought a cloud over our former pleasure.'

The next entry having reference to this painful subject is on the 12th of April, as follows: 'Annual fair day: the noise of which made my dear friend willing to seek a retreat with us till it should be over; and now he is here, he seems desirous to stay. So he and Mrs Unwin will now be with us for a time, and I hope the Lord will give him deliverance here. We long and pray for the event.' This visit, as we shall see, was prolonged till the end of May in the following year.

Things seem to have gone on without any radical improvement till the month of October. Yet was there a little diversion from the intensity of his gloom, for Mr Cowper was willing to amuse himself with gardening, of which he was always fond; but still the cloud did not disperse. And when, in the early part of this month, Mr Newton returned from a journey into Warwickshire, he says: 'We met an intimation on the road that greatly alarmed us — never returned home under such anxiety of spirit. Had a startling account, but found the Lord had mercifully interposed. Yet our trial in our dear friend, far from being removed, seems likely to increase, and he is rather worse than better.' A few days after: 'My mind much embarrassed about my friend, whose disorder has become much more tumultuous and troublesome.'

We have thus brought together all the passages relating to this melancholy story; but we must not leave it without an attempt to explain several points of importance in connection with it. Some of them affect the very unjust imputations which have been cast upon the wisdom, to say the least, of Mr Newton's treatment of Cowper.

In describing the malady of Mr Cowper, it will have been observed that reference is repeatedly made to the fearful temptation which assailed him. It was a temptation to commit self-destruction. And thenceforth to the end of his days, while perfectly sane in all other respects, he laboured under the most extraordinary and terrible hallucination that he had received a command from Heaven to execute this deed, and that his disobedience to that command had for ever shut him out from the hope of mercy. He thought that there was salvation for every man who would accept it but himself, and that consequently it was a sin for him to engage in any religious act. This melancholy view of his case is stated nine years afterwards, with all the force and beauty of diction so peculiar to him, in a letter to his friend, the Rev. William Bull.*

Mr Cowper's case was one which medicines were not likely to alleviate; indeed, he himself at first absolutely refused them. Mr Newton also evidently thought that little was to be effected in this way, though, in accordance with the suggestions of Mrs Madan, aunt of Mr Cowper, and whom he had fully informed of all that had taken place, they were pressed upon the sufferer. In the month of August Dr Cotton of St Albans was consulted, and Mr Cowper was then

---

* See *Memorials of the Rev. W. Bull*, p. 112; and Southey's *Works of Cowper*, iv. 235.

induced to take the medicines prescribed; and though for a time they appeared beneficial, they afterwards seemed in some respects to aggravate the malady, and their use was abandoned.

It may also be added that it occurred to Mr Newton to try on this friend the effect of electric shock, and this he did, but without any salutary result. We have mentioned these facts, because it is thought in some quarters that Mr Newton did not at once use all the means that might have been at least tried for Mr Cowper's recovery.

This may introduce consideration of a wider question of dispute or misapprehension in connection with this subject. In accounting for the causes which induced the return of this fearful malady, we think blame has been very unjustly cast upon Mr Newton. Those statements which have appeared in some quarters, involving the charge of exaction, severity, tyranny, and the like, in the previous conduct of Mr Newton neither need nor deserve reply. They simply betray ignorance of the man and the facts. But surely those biographers of Cowper and their sympathising readers are also at fault, who, while expressing all due respect to Mr Newton's character and motives, still insinuate that the manner of life to which his friend had been introduced was calculated to increase the morbid tendency in his frame, and to lead to the return of his fearful malady. His visiting the poor and sick, and ministering to their necessities, his offering prayer in public, the number of religious exercises in which he engaged — these things, it is affirmed, were neither proper nor wholesome for him. In reference to his part in the *Olney Hymns*, it is urged that the intense zeal with which he engaged in this fascinating pursuit must have been injurious. And so it is affirmed that there is the strongest reason to conclude that these engagements at length accelerated the recurrence of the disease.

Now, it is evident that a great deal of what is thus said and implied will take its complexion from the views the objectors entertain of spiritual religion — views which will not be held by evangelical Christians in general. They believe spiritual religion to be a reality, its truths and duties to be a source of true happiness, and eminently calculated to afford solace and comfort to the mind in the hour of sorrow and depression. It is easy to give such a distorted representation — we do not mean intentionally, but from misapprehension — of Mr Cowper's life at Olney, as to convey a very mistaken idea of it. Yet may we not ask, how was it that for five long years Mr Cowper's calm was undisturbed by storms, that he himself speaks of it as a season of the greatest happiness? Did not his religious life, his Christian experience and exercises avert for that time, rather than accelerate, the evil that came at last?

How was it, again, that he was supported through the trying scene of his brother's death — two years and nine months before the return of the malady? Why, on the other hand, at a subsequent period did the death of a friend induce a relapse after a partial recovery? Was it not because in this latter case his monomania robbed him of the consolations he formerly enjoyed? And yet again, is it not somewhat absurd to talk of the ill effects on Mr Cowper's mind of writing between sixty and seventy hymns perhaps in the course of two years? And what though some are sorrowful, others are full of joy and gladness — just the chequer-work of all true Christian experience?

And, not to multiply these queries further, we ask, is it likely, whatever Mr Newton's religious views, that seeing he was a man of a most genial, loving nature, a man of good sense, a man of experience, and perfectly acquainted with Mr Cowper's past history and mental temperament, is it likely, even possible, that he would have urged him, against his will, to duties and exercises palpably and manifestly injurious? This matter may best be set in its true light by the quotation of an account of Mr Cowper's life at Olney, written by Mr Newton, and found in the document from which we have already quoted, the fragmentary memorial of 1800. This, after all, may be the best answer to the objections above referred to. It is as follows:

'We were, as I have said, very much together; for, besides our frequent walks and visits home, occasional journeys seldom parted us.

We usually travelled together. He was soon known in many places, and everywhere admired by competent judges as a gentleman and scholar. He was a great blessing to the Lord's poor and afflicted people at Olney in the still higher and more important character of an eminent and exemplary Christian. For he had drunk deeply into the spirit of his Lord; he loved the poor, often visited them in their cottages, conversed with them in the most condescending manner, sympathised with them, counselled and comforted them in their distresses, and those who were seriously disposed were often cheered and animated by his prayers.

'While I remained at Olney we had meetings two or three times in a week for prayer. These he constantly attended with me. For a time his natural constitutional unwillingness to be noticed in public kept him in silence. But it was not very long before the ardency of his love to the Saviour, and his desire of being useful to others broke through every restraint. He frequently felt a difficulty and trepidation in the attempt, but when he had once begun all difficulty vanished, and he seemed to speak, though with self-abasement and humiliation of spirit, yet with that freedom and fervency, as if he saw the Lord whom he addressed face to face.

'The wisdom which is from above, which is pure and peaceable, gentle and easy to be entreated, full of mercy and good works, without partiality and without hypocrisy, possessed and filled his heart. The wonders and riches of redeeming love, as manifested by the glorious gospel of the blessed God, were the food of his soul, the source of his joys, the habitual subject of his study, and suggested the leading topics of his conversation. Like the apostle, he was determined to know nothing comparatively but Jesus Christ and Him crucified, and to do nothing but in dependence upon His strength, and ——'

Here the account abruptly terminates.

It will thus be seen that Mr Cowper's life was not, after all, as some would think it, a mere dull round of religious services and meditations, nor was he confined to the sole companionship of Mr Newton. Many intelligent visitors were constantly at the vicarage; and it is evident that their society was another source of pleasure to him. 'Sir Cowper' is constantly referred to in terms of kindest remembrance in the letters addressed to Mr Newton by such visitors. It appears to us that Mr Newton showed his discretion in not urging his friend to any exciting literary labours — the hymns surely were not such, but rather a pleasant recreation. One work, however, Mr Cowper did commence, whether at Mr Newton's suggestion or not, it is impossible to say — a brief comment on the Gospel of St John. Only the first chapter was completed. It is in Mr Cowper's handwriting, and manifestly his own production, for it has just the simplicity and beauty both of thought and style which we should expect from such a source. We find it in the commencement of a folio volume afterwards used by Mr Newton for his diary. The work was probably interrupted by the illness of its author.

Mr Cecil, in his life of Newton, referring to Mr Cowper's attack of illness, justly observes 'that the mind of the latter received the first consolation it ever tasted from evangelical truths under the care of Dr Cotton. Here also he received that settled tranquillity and peace which he enjoyed for several years afterwards. So far, therefore, was his constitutional malady from being produced or increased by his evangelical connections, either at St Albans or at Olney, that he seems never to have had any settled peace but from the truths he learned in these societies. It appears that among them alone he found the only sunshine he ever enjoyed through the cloudy day of his afflicted life!'

And to add another testimony. In his reminiscences of Mr Newton, the Rev. W. Jay, of Bath, speaks in the following terms: 'Some have thought the divine was hurtful to the poet. How mistaken were they! He was the very man, of all others, I should have chosen for him. He was not rigid in his creed. His views of the gospel were most free and encouraging. He had the tenderest disposition; and always judiciously regarded his friend's depression and despondency as a physical effect, for the removal of which he prayed, but never reasoned or argued with him concerning it.'

There is one other point upon which we must speak before leaving this subject, even though it may seem not to be quite relevant to our direct object. Dr Southey observes: 'Another cause, however, has been assigned for the return of Mr Cowper's malady. It has been said that he proposed marriage to Mrs Unwin; that the proposal was accepted and the time fixed; that prudential considerations were then thought to preponderate against it; and that his mind was overthrown by the anxieties consequent upon such an engagement. This I believe to be utterly unfounded; for that no such engagement was either known or suspected by Mr Newton I am enabled to assert; and who can suppose that it would have been concealed from him?'

This is unquestionably a mistake, although thus strongly put. Nothing, it is obvious, was more natural or becoming than a marriage between two persons thus providentially brought to reside with each other. Nor was there, as is perhaps generally supposed, any great disparity of years between Mr Cowper and Mrs Unwin. Now the editor of this volume is able to state that he has again and again heard his father say that Mr Cowper and Mrs Unwin were betrothed and about to be married when the melancholy return of Mr Cowper's malady in 1773 prevented the accomplishment of their purpose; and, moreover, that it was Mrs Unwin herself who made this statement to his grandfather.

But what Mr Newton has said in his unfinished sketch is even still more to the purpose, and must for ever settle this question. We copy from the original before us: 'They were congenial spirits, united in the faith and hope of the gospel, and their intimate and growing friendship led them in the course of four or five years to an engagement for marriage, which was well known to me, and to most of their and my friends, and was to have taken place in a few months, but was prevented by the terrible malady which seized him about that time.'

8: OLNEY
(1773–5)

A nd now to return to the history of Mr Newton's daily life. In March he complains of indisposition; and he thus speaks of it in a letter to a friend: 'I suppose you have heard I have been ill; through mercy I am now well. But indeed I must further tell you that when I was sick I was well; and since the Lord has removed my illness I have been much worse. My illness was far from violent in itself, and was greatly sweetened by a calm, submissive frame the Lord gave me under it. My heart seemed more alive to Him then than it has done since my cough, fever, and deafness have been removed.'

In May Mr Newton went with a friend to Yelling, and had, he tells us, much agreeable discourse by the way, and spoke in the evening in Mr Venn's kitchen to about thirty people from Romans 8:1.

'Monday, 17th. Waited upon the Bishop at Newport with about fifty-five persons for confirmation — some of them, I hope, already devoted to the Lord, but others, I fear, too little sensible of the engagement they were to make, though I endeavour to keep such away. Dined with him, and had some talk about our prayer-meetings; but through the Lord's goodness all ended well.'

After speaking of two very interesting cases of persons at a distance to whom he was made useful Mr Newton tells us of a visit he received in July from the Milners, of Hull: 'Spent the day very agreeably with my two friends. Their various knowledge gave our conversation a larger scope than I have often opportunity for. Though few of the wise and learned are brought to account all things loss for Christ, praised be the Lord some are. Oh that I could take as much pleasure in drawing at the fountain as I do from cisterns. I find the best creature converse will not feed my soul like waiting upon the Lord.'

There was frequent intercourse and correspondence between the younger Mr Ryland (afterwards Dr Ryland) and Mr Newton. The former had written to Olney in a very desponding tone as to the state of things in the religious world. He speaks of error abounding on the one hand and lukewarmness on the other. He is staggered sometimes, and knows not what to think of things — either Satan or unbelief, or both, say, Christ is asleep, and cares not that the ship is going to the bottom. To these complaints Mr Newton thus pertinently replies: 'The ship was safe when Christ was in her, though he was *really* asleep. At present I can tell you good news, though you know it; He is wide awake, and His eyes are in every place. You and I, if we could be pounded together, might perhaps make two tolerable ones. You are too anxious, and I am too easy in some respects. Indeed, I cannot be too easy when I have a right thought that all is safe in His hands; but if your anxiety makes you pray, and my composure makes me careless, you have certainly the best of it. However, the ark is fixed upon an immovable foundation, and if we think we see it totter, it is owing to a swimming in our heads. Seriously, the times look dark and stormy, and call for much circumspection and prayer; but let us not forget that we have an infallible Pilot, and that the power, wisdom, and honour of God are embarked with us.'*

On his birthday (August 4th) Mr Newton wrote a long letter to Mr Thornton. It contains some particulars of Mr Newton's early history, which are not to be found elsewhere. We quote the following passages: 'As little remarkable has occurred since my last, permit me to fill up a part of this sheet about myself, and to indulge the train of thought which the return of this day has led me to. It is my birthday, and likewise the day on which, fifteen years ago, I solemnly devoted myself to the Lord's service in the ministry, if He would please to employ me. Some hours I have passed to-day (according to annual custom when the weather is fine) wandering in the fields, recollecting those early engagements, and endeavouring to praise the Lord for the wonderful and gracious manner in which He has since answered the prayers I offered in secret, and to humble myself for the much evil and defilement which have been mingled with my poor services. Perhaps the history of the whole Church does not afford an instance of one so totally abandoned, and to appearance so entirely cut off from the least probability of recovery, being called to preach the gospel. Banished to the dreadful wilds of Africa, from whence I am almost the only person (in the like circumstances) who ever returned. Then after having renounced Christianity I commenced idolater; and I doubt not, if the Lord had not snatched me away, I should in a little time have adopted the wildest infatuations of the blinded Negroes.

'I believe I never told you (nay, I think it has been locked up in my breast to this moment) that I conceived a strange sort of veneration of the *moon*, and laid myself for a while under a foolish restriction to sleep as little as possible while the moon was visible above the horizon. To such madness may the heart be seduced when it leaves the truth, and is left of God. At the very time when the ship

* *Cardiphonia*, ii. 160.

appeared so critically, and brought me off the coast, I had formed the horrid design of fighting a man who had affronted me (and who was too strong for me) with pistols, and in a few days should have put it in execution. I had likewise entered into such connections with the natives, that, had not the Lord wonderfully interposed by that power which He has over all hearts, I could not have left them. Nor should I ever have been sent for or inquired after again, if that ship had missed me. Many times afterwards I pushed myself into the extremest dangers, and was at last preserved from falling in the deep waters by a series of evident miracles. Such they appear to me now. I could have swelled my narrative almost to a folio had I given such a minute detail of my wickedness, misery, and hairbreadth escapes as my memory would have furnished me with.

'After all this I am alive, possessed of the happiness which I renounced, and preaching the faith which I laboured to destroy. And *after all this*, what ingratitude, lukewarmness, and perverseness am I to this day conscious of! Sure I may say again, there never was a case like mine. When the thought of the ministry first ran much in my mind I trembled at it: it seemed to be in me presumptuous and impossible. But the Lord has done it. A little dissenting congregation in an obscure corner was the height of my first proposal; but He has placed me upon a hill, made me happy in my situation, and acceptable to many. By ways which I could not have expected He has strengthened my hands, given me friends and favour, and set a hedge of protection around me on every side. How unlike am I now to that poor slave of the slaves who wandered almost naked, and like a hungry dog was glad to receive a morsel of food from any hand that offered it!'

It may be added to the above statement that in writing to Mr Coffin, in the year 1796, after referring to his *Narrative*, Mr Newton says: 'It chiefly relates to the misery of my situation. Had I given a detail of the wickedness of my heart and life, the book would have been too shocking to bear a reading.'

'Thursday, August 5th. Answered a letter which I received yesterday from a person in Moreton Hampstead, Devonshire, under conviction and distress, who has found some relief by reading my *Narrative*, and desired to hear further from me.'

Then followed some entries of the ordinary round of duties — of the help he received in preaching — of his reading, writing, visiting, walking, and his children's meetings, which were still continued.

In the month of August, writing to his friend Mr Brewer, he thus refers to the affliction of Mr Cowper, and also to his own circumstances:

'Heavy indeed is the trial with which the Lord has visited him, and, to appearance, no one needed it less. I can hardly form an idea of a closer walk with God than he uniformly maintained. Communion with God and the good of His people seemed to be the only objects he had in view from the beginning to the end of the year, and he was remarkably thriving and happy to the very hour when this trouble overtook him. But the Lord is wise. Mysterious as the dispensation seems, I dare not question its expediency, nor, though it continues so long, can I despond as to the event. In the meantime, it is upon many accounts a very great trial to me. But I hope I am learning (though I am a slow scholar) to silence all vain reasonings and unbelieving complaints with the consideration of the Lord's sovereignty, wisdom and love ... I have had some pinching experiences in my own soul, and have seen some hopeful plants sadly blighted by the arts of the enemy. It is well that the worm of self-importance should sometimes get a blow on the head. If I had not met some cutting things both within and without I should be like the fly in the fable, which said, when posted upon the axletree of a carriage, *"What a dust do I raise!"* Poor creature! the best that I can do is to sit and look on and wonder while the Lord works. What a mercy it is that He will take so many wise methods to hide pride from man!'

'Monday, August 23rd. In the evening Mr Rose of Oxford called. He is a remarkable instance of distinguishing grace, was one of the gayest and most dissipated youths in the University, but is now sitting at the feet of Jesus.'*

Friday, September 3rd, Mr Newton speaks of a happy season of retirement at the Great House, whither indeed he often resorted, and habitually on the sabbath morning to seek communion with God.

During the latter part of this year, Mr Newton was visited by various friends — of one of them he writes as follows: 'Accompanied Mrs Place to Bedford. She stayed much longer than she intended, but I hope the event has been happy. She goes from us not only much better in her health and spirits, but enlightened with views of the gospel which she had not before. I trust the Lord's hand was evident in her coming to Olney, as it was by a remarkable concurrence of providences. The visit has likewise been blessed to her maid.'

About the same time he also made the acquaintance of Mr Barham of Bedford, a large West Indian proprietor, and by religious profession a Moravian. He says: 'This new acquaintance which the Lord has given me, and this my first visit proved exceedingly pleasant. I was much pleased with him and Mrs B. and with their four daughters. All seemed to be awakened and to be seeking Jesus in a scriptural way.' Under the date November 30th, Mr Newton writes: 'Finished a hymn on the barren fig-tree.† I usually make one hymn a week to expound at the Great House.'

It appears that during this year Mr Newton was variously exercised, and he often expresses grief that he cannot get near access to God, and lamentation of the evil that is in him. Yet he says in one place: 'In the midst of all my conflicts peace is at the bottom, which He has not permitted to be shaken.' What Mr Newton says in a letter written to his friend Mr Symonds, in October, may, perhaps, not be inapplicable to his own circumstances: 'If the lives of the two

* Mr. Rose married one of the daughters of Mr Barham, of Bedford, and obtained the living of Beckenham, Kent.
† *Olney Hymns*, i. 103.

Henrys, and of other good men, were written by inspired men, you would not be so much discouraged at reading them. Depend upon it, they saw as much reason to be ashamed of themselves as we do. To us they appear in their best clothes, and we are told more of what the Lord wrought for them, than of the effects of indwelling sin under which they groaned. If I should outlive you, and I should have a call to write the life of the Rev. Mr Symonds of Bedford, I should perhaps find more to say in your favour than you are aware of; and if you would have the darker side known as well as the brighter, you must write it yourself.'

1774. New Year's day opens with suitable reflections, and amongst them an earnest prayer for his dear friend, who has now spent a whole year in the 'valley of the shadow of death'.

'February 24th. All my leisure taken up with talking and reading with Mr Gurdon, a valuable young man.* I think he is for judgment and spirit one of the first of the younger ministers. Great hindrances were thrown in his way at Oxford, but the Lord brought him happily through them.'

'March 11th. This evening received an account of the death of my friend Mr Talbot,† who might justly be numbered amongst the first worthies. Considering his character, abilities, and situation, the Church of God could hardly have sustained a heavier loss in the removal of one minister.'

During this month Mr Newton writes of his friend Mr Cowper, that he is still in the depths. He adds: 'In the beginning of his disorder, when he was more capable of conversing than he was sometimes afterwards, how often have I heard him adore and submit to the sovereignty of God, and declare, though in the most agonizing and inconceivable distress, he was so perfectly satisfied of the wisdom

---

* The Rev. Philip Gurdon, who was afterwards very useful at Cookham, in Berkshire, and subsequently became curate to Mr Cadogan, at St Giles's, Reading.
† The Rev. W. Talbot of Reading. There are four letters addressed to Mrs Talbot in the second volume of *Cardiphonia*.

and rectitude of the Lord's appointments, that if he was sure of relieving himself only by stretching out his hand, he would not do it, unless he was equally sure it was agreeable to His will that he should do it.'

'April 27th. At the visitation. I had a call of duty, otherwise I need not wish to pass a day to less purpose. We had a sermon on contending earnestly for the faith; but, alas! the true faith was opposed and reviled. At dinner nothing spiritual or even serious, though forty persons or upwards who bear the name of ministers of Christ'

'May 24th. Began the Epistle to the Colossians at the Great House.'

It was on the 28th of May that Mrs Unwin and Mr Cowper left the vicarage, after having been there some fourteen months. Mr Newton thus speaks of this circumstance: 'My dear friends Mrs Unwin and Mr Cowper, who have been our guests since 12th April last year, this day returned to their own house. This is a proof that he is in some respects better; for till very lately he could not bear the proposal of going home. When Mrs Unwin used every means to urge his return he would weep and plead to stay. The Lord has graciously interposed in this business. Reports and misconstructions have for some time made me uneasy. My friends were ready to blame me. I endeavoured to satisfy myself that however chargeable with shame before the Lord in many respects, yet in this point my heart was upright in His sight. I could not relieve myself, but He has mercifully relieved me.

'I can see much of His wisdom and goodness in sending him under my roof, and now I see His goodness in removing him. Upon the whole, I have not been weary of my cross. Besides the submission I owe to the Lord, I think I can hardly do or suffer too much for such a friend, yet sometimes my heart has been impatient and rebellious. His health is better; he works almost incessantly in the garden, and while employed is tolerably easy; but as soon as he leaves off he is instantly swallowed up by the most gloomy apprehensions, though in everything that does not concern his own peace he is as sensible and discovers as quick a judgment as ever.'

'Wednesday, June 8th. This morning Mr and Mrs Trinder, with about a dozen more of their company, called and breakfasted with us on the way to Carlton, to the Baptist Association. I hear there was a very large assembly there. Some hundreds, I suppose, went from Olney. I should have liked to have gone myself, but thought my presence would not be agreeable to some. Ere long the effects of bigotry and a party spirit will cease.'

Writing about this time to his sister-in-law, Mrs Cunningham, who had removed to Scotland, he sends her a copy of his hymn, entitled 'Jacob's Ladder,'* saying: 'Your removal led my thoughts to the subject of the following hymn, and therefore you ought to have a copy.'

The same month Mr Newton was at Bedford at the house of Mr Symonds. In the diary we find this sentence: 'My visit at Mr Symonds's not disagreeable. Yet I have reason to be ashamed of evil discovered in my heart, and mistakes in conversation. It was my fault that the time was not better improved.'

The reference of this last sentence will be seen in the following extract from a letter written to Mr Symonds two days after this visit. It is a beautiful illustration of that true refinement of Christian feeling which was always conspicuous in Mr Newton: 'Though I was very glad to see you and our friends at your house, I was not pleased with myself when there. Particularly, I was sorry I gave way to the discourse about baptism, which, as we all seemed well persuaded in our own minds, was little better than idle talk. When tea was almost over, it occurred to me how easily I might have turned it to a more profitable subject; but then it was too late. Methinks it did not require much study to find out that we were but poorly employed. Perhaps I may be wiser hereafter; but one word draws upon another so strangely, that we are liable to be entangled before we are aware, for Mr Self loves to speak last.'

* *Olney Hymns*, i. 9.

'Sunday, 26th. Spoke in the evening from a hymn on the day of judgment.'* This hymn, he says previously, took him the most of two days to finish.

'Thursday, July 6th. [*sic:* July 6, 1774, was a Wednesday] *Omicron's Letters* are now published. May the Lord accompany them with His blessing. In reading them, I could not but observe how different I appear on paper from what I know myself to be. If the Lord has enabled me to express myself with some propriety upon any of the important subjects of the gospel, instead of assuming anything to myself on this account, I ought to be covered with shame and confusion to think how lamentably I fall short.'

These letters are on a variety of important religious topics. They are twenty-six in number, and were written at various times for the *Gospel Magazine*. A few of them were addressed to Mr Newton's friends — in some cases, through the press. Thus, in the seventeenth letter he says: 'I send these thoughts to you, not by the post, but through the press, because the exercise of which you speak is not peculiar to you or me, but more or less the burden of all who are spiritually minded.'†

To this edition are appended several hymns, which afterwards appeared in the Olney collection, two of them by Mr Cowper, and also the piece on 'The Kite; or Pride must have a Fall.'

One of Mr Newton's lady correspondents asked him the meaning of the term 'Omicron'; and for any who may still desire that information, we may observe that it is a modest and ingenious *nom de plume* [pen-name] borrowed from the Greek alphabet — *omicron*, short or little O.

From the beginning of the present year Mr Newton adopted another signature subscribing himself 'Vigil' or Watchful. Fifteen

* 'Day of Judgment, day of wonders,' ii. 77.
† In a presentation copy to the Rev. W. Bull, we find the following MS. note: 'Letters 1 and 2, Mr. Symonds; 3 and 7, Mr. Jones of Hull; 9, Mr. Milner of Hull; 10, 11, 12, Mr. Thornton; 14, Mr. Cooper (query, Cowper); 17, Mr. John Ryland; 18, the people of Olney. The rest addressed to no one in particular.'

papers appear under this name. He tells one of his correspondents there were also some few other things of his in that publication, particularly verses entitled *Spider and Toad*, to which there is no name subjoined.

From a communication to Mr Newton by his young friend, Mr Ryland of Northampton, written August, 1776, we learn that *Omicron's Letters* had been translated into Dutch, and that the *Narrative* of his life had appeared in that language nine years before.

Mr Newton visited Bedford this year, and speaks with the greatest pleasure of his stay at Mr Barham's. 'Such a happy family,' he says, 'perhaps I never saw, where the peace and love of God seem to dwell in every heart. I spoke every morning after breakfast, and attended chapel (Moravian) every evening. On Thursday,' he adds, 'we paid a morning visit to Mr Howard of Cardington, when we had some interesting conversation. May the Lord bless it. I presented him with an *Omicron*.' The great philanthropist had the previous year commenced his visitation of English prisons, and in 1775 (the year following) undertook his first journey abroad.

At the beginning of September the Rev. Dr and Mrs Ford were guests at Olney. Dr Ford was there on his way to settle at Melton Mowbray: 'a very dark place,' says Mr Newton. 'May they soon rejoice in the light.'

Some days after Mr Newton was at Northampton: 'Preached four times in Mrs Trinder's house. The last,' he says, 'was a favoured season, and I trust many received a blessing. The Lord is pleased to own me to the comfort of the serious young persons in Mrs Trinder's school, of whom I conversed with about twelve this time, who seem very promising.' It was probably on his return from this visit (for the letter is without date), that Mr Newton received a brief communication, signed by fifteen of Mrs Trinder's pupils, expressing the benefit they had derived from his services, and hoping that he would soon come amongst them again. 'I hope I got something for myself likewise,' he adds. 'Heard Mr Ryland twice and Mr Winter. The Lord's work seems to flourish. Mr Ryland, amidst the many particularities which give him an originality of character beyond most men I ever knew, appears to me to greater advantage every time I see him.'

The following quotation will show to what an extent all the events of life were sanctified by the Word of God and prayer in the circle of which Mr Newton formed so important a member, and how many of his friends especially valued his supplications at the throne of grace. It is from a clergyman, who was to be married: 'As I would have many of the Lord's people holding up their hands and hearts to Him for us on the day of our approaching marriage, I am sure I know of none whose prayers I would sooner desire than yours. I therefore must entreat you to meet us on Thursday, October 6th. And to whomsoever else you shall choose to communicate this, beg likewise their charity toward us. 'Tis thus I would enter the holy state, and shall count it my great privilege. It will comfort us much to consider that we have so many children of the Lord imploring His blessing on us.'

On Sunday, October 2nd, we have this entry: 'For several weeks past the Sabbath has found me unprepared of subjects for preaching; yet I believe, provided my time was properly filled up in other services, this would be no disadvantage to speak freely and simply, without previous plans, upon any suitable passage of Scripture that should occur.'

At a later period Mr Newton writes: 'In the morning I had not a single subject in view. Lord, I am empty indeed, but, oh, the happiness of feeling some dependence upon Thee, and of receiving out of Thy fulness in measure and in season as services and occasions occur. Surely this is the more excellent way, and better than hoarding up upon paper, or in the memory, notions of truth, which are apt to breed the worms of self-admiration and self-dependence. I conceive a ripeness in ministerial abilities to consist much in a gracious power of trusting in Thee for a readiness to bring out things new and old that shall be suitable to the subject and the auditory.'

Mr Venn, when congratulating his friend on his appointment to St Mary Woolnoth, in 1779, alludes to their difference of opinion on this point, and urges Mr Newton to its reconsideration. Mr Newton's judgment, as Mr Cecil justly observes, was certainly deficient in this matter.

In consequence of a bad harvest and other threatening appearances the state of things in the country was serious; and on this account Mr Newton commenced an early morning prayer-meeting on Tuesday, October 3rd. [*sic:* October 3, 1774, was a Monday] As a proof of the scarcity that prevailed, it is mentioned that on Saturday 14th [*sic:* October 14, 1774, was a Friday] a wagon laden with flour was attacked, and in great danger of being plundered by a mob assembled for that purpose about the Bull Inn; but the robbery was happily prevented.

In December, Mrs Newton lost by death her brother, Mr George Catlett. This rendered a journey to London necessary. They stopped at Whetstone for the night, 'and,' says Mr Newton, 'had an agreeable family meeting. Expounded the 23rd Psalm, and prayed with the master and mistress of the inn.'

'My brother,' says Mr Newton, 'has left a sweet orphan girl about five years old (her mother died two years ago), which we now, in dependence upon the Lord, and the clear call of His providence, cheerfully adopt for our own. Oh, may He by His grace adopt her into His chosen family!'

In reference to Mr Cowper, Mr Newton says: 'My dear friend is better in many respects than he was this time twelve-month. Some of his most dreadful temptations removed; his spirit more at liberty to attend to common incidents; yet the main stress of his disorder still remains.'

1775. Mr Newton regrets, to one of his friends, that his correspondence was so enlarged year by year, that he found great difficulty in meeting its demands. He was, therefore, very busy this month (January) in letter writing. In one of these communications he thus gives his opinion of [Richard] Baxter. He had been reading one of his sermons in the *Morning Exercises*; and, after speaking of some of his theological sentiments as rather cloudy, he adds: 'But by what I have read of him, where he is quiet and not ruffled by controversy, he appears to me, notwithstanding some mistakes, to have been one of the greatest men of his age, and perhaps in fervour, spirituality, and success, more than equal both as a minister and a Christian to some twenty taken together, of those who affect to undervalue him in this present day. There is a spirit in some passages of his *Saints' Rest*, his *Dying Thoughts*, and other of his practical treatises, compared with which many modern compositions, though well written and well meant, appear to me to a great disadvantage.'

A hymn was now made for every Sunday evening's service at the Great House. Thus, on the 22nd January, the hymn on the Queen of Sheba was written: on the 29th, the Withered Fig Tree. The hymns entitled 'The Lord will provide' and 'Lazarus,' were written in February, and on March 5th the hymn, 'I would but cannot sing.'*

In the month of March Mr and Mrs Newton spent a week in Leicestershire, visited Mr Robinson,† and Dr Ford at Melton. Mr Newton was engaged nearly the whole time in various religious exercises, preaching to crowded congregations, especially at Leicester.

He thus speaks of this journey, when in prospect, to his friend Mr Bowman: 'I am going (if the Lord please) into Leicestershire on Friday. This was lately such a dark place as you describe your country to be, and much of it is so still; but the Lord has visited three of the principal towns with gospel light. I have a desire of visiting these brethren in the vineyard, to bear my poor testimony to the truths they preach, and to catch, if I may, a little fire and fervour among them.'

* *Olney Hymns*, i. 34; i. 97; i. 7; ii. 105; i. 126.
† Afterwards vicar of St Mary's, Leicester, and author of *The Christian System*, *Scripture Characters*, etc.

There is no particular record in the month of April; but an interesting letter on the doctrines of free grace was written to Mr Newton by the Rev. Mr Woodman, of Thorn, from which we give the following sentences: 'Some time last summer I had an opportunity to read (as lent to me) Mr Fletcher's *Four Checks to Antinomianism.* I hope they were some use to me. I fear those on our side have often delivered truths in a raw, unguarded manner. I think he is sincere in his concern for the interests of holiness; but I wish he was more sensible than I fear he is of our obligations to grace; yet this, I think, he has a real regard for too. I know not how to account for several things relating to the controversy between the Predestinarians and Universalists, which have been remarked by me more of late than in former years . . . I heartily join with Mr Fletcher in his wish expressed somewhere in a large note, I think in the *Second Check*, that some person equal to the undertaking would stand forth and settle this matter between those advocates for grace and works. I know no one so well qualified as 'Omicron' or 'Vigil.'

'I cannot with Mr Fletcher think Judas was ever truly pious: that word, 'I *never* knew you, NEVER approved of you', is full proof to me apostates were never pious. I would have the practical part of religion firmly adhered to; yet God's children should not be robbed of their comfort nor God of His glory to humour meritmongers, or because dogs will snatch at the children's bread.'

In May we find a mention of Mr Teedon, a schoolmaster of Bedford, who came to Olney about this time, and in whom Mr Newton interested himself. His name will be remembered by the readers of Mr Cowper's life. On the 13th Mr Newton was surprised by a visit from an old friend, Mr Whitford. The sight of him revived the remembrance of many incidents long since past. It is a singular circumstance that, Mr Drake being soon afterwards removed by death, Mr Whitford succeeded him as the Independent minister at Olney, and as long as Mr Newton remained their old intimacy continued unimpaired.

On the 18th May there is this important entry: 'Received an unexpected letter from Mr Scott,* my brother curate near me, very long and frank. It seems dictated by a spirit in search of the truth.' Of what importance this intercourse was in its results is well known, and it will be interesting as we proceed to read Mr Newton's various notices of its progress and issues.

'31st. The paper this evening brought an account of the commencement of hostilities in New England [the outbreak of the American Revolutionary War], and many killed on both sides. These things I fear are the beginning of sorrows. Oh, that I could be suitably affected with what I see and hear.'

A few days afterwards Mr Newton says that, 'having proposed an extraordinary meeting for prayer weekly on account of the times, we began this morning; and, though we met at five o'clock, more people were present than we usually have in the evening.'

'Sunday, June 11th. In the evening I gave a brief sketch of the past and present state of the nation, with a view to engage the people to attendance on our Tuesday morning meetings by apprising them of the importance of the present crisis. Hymn 207 was composed for this service.'†

'Friday, 16th. I have done little with my pen this week, but made a hymn, and answered Mr Scott's last letter, which, after many interruptions, I could only finish tonight. Then went to hear Mr Ashburner.' This letter to Mr Scott is one of great wisdom, and breathes a most Christian spirit. After speaking on the topics on which Mr Scott's mind was wavering, Mr Newton concludes with these words: 'I set a great value upon your offer of friendship, which I trust will not be interrupted on either side by the freedom with which we

---

* The Rev. Thomas Scott, the commentator.
† The hymns have been spoken of several times, but only described by their numbers — a temporary mode of reference — they being subsequently arranged upon another principle. The hymn commences, 'The gathering clouds, with aspect dark,' ii. 64.

mutually express our difference of sentiments when we are constrained to differ.'

'Monday, 19th. In the afternoon Mr Robinson, of Leicester, called. We soon set the bells ringing to give notice of preaching.'

Tuesday, 20th, Mr Newton speaks of a meeting of the Baptist Association at Olney. Of one of the sermons he heard on that occasion he says: 'It was an excellent discourse indeed, and the Lord was pleased to give me some softenings and relentings of heart. It is long since I had such an opportunity. O Lord, soften me yet more, and enable me to rejoice in Thy peace.' Four of the Baptist ministers dined with him the same day.

'Monday, July 3rd. Took the Miss Barhams to see Hannah Markham. She has walked honourably several years; and I have long looked upon her as the most eminent and exemplary Christian among us. She is now upon her dying bed, worn out with age and infirmities, but perfectly composed and happy — waiting the happy moment of her dismission with warm desire, tempered with unreserved submission to the will of the Lord.'

'Wednesday, 5th. Mr Brire, a student at Dr Conder's academy, called upon me, prompted, as he said, by reading my *Narrative*. Alas! that I should be no more affected by my wonderful case, when it has made such an impression on the hearts of many strangers. He went with me to Cranfield, where I preached, upon a sudden emergency, in Mr Goodman's house, to a large number of people. The Lord gave me a pleasant journey and liberty in speaking.'

'Sunday, July 23rd. I found on my return from service a present from my dear friend (Mr Thornton), which I begged him to procure for me at Paris — the *Essais de Morale* of M. Nicole. They proved to be twenty-five volumes, the last being the life of the author. A voluminous writer, yet wonderfully exact, and though in many things strongly tinctured with the mistakes and prejudices of the Romish Church, yet expresses a savour and spirit of Divine truth which would do honour to a Protestant pen.'

'Saturday, 29th. At Mr Thornton's request drew up a short preface for his new edition of the first part of *Pilgrim's Progress*.'

In a letter to Mr Stillingfleet on the 26th, Mr Newton makes the following judicious observation on the subject of Calvinism: 'I am an avowed Calvinist; the points which are usually comprised in that term seem to me so consonant to Scripture, reason (when enlightened), and experience, that I have not the shadow of a doubt about them. But I cannot dispute; I dare not speculate. What is by some called High Calvinism [or Hyper-Calvinism] I dread. I feel much more union of spirit with some Arminians than I could with some Calvinists; and if I thought a person feared sin, loved the Word of God, and was seeking after Jesus, I would not walk the length of my study to proselyte him to the Calvinist doctrines. Not because I think them mere opinions, or of little importance to a believer — I think the contrary; but because I believe these doctrines will do no one any good till he is taught them of God. I believe a too hasty assent to Calvinistic principles, before a person is duly acquainted with the plague of his own heart, is one principal cause of that lightness of profession which so lamentably abounds in this day, a chief reason why many professors are rash, heady, high-minded, contentious about words, and sadly remiss as to the means of Divine appointment. For this reason, I suppose, though I never preached a sermon in which the tincture of Calvinism may not be easily discerned by a judicious hearer, yet I very seldom insist expressly upon those points, unless they fairly and necessarily lie in my way.'

'Thursday, 10th [August]. Wrote a long letter to Mr Scott.' Mr Newton had written the previous month. In these letters he discusses various topics relating to the great principles of gospel truth, and he concludes the above letter with these words: 'I feel myself much interested in your concerns. And your unexpected frank application to me (though you well know the light in which I appear to some people) I consider as a providential call, which binds me to your service. I hope our correspondence will be productive of happy effects, and that we shall both one day rejoice in it.'

About the middle of this month Mr Newton went to London, and while there the living of Deptford became vacant. 'I had,' he says, 'the second offer, which caused me some serious thoughts; but Dr Conyers accepted it. All my friends seemed to think I ought to have accepted it had it come before me, and I believe I should; yet surely, as to my own concernments, I have a thousand reasons for wishing to remain where I am.'

Again, he says: 'Mr Thornton thinks I am designed for Halifax. It seems to be impossible, for many reasons besides my own unworthiness. Yet there are some faint reasons on the other side. Let me not desire it; but should it be so, may the Lord clearly shine on my path, and suffer me not to mistake His voice or to have a will of my own.'

It is proof of the political excitement that prevailed at this time, that, on the 28th, Mr Samuel Thornton, writing to Mr Newton, says: 'A king's messenger has been down to Northampton for Mr Ryland, who was reprimanded for speaking too freely in the pulpit upon the present American disputes. It was reported, and almost universally believed for two or three days, that they had put him into Newgate; but that proves a falsity, as a gentleman saw him in the streets yesterday.' The Rev. Robert Hall relates to a circumstance which will confirm the above statement. He says: 'When I was quite a lad my father took me to Mr Ryland's school at Northampton. Mr Ryland was then violently against the American war. The subject being mentioned, he rose and said, with a fierce countenance and a loud voice: "If I were General Washington I would summon all my officers around me, and make them draw blood from their arms into a basin, and, dipping their swords into it, swear that they would not sheath them till America had gained her independence."'

'Thursday, 18th. Much of my leisure since I have been alone* has been employed in writing to Mr Scott. This correspondence takes

* Mrs. Newton was from home, in consequence of her father's illness.

up much time, and hitherto I seem to get but little ground. It is Thy prerogative to enlighten and awake the heart. In dependence upon Thy blessing I persevere.'

'Sunday, Nov. 19th. The hymn written for this day was "Afflictions do not come alone."'*

Speaking of his friend Mr Bull, on the 30th, Mr Newton says: 'He has just called and spent an hour with me. I seem to shrink into nothing when before him, to be a poor, empty, superficial creature. I could sit silent half a day to listen to him, and am almost unwilling to speak a word for fear of preventing him.' Again, some days afterwards: '. . . For myself, as I had been chiefly sedentary, I thought a little exercise would do me good, and therefore walked to Newport to breakfast with Mr Bull; stayed near three o'clock. My visit was very pleasant. I admire Mr Bull, so humble, so spiritual, so judicious, and so savoury. He seems well pleased with me, though surely not with the same reason. However, I rejoice in what the Lord has done for him, and I think he will be my most profitable companion in these parts.'

December 5th, he attends the meeting of Baptist ministers, and expresses his pleasure in uniting with them.

'11th. Much of my leisure employed this week in finishing a long letter to Mr Scott, which will probably close our correspondence, unless the Lord is pleased to work upon his heart by what I have already sent, or by some other means.'†

'13th. My mind sadly filled with idle thoughts about Halifax. It is against probability, and most likely such an event would plunge me in trouble for the rest of my life. What I hear from Mr Hall (of Arnsby) is well suited to rebuke and shame me for my vanity and fickleness. I see one whom I have reason both as a Christian and a minister to prefer to myself supplied with a very slender provision, and yet content, while I am seeking, or at least desiring great things

* *Olney Hymns*, i. 135.
† See *Cardiphonia*, i. 208.

for myself. Lord forgive me, I pray Thee, and cure this weakness, this wickedness.' The letter referred to describes Mr Hall's difficulties, which, through Mr Newton's intervention, were subsequently relieved by Mr Thornton's generous assistance.

22nd, another entry about Mr Scott. 'My debate with him seems closed for the present. He writes in a very friendly spirit, and I shall wait in hope of a blessing attending my occasional intercourse with him. He has sincerity (if I mistake not) in such a sense as he could not have if the Lord had not in some degree visited his heart. May He be pleased to lead him gently on, and to reveal His salvation to him.'

In a letter to Mrs Newton on the 26th, he says: 'Yesterday was a busy time . . . I am sufficiently indulgent to Mr Self. Do not fear my pinching or overworking him. I need a spur more than a bridle. You often think I do too much. I much oftener see cause to confess myself — comparatively, at least — a slothful and unprofitable servant. In the concerns of immortal souls, with eternity in view, and so much depending upon the present moment, what assiduity or importunity can be proportioned to the case? I ought to be always on the wing, seizing any opportunity of aiming to be useful, whether by word or pen, and much more careful and diligent than I am to redeem the time.'

At the close of the year Mr. and Mrs. Trinder paid their annual visit to Olney. The last day of the year was a Sabbath, and is closed with appropriate reflections.

9: OLNEY
(1776–9)

Severe Weather – Charge of meddling with politics – Mr Scott – Baptist Association – Eclipse of the Moon – Ordination of Mr Sutcliff – Mr Barham – Surgical Operation – Probable Removal to Hull – Dr Dodd – Journey into Warwickshire and Leicestershire – Cook's Voyages – Visitors – Death of Mr Catlett – Visit to London – Fire at Olney – Mr Cecil – Foote – The Theatre – Fifth of November – Reflections – Letter to Mrs Cunningham – Confirmation – Letter to Mr Bull – A Lion at Olney – Rowland Hill at Olney – State of the Country – Allegorical Preaching – Mr Barham – *Olney Hymns* – Scott's *Force of Truth* – Journey into Leicestershire – Illness of Mr Scott – *Cardiphonia* – Law's writings – Prospect of Removal – The Living of St Mary Woolnoth accepted – Regrets.

At the opening of the new year (1776) Mr Newton expresses his thankfulness that he was aided in preaching his new year's sermon to the young, and prays that the other ministers who were to preach on the following evenings might be instruments for good.

Early in January it was Mr Newton's intention to go to London, Mrs Newton having been there for some weeks; but a heavy snowstorm rendered the roads impassable. Very beautifully he speaks of this circumstance in the following sentences: 'I desire to rest not only quiet but satisfied with Thy will. I often feel my weakness and my wickedness in a secret dissatisfaction with the weather, especially when I or mine have a journey in view, as if God's great plan should conform to my narrow views. Oh, to believe that not a worm or a leaf can move but by Thee; and to live in a cheerful persuasion that Thou doest all things well!'

Such was the state of the weather that the post became irregular, travelling was to a great extent prevented, and in every way there was much inconvenience and suffering. We glean the following particulars from the notes and letters of Mr Newton.

On the 9th, Mr Newton writes: 'I hope you will not say, "Ah, this naughty snow, to prolong our separation." Every flake of it fell by the Lord's direction as to the time and spot. And He times our affairs; or the snow might have caught your father upon the road, as it did some company between Woburn and Newport on Sunday, so that they could get neither backward or forward. At last, after six hours' toil in jeopardy (the distance is but five miles), they reached Broughton, and thought it an escape as from shipwreck. Come, all is well. We are indeed asunder, but I am not in Guinea. I allow I feel it to be a cross, but we might have had a heavier. And the Lord can — I trust will — do us good by this.'

Two days later: 'The great fall of snow today has blocked up the roads. I believe no stage has passed this week either up or down, and we have had no post since Monday' (this was Friday). 'I hear that at Woburn and Brickhill the places are so full of passengers that can get no farther any way that hardly a bed can be procured for money.'

Again, on the 16th: 'I suppose there has hardly been such a stop upon the road in the memory of man. The road from Dunstable to Newport is said to be hardly passable for a horse.'

On the 27th, Mr Newton writes: 'As Dr Ford officiated the three last Sunday evenings, we have not had a new hymn since the new year began. That which is for tomorrow I will send on the other side.* This sharp frost is as a lion to many of our poor people, but the Lord who sent it can sanctify it, and teach them to get honey from it'.

On the 6th February, Mr Newton mentions the arrival of his father-in-law, Mr Catlett, at Olney, who, though a great invalid, arrived in a chaise without injury, though the postboy could hardly get off his horse, and declared he thought he could not possibly have gone two miles farther. He adds: 'I wrote to Lord Dartmouth for the

* The hymn begins, 'The lion that on Samson roared,' i. 24.

poor, and received a kind letter with twenty pounds. We are trying to get the town to make a collection.'

On the 8th, Mrs Newton reached home in safety, after an absence of twelve weeks. To Mr Newton's affectionate, loving heart this separation had been a great trial.

'13th. A little writing to-day. O Lord, do Thou guide my pen, and renew my diligence in improving time. Let me stir up the gifts Thou hast favoured me with, and not tarnish them for want of exercise.'

Under the date of February 16th he addressed a letter to Mrs Thornton, on the Divinity of Christ, being a continuation of a former letter on the same subject in the previous November.*

'17th. Wrote to Lord Dartmouth to exculpate myself from a charge I found entertained against me of meddling with politics, and ranking myself on the side of the complainers. I trust the Lord has given me a love to peace and submission, and I wish to be found amongst those that are quiet in the land.' It may be observed that the most absurd rumours were in circulation in consequence of the establishment of the prayer-meeting already referred to.

On the 25th, Mr Newton says: 'Through the goodness of a gracious God I have received letters from Lord Dartmouth and Mr Serle' (who had written to him on the subject) 'making me easy about the late charge. It is Thou, O Lord, who preservest my character and givest me favour in the eyes of men.'

Writing in the month of May to his friend Mr West, Mr Newton says: 'I trust the Lord has not wholly withdrawn from us. We walk in peace, and have some seasons of refreshment; now and then we hear of a new inquirer. I would be thankful when as an angler I catch a single fish. But oh that the Lord would put His great net in my hand, and fill it with a shoal!'

'Thursday, 9th. Mr Scott dined and spent the afternoon with me and stayed [for] church. We had some free conversation; and though

* *Cardiphonia*, ii. 12.

he does not see things clearly, I have reason to hope the Lord has begun a good work in his heart. Lord, confirm my hopes, and teach him, that he may be a blessed instrument of teaching others.'

May 27th, Sir Harry Trelawny writes to Mr Newton, saying he has two years before he can take orders; and not having much business at Oxford he wished to reside at Olney and put himself under Mr Newton's direction.

On the 29th, he speaks of the meeting of the Baptist Association, and of his great interest in the services. Mr Newton's house was full of company. He preached himself on the following evening, when five or six of the ministers who remained in town came to church. The next morning they breakfasted with him, and, as he says, 'We seemed all mutually pleased.'

On the 4th of June he was visited by Dr and Mrs Ford. On the 19th of the same month Mr Newton was present at the settlement of his old friend Mr Whitford over the Independent church at Olney.

At the end of the month, being in London, he tells us he was at Clapham, and obtained assistance for Mr Whitford.

'July 30th. To-night I attended (*sic*) an eclipse of the moon. How great, O Lord, are Thy works! with what punctuality do the heavenly bodies fulfil their courses and observe the seasons to a moment! All things obey Thee but fallen angels and fallen man. My thoughts would have taken a serious turn, but I was not alone. I thought, my Lord, of Thine eclipse. The horrible darkness which overwhelmed Thy mind when Thou saidst, "Why hast Thou forsaken Me?" Ah, sin was the cause — my sins — yet I do not hate sin nor loathe myself as I ought.'

'31st. Dined at the mill' (Lavendon) 'with Mr Bull. In the evening walked to the village. Mr Bull preached, and I heard with some pleasure. Do Thou, Lord, command a blessing. A pleasant walk home.'

On the 3rd of August, Mr Newton committed his little orphan niece, Miss Catlett, to the care of his friend Mrs Trinder of

Northampton, and he expresses his earnest desire that she may be an early partaker of spiritual blessings.

On the 7th, Mr Sutcliff was ordained over the Baptist church at Olney. Mr Newton was present, and gives a full account of the services.

In September, Mr and Mrs Newton paid their annual visit to Northampton. 'Preached the four mornings of my stay, and on Friday evening, when there was as large a company as the house would hold. The Lord puts great honour upon Mrs Trinder in owning her prayers and discourses to the awakening of many of her scholars. Oh may my child share the blessing. Heard Mr Ryland. He is always instructive and savoury.'

In November, Mr Newton underwent an operation for a tumour in his thigh. He was mercifully brought through it, and was very soon able to resume his ordinary duties. On this occasion he composed the 71st Hymn, Book ii. in the *Olney Hymns*.

About this time Mr Newton addressed a letter to Lord Dartmouth, in which may be found some very judicious remarks on the subject of things lawful, but not expedient, and which have a very striking application to the circumstances of the present times.*

Writing to his friend Mr Rose, on the 21st, he congratulates him on having obtained a living, 'especially because I believe God has given you a desire to be useful to souls. Church preferment, in any other view, is dreadful; and I would as soon congratulate a man upon seeing a millstone tied about his neck, to sink him into the depths of the sea, as upon his obtaining what is called a good living, except I thought him determined to spend and be spent in the cause of the gospel. A parish is an awful millstone indeed to those who see nothing valuable in the flock but the fleece.'

1777. The services at the beginning of the year were as usual. In March there seemed a great probability of Mr Newton's removal

* *Cardiphonia*, i. 138.

to Hull, but just when everything appeared to be settled another clergyman was appointed. 'There was much grief,' says Mr Newton, 'amongst the people;' and he adds: 'The 1st March is now to supersede the annual commemoration of the 1st of February. It is to be a Hull instead of a Cottenham day, which was growing old. The Lord make us thankful and fruitful.'

Mr Newton mentions the case of the unhappy Dr Dodd, and says how much it affected him. 'How downhill,' he observes, 'is the road to sin! How powerful Satan when the soul is once entangled! He once preached the truth and began to meet the cross, but, alas! the fear of man and the hope of preferment turned him aside. For a while he appeared to succeed, obtained titles, livings, a prebend — was publicly disgraced some years ago for an attempt to gain a living by money, and is now likely to lose his life by a public execution.' We find under a subsequent date, in a communication from Mr Barham, that Mr La Trobe had visited Dr Dodd, and felt satisfied that he died a real penitent.

In April we are told that Mr Samuel and Mr Robert Thornton visited Olney on their way to Yorkshire, and then follow these words: 'My Lord, forgive me that, besides many other things wrong in me, I have not bridled my tongue. I profess to abhor evil speaking of another, yet I fear I have been guilty of it in a rash and needless censure of Mr De Courcy — was ensared in other respects with levity, from a foolish desire of pleasing. Oh pardon me, and teach me to avoid the like evils in future.'

Mr Newton being asked by Mr Ryland to preach his annual sermons at Birmingham, availed himself of the opportunity to make a brief tour by way of Melton, Leicester, and elsewhere, and preached not less than nineteen times, being absent about three weeks. He was refused the pulpit at Lutterworth; 'but God,' he says, 'opened a door for me at a neighbouring village — Bitteswell, where I preached Thursday evening and the next morning to large auditories, and with much apparent acceptance.'

Upon reading the voyages of Captain Cook in the Southern Ocean, great concern is expressed for the spiritual condition of the inhabitants. 'Lord,' he says, 'hast Thou not a time for these poor benighted souls, when Thou wilt arise and shine upon them?' That time was soon to come.

On the 15th June, Mr Newton speaks of several visitors, and then adds: 'In the evening, O Lord, I felt my vain heart presumptuously and feloniously trading for itself upon Thy stock. Because Thou gavest me some undeserved liberty, I was led to indulge the thought that some present would think I spoke well.'

About this time two young men preparing for the church settled for some time at Olney, to avail themselves of Mr Newton's instructions in theology.

Mrs Newton's father had resided at Olney from the commencement of the year preceding, and at the beginning of August it pleased God to remove him. His last days were happy and peaceful, and he died in the hope of the gospel. Mr Newton thus writes to Mrs Cunningham in reference to it: 'Mr Romaine came hither on Sunday. My father was much rejoiced to see him, and expressed himself to him very comfortably. Mr Romaine conversed and prayed with him two or three times, and was one of the last persons to whom he spoke on Friday evening. I thought it providential that the only gospel minister whom he knew, and had formerly heard, should be sent, as it were, on purpose to close his eyes, and receive his dying testimony . . . Considering what he endured, and the comfortable hope in Christ which he possessed unshaken in life and in death, I cannot consider his removal a subject for grief.'

'September 2nd. A visit from Mr Scott yesterday morning. O my Lord, I thank Thee for Thy goodness to him; I think he gets forward into the light of Thy truth.'

'8th. A talking day. We went, a large company, to see Mr Bull. We went, O Lord, in Thy name. Met T. Priestly, from Manchester, a lively, active spirit. Some things he said called for notice. How different from his brother! It is Thy grace makes us to differ.'

'15th. Drank tea yesterday with Mr Scott. Was rejoiced to see how Thy goodness has confirmed the hopes I conceived two years ago when we corresponded for some months. Though his views were then very dark, and he objected to almost every point proposed, yet I could perceive Thou hadst given him a sincerity, which I looked upon as a token of Thy further favour. And now he seems enlightened and established in the most important parts of the gospel, and will I trust prove an instrument of usefulness in Thy hand.'

During the greater part of October Mr Newton was in London; but he was not idle, for during that time he preached and expounded between thirty and forty times. He says: 'Mr Scott preached twice in my absence with much acceptance.'

While Mr Newton was away on this occasion a fire broke out in Olney, which did considerable damage. Not less than £200 was contributed by his friends in London for the relief of the sufferers.

In a letter addressed to Mrs Newton, her husband thus writes of Mr Cecil: 'I heard him at St Antholin's. He is a good speaker and a good preacher for a young man — for young men, not having had time to be duly acquainted with the depths of the heart and the depths of Satan, cannot ordinarily be expected to speak with so much feeling and experience as they who have been in many conflicts and exercises. I love young preachers, for they are sprightly, warm and earnest. I love old preachers, for they are solid, savoury and experimental. So I love them all, and am glad to hear all as occasion offers. But I own I like the old wine best. It is a mercy that the Lord not only gives us food, but such a variety that every one may in his turn have his palate pleased if he be not quite unreasonable and dainty indeed.'

'November 1st. The late death of Mr Foote ought to affect me. The papers abound with accounts of his gaiety a few hours before he was snatched into eternity. How awful, to spend a life in disseminating folly and wickedness, and then to be summoned without time or heart to ask for mercy! Thou wilt have mercy on whom Thou wilt; Thou art sovereign. I equalled him in inclination, however I fell short of him in ability and opportunity for mischief. But I was spared, and he was hardened.'

It was in a letter written some time during this year that Mr Newton thus expresses himself on the subject of theatrical entertainments, and it may be fitly introduced after the above remarks: 'If there is any practice in this land sinful, attendance on the play-house is properly and eminently so. The theatres are fountains and means of vice; I had almost said in the same manner and degree as the ordinances of the gospel are the means of grace; and I can hardly think there is a Christian upon earth who would dare to be seen there, if the nature and effects of the theatre were properly set before him. Dr Witherspoon, of Scotland, has written an excellent piece upon the Stage, or, rather, against it, which I wish every person who makes the least pretence to fear God had an opportunity of perusing. I cannot judge much more favourably of Ranelagh, Vauxhall, and all the innumerable train of dissipations by which the god of this world blinds the eyes of multitudes, lest the light of the glorious gospel should shine in upon them.'

'Sunday, 2nd. Spoke on the subject of the fire in the evening from a hymn I composed on the occasion.'*

An attempt was made on the 5th of November to restrain the excesses that usually prevailed on that day, and especially with a view to lessen the probability of fire. This gave rise to a great deal of opposition. The excitement was so great that Mr Newton's house was threatened. 'My heart,' says the good man, 'is deceitful, but I hope I bear no resentment against any. I pray that all who have acted in a wrong spirit may be forgiven.'

This affair was a great grief to him; and it is recorded that he said afterwards that he believed he should never have left Olney had not

* 'Wearied by day with toils and cares,' ii. 63.

so incorrigible a spirit prevailed in a parish he had long laboured to reform.

On the 10th, Mr Scott's name occurs again: 'Breakfasted yesterday with Mr Scott. The Lord has answered my desires, and exceeded my expectation in him. How gradually and yet how clearly has he been taught of God the truth of the gospel, and favoured with a single eye to seek that truth above all! I hope to see him (if my life is spared) eminent in knowledge, power, and usefulness. What an honour and mercy should I esteem it to be any way instrumental in this good work! All the praise be to God!'

On the 31st December we have, amongst other appropriate reflections for the close of the year, the expression of his old liberality: 'In the evening heard Mr Whitford's sermon to the young people. He was very faithful and earnest. May Thy blessing crown this threefold service. Help me to entreat Thy presence with the other ministers equally with myself. I beg that good may be done, and to be well pleased that all who serve Thee in the gospel may have a share in it as instruments in Thy hands, without limiting my regard to names, parties or persons. Such a spirit would be the best token for comfort and success to myself.'

1778. January 22nd, Mr Scott came to hear. From this time we find him frequently at Mr Newton's week-day services at church and at the Great House. On his preaching for him on one of these occasions, Mr Newton says: 'My heart rejoiced and wondered. O my Lord, what a teacher art Thou! How soon, clearly and solidly is he established in the knowledge and experience of Thy gospel, who but lately was a disputer against every point! I praise Thee for him. Often in my faint manner have I prayed to see some of my neighbours of the clergy awakened. Thou hast answered prayer. Oh may it please Thee yet to add to the number.'

Writing to Mrs Cunningham in February, after having made some necessary allusion to Mr Catlett's will, he adds: 'Let us praise the Lord Jesus that before He died He made His will, and He remembered us in it. By His death the will was valid (*Heb.* 9:16). And He is now risen, and is the executor of His own will, so that it is not possible we can be defrauded of what He has bequeathed us. The chief articles are tribulation, peace, and a kingdom.'

'March 19th. News of more trouble. War with France is inevitable. All seems disastrous abroad and at home. These are, I fear, the beginnings of sorrow. For, though the Lord's hand is lifted up, men will not see.'

On the 23rd of May, Mr Thornton, 'his best friend,' and Dr Conyers visited Olney.

'24th. I preached with a view to the approaching confirmation, an institution which, as generally managed amongst us, is little better than trifling with holy things. But Thou, Lord, canst overrule and make it an occasion for good. I pray Thee to prepare the hearts of those who are inclined to go, and give me wisdom and faithfulness to speak to them who apply to me.'

'June 9th. At the Bishop's visitation. Captain Scott came home with me, and preached in the evening from Psalm 34:8; a warm experimental discourse.'

In reference to the above statements, Mr Newton thus playfully writes to his friend Mr Bull on the 6th: 'Herewith I send you my sheep's clothing, as an earnest of my purpose to follow it on Tuesday morning to beg a breakfast with you, if the Lord permit. My friend Captain Scott will pass through Newport on his way to Olney on Tuesday. As it is possible I may be engaged with my betters, and as such persons as he and you must not dine with "we preachers" of the Establishment when we meet *in pontificalibus* [in the robes of a bishop or cardinal] I have invited him to quarter an hour or two at your house, till I am at liberty to call for him, and escort him home.'

'30th. Went to see a lion that was brought into town.' Thus piously and ingeniously Mr Newton refers to this circumstance in a letter written a few days afterwards to Mr Bull: 'Last week we had a lion in town. I went to see him. He was wonderfully tame, as familiar with his keeper, and as docile and obedient as a spaniel; yet the man told me he had his surly fits, when they dare not touch him. No looking glass could express my face more justly than this lion did my heart. I could trace every feature. As wild and fierce by nature, yea, much more so, but grace has in some measure tamed me. I know and love my Keeper, and sometimes watch His looks, that I may learn His will. But, oh! I have my surly fits, too — seasons when I relapse into the savage again, as though I had forgotten all. I got a hymn out of this lion, which you shall see when you come to Olney if you please me.'*

There was now much intercourse between Mr Newton and Mr Scott. Mr Newton going to Weston (Mr Scott's curacy), says: 'It is the first time I have heard him since he began to preach *extempore*. His discourse was clear, copious, judicious, and animated.'

July 28th, Mr Newton writes to Mr Bull:

'Mr Rowland Hill will be here on Monday. If agreeable to you and Mr Barton to come and dine with him, you will find some roast beef and a hearty welcome. You may tell it at Newport and publish it at Lathbury that the celebrated and original Mr Rowley Hill will preach at Olney Church on Monday evening at half-past six.'

Soon after follows another brief letter of a similar character:

'Bucks to wit. You are hereby required and enjoined to appear personally at our Episcopal seat in Olney on the present Wednesday, 19th August, to dine with the Rev. Henry Venn and with us. And hereof you are not to fail.

Given at our den — die supra dicto,

John Newton.'

Again, later in the month: '. . . If the Lord affords health — if the weather be tolerable — if no unforeseen change takes place — if no company comes in upon me tonight (which sometimes unexpectedly happens) — with these provisos, Mr Scott and I have engaged to travel to Newport on Monday next, and hope to be with you by eleven o'clock . . . Pray for a blessing on our coming together. It

* 'A lion though by nature wild,' ii. 93.

would be a pity to walk ten miles to pick straws, or to come back with our empty vessels upon our heads, saying, "We have found no water."'

'August 4th. Anniversary of my birthday. Had a pleasant walk to the temple (at Weston), a spot where I have often presented prayer, which God has mercifully answered. I essayed to take a review of past mercies, to humble myself for my ingratitude and sin, and to commit my future path to the Divine care and direction.'

Speaking of the gloomy prospects of the country, under the same date, Mr Newton writes: 'Our great fleet returned, having done but little. A war with France and Spain at the door. America gone. Surely the Lord has a controversy with this sinful land. Therefore our counsels are infatuated and our plans rendered abortive.'

To Mr Thornton he says: 'Our disunion from America is an event of such great importance, so suddenly and irretrievably brought about that it seems to me like a dream, and I can hardly persuade myself it is true; but we must abide by the consequence. Well, if we get to heaven at last all will be well. And I know that even at present they who fear the Lord have no great cause to be alarmed for themselves. If He brings a cloud over the land His covenant rainbow will be seen in it. He knows His own people, where they are, what they need, how to protect, provide for, and support them. And if He permits them to share in general troubles He can give them strength according to their day, and make them joyful in tribulation.'

'Sunday, October 11th. Some breathings of soul after the Lord, and some liberty in service for Him.' Mr Page, of Clifton, preached in the evening. Mr Newton wonders he should be preferred to Mr Scott. A week afterwards he heard him again, and very justly questions his taste when, preaching from Genesis 35:8, he endeavoured to show that Deborah signified the law, Rebekah the church, the oak the cross of Christ, under which the power of the law dies and is buried as to believers. 'Some admire,' he says, 'the ingenuity of those who can find what they please in such quaint texts, which is perhaps a temptation to preachers to give in to this way. Simple people may get benefit, but those of more knowledge are disgusted. I am quite a mole,' adds Mr Newton, writing of this to Mr Bull, 'when compared to these eagle-eyed divines, and must often content myself with plodding upon the lower ground of accommodation and allusion, except when the New Testament writers assure me what the mind of the Holy Ghost was.'

On the 25th he thus speaks of his correspondence with Mr Barlass: 'Much of my leisure yesterday employed in writing to Scotland. Mr B. has entered upon the ministry. His application to me was unexpected, I hope providential. He says the Lord makes me useful to him. It may be so; but the terms in which he speaks of me should rather fill me with shame than make me proud.'

This correspondence was commenced a year or two before, and a volume of letters from Mr Newton to Mr Barlass has been published.

There is a letter of the present date, addressed to Mrs Thornton, containing some curious observations on the influence of separate spirits. It will be found in *Cardiphonia*, vol. ii. p. 34.

Mr Newton was visited during the latter part of this month by Mr Watts Wilkinson, then a student at Oxford, afterwards well known as a popular clergyman in London.

'December 11th. Breakfasted with Mr Scott. Heard him read a narrative of his conversion (*The Force of Truth*) which he has drawn up for publication. It is striking and judicious, and will I hope by the Divine blessing be very useful. I think I can see that he has got before me already. Lord, if I have been useful to him, do Thou, I beseech Thee make him now useful to me.'

'December 22nd. The poor are likely to be in great distress by the failure of their staple business, the lace. O Lord, bless the poor that trust in Thee, and cause all to work together for good.'

'1779. January 1st . . . Last night heard my friend Scott preach at Weston from 1 Timothy 4:8. How should I wonder and rejoice!

Surely when Thou wilt work none can let it. What liberty, power, and judgment in so young a preacher! May Thy comforts fill his heart and Thy blessing crown his labours.'

As usual, Mr Newton attended the sermons to the young at the two dissenting chapels.

'12th. At the Great House concluded the First Epistle of Peter, which I began to expound from November 19, 1776.'

In February the Sunday-evening service was removed from the Great House to the church, Mr Newton expressing his hope that strength might be afforded him for this additional labour. He had now three full services on the Lord's-day.

Mr Newton had been often requested to print his hymns and those of his friend Mr Cowper. To these wishes he yielded, and the *Olney Hymns* were sent to the press in February of this year. We may here be allowed to a few words on this now well-known and popular work. In the preface Mr Newton says: 'A desire of promoting the faith and comfort of sincere Christians, though the principal, was not the only motive of this undertaking. It was likewise intended as a monument to perpetuate the remembrance of an intimate and endeared friendship. With this pleasing view I entered upon my part, which would have been much smaller than it is, and the book would have appeared much sooner and in a very different form, if the wise though mysterious providence of God had not seen fit to cross my wishes. We had not proceeded far upon our proposed plan before my dear friend was prevented by a long and afflicting indisposition from according me any further assistance. My grief and disappointment were great. I hung my harp upon the willows, and for some time determined to proceed no further without him. Yet I was afterwards led to resume the service, and in the course of years the hymns amounted to a considerable number. Deference to the judgment and desires of others has at length overcome the reluctance I long felt to see them in print while I had so few of my friend's hymns to insert in the collection.'

The total number of hymns contributed by Mr Cowper was sixty-eight, so that Mr Newton furnished not less than two hundred and eighty.

In the introductory essay to Collins's edition of the hymns, by Montgomery, it is justly observed that by enlisting Cowper as his coadjutor in the *Olney Hymns*, Newton gave to the poet's mind both the bias and the impulse which ever afterwards directed its course. In speaking of the comparative poetical merit of their several productions the same writer observes that it was no discredit to Newton to be distanced by Cowper in such a race. While he complains of the pulpit idioms, the bald phraseology, and the conversational cadence of his lines, he yet allows that even persons of superior discernment who are at the same time spiritually-minded will highly esteem the labours of Newton in this department. He goes on to say: 'The collection has become a standard book among devout readers of every evangelical denomination, and by the decision of posterity — for the present generation is posterity to the authors — this volume may now safely abide whatever imperfections or offences against good taste may be found in its very numerous and very unequal compositions.'

Acknowledging to a great extent the truth of this criticism, we yet venture to think that justice is hardly done to Mr Newton. With much that is certainly prosaic and halting, the pieces, 'Glorious things of Thee are spoken,' 'Day of judgment, day of wonders,' 'Let us love and sing and wonder,' with some others, are not wanting in the poetry of the imagination, while we have in abundant measure the poetry of feeling — the language that speaks to the heart — in such hymns as, 'Begone, unbelief,' 'How sweet the name of Jesus sounds,' 'Approach, my soul, the mercy seat,' 'Come, my soul, thy suit prepare', and many others.

The volume is divided into three books, the first consisting of select portions of the Old and New Testaments — unquestionably a most difficult exercise of the poetic gift; the second book, on occasional subjects, seasons, ordinances, providence, and creation; the third, on the various aspects of the spiritual life. 'These,' says Montgomery, 'are frequently in a higher tone of poetry, with deeper pathos and more ardent expression, than the average strain of pieces in the foregoing books.'

And now to return to the journal. In the month of March, Mr Scott's *Narrative*, having been revised by Mr Newton, was sent to London to be printed.

In April, Mr and Mrs Newton travelled into Leicestershire, Mr Newton everywhere sympathizing with his friends in their religious efforts, and in every way seeking to strengthen their hands. He preached not less than twenty-seven times during this visit; and in a letter to Mrs Unwin we have the following account of one of these services:

'You can form an idea of the rushing of many waters when a bank breaks in the fens. Such was the rushing into Creaton Church on Wednesday when the doors were opened. The waves soon overflowed the floor, mounted the gallery, covered the windows, walls, and beams. What the church could not contain diffused itself round the walls, so that it was an island surrounded with a sea of heads. We had a good opportunity, I hope. I returned very weary to Northampton, for I went on horseback, and refreshed myself by preaching an hour and a quarter at Mrs Trinder's that evening.'

As a specimen of Mr Thornton's liberality and consideration for his friend, we find in a letter addressed to Mr Newton previous to his journey into Leicestershire the following sentence: 'I wish you and Mrs Newton a good journey to Melton Mowbray, and I enclose you a twenty-pound note to pay charges.'

On the 22nd Mr Newton writes that Mrs Newton was ill again, and that Mr Scott was laid up with fever. 'He caught it,' writes Mr Newton to Mr Bull, 'by attendance on the sick poor. A noble wound! Shall soldiers risk their lives and stand as a mark for great guns for sixpence a day, or for the word of Honour? And is it not worth venturing something in imitation of Him who went about doing good, and when the good we aim at is for His sake?'

Several friends visited Olney about this time — Mrs Wilberforce, Mr Barham, Mr Symonds, and others.

'Tuesday, 25th [May]. Mr Bull spoke excellently at the Great House tonight. It was the first time of his appearance there, but I hope it will not be the last.'

On the 24th of July we find the first thought of *Cardiphonia*: 'Have been employed in revising my letters, which, if the Lord sees fit, are to be my next publication. In reading them over (the originals returned, or copies of them) what cause have I for humiliation! Alas! how faintly am I impressed with those truths which I can easily descant upon to others! How defective in observing myself the rules and cautions I propose to others!'

'August 16th. Met the children. I am fearful lest this stated service should become formal. I see but little effect from it. But it is not necessary I should know. Perhaps the seeds I am now sowing may hereafter, when I am no more in this world, by God's blessing spring up and yield increase. Give me, O Lord, that solicitude in every part of my ministerial business as may engage my prayers and diligence, and then may I submit the event to Thee.'

In the course of this month we have a letter addressed by Mr Newton to his old friend Dr Dixon, in which he gives his opinion of Mr Law's writings. He speaks of his genius, and of the many striking passages to be found in his works, and tells his correspondent that he was once a great admirer of him. He then refers to the necessity of an atonement — 'of something to be done for me as well as in me, and of holiness as utterly unattainable without that. The essence of that holiness I thirst after I conceive to be love and devotedness to God; but how can I love Him till I have hope that His anger is turned away from me, or at least till I can see a solid foundation for that hope? Here Mr Law's scheme fails me, and the gospel gives me relief.'

Mr Newton had now resided at Olney rather more than fifteen years. On several occasions there had been some prospect of change; but hitherto it had been the will of God that he should remain where he was. Now, however, Divine providence seemed very clearly to intimate that the time was come for his removal. And on the 19th of this month we have the following entry in the diary: 'The post has thrown me into a hurry of spirit by the kind offer of my dear friend (the offer by Mr Thornton of the presentation to the parish of St Mary Woolnoth, in London). I look up to Thee, my God, for Thy blessing on the acceptance of it. Thou knowest my heart. I know it not myself. But surely I love this people, and have often wished and prayed to live and die here. If other thoughts of late have sometimes had place, they have rather been transient and involuntary than allowed. Yet I think I see mercy in this new appointment. The trial will be great, but at my time of life a settlement might seem desirable. O my Lord, let me not be deceived in thinking it is Thy call. If Thy presence go not with us still I would pray, Carry us not up hence.' Mr Newton then speaks of some coldness and declension on the part of his parishioners. Yet he prays that God would provide for his poor people, and sanctify this breach to them.

The following is Mr Thornton's characteristic letter on this occasion:

'Dear Sir, I read in the papers today of the death of Dr Plumptree; and as I know of no one who will so well fill his place as the curate of Olney, I should be glad to know whether I may fill up the presentation of St Mary Woolnoth in that name, and have all ready for your translation when you purpose being resident at London and Mr Foster takes care of your church. With respects to Mrs Newton and our friends at Orchard Side,

'I am, dear Sir,
'Your much devoted Friend, etc.,
John Thornton
'Clapham: 18th September, 1779.'

'21st. Wrote to my dear friend, signifying my thankful acceptance of his offer. I trust I can do it in faith. My own sentiment is likewise confirmed by the judgment of my dear Mrs Unwin and Mr Cowper, who, though they feel interested in the case and concerned that we must be parted, are satisfied that this call is from God and that I ought to obey.'

Mr Newton thus writes on the subject to his friend Mr Bull: 'My race at Olney is nearly finished. I am about to form a connection for life with one Mary Woolnoth, a reputed London saint in Lombard Street. I hope you will not blame me. I think you would not if you knew all circumstances. I am not elated at what the world calls preferment. London is the last situation I should have chosen for myself. The throng and hurry of the busy world, and noise and party contentions of the religious world, are very disagreeable to me. I love woods and fields and streams and trees — to hear the birds sing and the sheep bleat. I thank the Lord for His goodness to me here. Here I have rejoiced to live — here I have often wished and prayed that I might die. I am sure no outward change can make me happier, but it becomes not a soldier to choose his own post.'

'Thursday, 23rd September. Mr Wilkinson preached. I spoke a few words to the people after sermon, and told them I was going. There are many weepers. May Thy gracious hand, my Lord, wipe away their tears, and turn their mourning into joy. I trust it shall be so if Thou art pleased to favour my wishes and endeavours for Mr Scott to supply my place, which he is willing to do, if Thou art pleased to appoint him.'

'Sunday, 26th. My subjects had a view to the present trial of the people. My heart is sometimes pinched at the prospect before me, but in the main I am peaceful, and trust that the event will prove it is the Lord's appointment.'

'Monday, 27th. Had the meeting tonight. I opened my heart freely respecting the past and the future, gave them my best advice, and commended them to the blessing of the Lord.'

'30th. Received a favourable answer from Mr Browne,* to my recommendation of Mr Scott.'

'October, 2nd. To my surprise and grief, I have found a strong opposition against Mr Scott, so that he has given up the thought of coming. I have seen much of a wrong spirit in the business where I expected better things. Contempt has been cast upon one whom God has honoured, and my care for their prosperity has given offence and provoked anger. Lord, enable me to bear it as I ought, to pray for them, to continue to love, and to endeavour to save them. Let not my spirit be hurt, and pity and provide for the faithful few who would have rejoiced in such a minister.'

'5th. A day of trial in taking leave of the people.'

Wednesday, December 22nd, Mr Newton states that he had been to London, and that, after some delay, through the interposition of a *caveat*, he had received his institution to St Mary Woolnoth, and had preached his first sermon there on the Sunday preceding.

'December 31st. Brought by Thy mercy to the close of another year; a memorable year for the change which it has brought me. A few changes more, and the great change will come. Lord, prepare me for it, and teach me to have it always in my view.'

Mr Newton's last sermon at Olney was preached at the Great House, on Tuesday evening, January 11, 1780. The text, Jeremiah 17:8.

On Thursday, January 13th, we have the following entry, the last made at Olney:

'This evening service is to terminate my connection with Olney. Tomorrow I return to London. My gracious Lord, bless the people from whom Thou removest me. Oh, give me a heart to praise Thee for the years of mercies I have known in this place, provision, protection, support, acceptance, and, I hope, usefulness. If we have had trials, comforts have more abounded. Prepare us a habitation, and

* The Rev. Moses Browne, vicar of Olney.

oh, above all, prepare our hearts a habitation for Thyself. Sanctify this removal, and fit us for our great change, our final removal from a world of sin and sorrow, that we may be with Thee for ever. Amen and Amen.'

Thus at length Mr Newton left Olney, where he had spent so many happy and useful years of his ministerial life. In his own opinion and in that of his most judicious friends he was following the leadings of Divine providence. Nevertheless, like all such changes, it was accompanied with many regrets. 'Oh, my beloved leisure,' exclaims Mr Newton, when settled in London, 'my sweet retirements, how I should regret your loss, if I were not checked by the thought that the post I am in must needs be the best upon the whole, because the Lord has assigned it for me! . . . I loved the people so that it was in my heart and in my prayers to live and die with them.' Then he adds, as giving some of his reasons for leaving: 'Our privileges were great; and the enjoyment of them for a long course of years without interruption made them seem to too many as a matter of course. Weeds sprang up, offences appeared. I hope it was in mercy to them, as well in mercy to me that the Lord removed me.'

Some of his friends thought, not without reason, that Mr Newton's real influence at Olney had suffered by over-much familiarity on his part, and from an excess of charitable feeling by which his judgment was sometimes led astray; that thus, in some instances, he lost that esteem and love to which he had really so good a title. It was, moreover, his own conviction, as expressed by him on a review of this period, that he had encouraged his people in a liberty in the exercise of their gifts which, in the end, he could not control, and which became a source of uneasiness to him.

It may be well supposed that Mr Newton's loss was deeply felt, not only by many of his people at Olney, but by those of his more immediate neighbours, who best knew and appreciated him. How pathetically does Mr Cowper write on the subject: 'The vicarage house became a melancholy object as soon as Mr Newton left it. As

I walked in the garden this evening I saw the smoke issue from the study chimney, and said to myself, "That used to be a sign that Mr Newton was there;" but it is so no longer. The walls of the house know nothing of the change that has taken place; the bolt of the chamber door sounds just as it used to do; and when Mr Page goes up stairs, for aught I know, or ever shall know, the fall of his foot could hardly, perhaps, be distinguished from that of Mr Newton. But Mr Newton's foot will never be heard upon that staircase again. These reflections and such as these, occurred to me upon the occasion. Such are my thoughts about the matter. Others are more deeply affected, and by more weighty considerations, having been many years the objects of a ministry which they had reason to account themselves happy in the possession of.'

Writing to Mr. Newton soon after he left the neighbourhood, Mr Bull speaks of his removal as one of the greatest trials he ever met with: 'I rode to Olney this week. I believe it is only the second time since you left it. The name of the place seems quite to have altered its signification, and the once dear Mr Newton is (in a great measure) to me no more.' And not long afterwards: 'I have this week had again to lament your absence from Olney. On Wednesday night I preached there. I believe almost every one of your serious friends came to the meeting, and, indeed, I may say, I think that they seemed to love you in me.'

PART THREE

MR NEWTON RECTOR
OF ST MARY WOOLNOTH

10: LONDON
(1780–2)

Mr Newton's reflections on his new position – An accident – Declaring the Parish Boundaries – 'No Popery' Riots – *Thelyph-thora* – Ramsgate – *Cardiphonia* – State of the times – Fast Sermon – Preface to Cowper's Poems – Visit to Olney – Address to his Parishoners – Plan of academical preparation for the ministry – Growing popularity – At Hastings.

And now we have to follow Mr Newton in his career as a London rector; and though filling a more important, and in many respects a more congenial sphere, we still find him the same humble, devout, laborious, and useful man. He is not spoiled by the attentions of the great and good, by the many testimonies to the singular success of his labours, or by the application of persons in almost all circumstances to him for counsel or help. His largeness of heart seemed but to increase with the demands made upon it. To impart to others by every means in his power, or, in Scripture phrase, 'to do good to all men as he had opportunity' was his daily occupation and his daily delight.

At the time Mr Newton went to London he thus speaks of the state of religion in the Establishment, in a letter to his friend, Mr Barlass: 'There are,' he says, 'but two gospel ministers who have churches of their own, Mr Romaine and myself. But we have about ten clergymen, who, either as morning preachers or lecturers, preach either on the Lord's Day or at different times of the week in, perhaps, fifteen or sixteen churches. There is likewise the Lock, and another chapel in Westminster; the former served chiefly by Mr Coetlogen, the latter by Mr Peckwell — well attended.'

January 19th, Mr Newton writes to Mr Bull: 'My entrance to St Mary Woolnoth is hitherto as favourable as I could expect; indeed more so. Some of my new parishioners are rather pleased, and some who do not quite relish what I say seem to believe that, at least, I speak from my heart, and mean well.'

Elsewhere Mr Newton says: 'I am wonderfully at peace in my new settlement, and I hope not unuseful. My lecture on the Lord's Day evening was much crowded. My dispensation likewise seems to be peace. My congregation is made up from various and discordant parties, who, in the midst of differences can agree in one point — to hear patiently a man who is of no party. I say little to my hearers of the things wherein they differ, but aim to lead them all to a growing and more experimental knowledge of the Son of God and a life of faith in Him.'

Many strangers came to hear Mr Newton, so that the parishioners complained that their seats were either taken, or that they could not get to them for the crowd in the aisle. He relates all this in a letter to his wife, still at Olney, and after saying that he told the church-warden who made this complaint how sorry he was, but knew not how to prevent it, adds, with quiet humour: 'He proposed with many apologies my letting another clergyman preach now and then for me; hinted that it should be no expense to me, and thought that if it was uncertain whether I preached or no the people would not throng the church so much. I could not but admire the scheme. I thought it would exactly answer the design. But I said I could not possibly comply with it. If he pleased, I would speak to the people from the desk. He wished I would; therefore I shall, and add a word to the parishioners to dispose them to be good-humoured to the strangers. Some little difficulty upon this head must be expected, but I hope it will subside by degrees.'

In April Mr Newton had a fall and dislocated his shoulder, the only time, he says, of his receiving any hurt, though he had travelled so many leagues by land and water. 'I was standing at my own door, put my foot carelessly back against the stone, which tripped me up, and threw me over a short post.'

Writing some days afterwards to Mr Cowper, he thus speaks of the accident in his own peculiar vein: 'I consider it as a chastisement, though of a gentle and merciful kind. A sinner need not spend much time in searching out the cause of an affliction; but that the afflictions of such a sinner as I should be so seldom, so moderate, so soon removed, depends upon reasons which I should never have known, but by the Word of God. There I am taught to spell His name, "The Lord, the Lord God, long-suffering, abundant in mercy, forgiving iniquity, transgression, and sin;" and thus I read the reason why I am not consumed.'

In the same letter Mr Newton speaks of the advance of spring, and tells Mr Cowper how he substitutes in imagination the various objects around him for the old familiar scenes of Olney, observing, however, that his attainment in this art is unequal to the supposition that any persons can be like the friends at Orchard Side. He then goes on to say: 'In other respects, our situation is, upon the whole, so well that I may apply to either of you —

Excepto quod non simul esses, cætera lætus
[Happy on all accounts, except that you are not with me].

But indeed, a removal from two such dear friends is a dislocation, and gives me at times a mental feeling something analogous to what my body felt when my arm was forced from its socket. I live in hopes that this mental dislocation will one day be happily reduced likewise, and that we shall come together again *as bone to its bone.'*

On May Day Mr Newton preached for Mr Romaine a sermon to young people, reminding him, he says, a little of his annual New Years' sermons at Olney, though he felt a difference between speaking to his own children and those of another.

The same month, writing to Mr Cowper, Mr Newton gives an amusing account of his taking part, on Ascension Day, at the annual farce of declaring parish boundaries: 'I am afraid my overture is very dull, but if you could suppose it the translation of a fragment dug out of Herculaneum, giving an account of some custom that obtained (*mutatis mutandis*) in ancient Rome, then both the ears of your classical attention would doubtless be nailed to the subject.'

In June 1780 occurred the 'No Popery' riots, of which Mr Newton thus speaks:

'We have had a terrible storm, but our infallible Pilot has supported and brought us, thus far, safely through. Now all is calm. Charles Square' (Hoxton, the place of Mr Newton's residence,) 'was full of people on Monday the 5th, but they behaved peaceably, made a few inquiries, and soon went away. The devastations on Tuesday and Wednesday nights were horrible. We could count from our back windows six or seven terrible fires each night. On Wednesday night and Thursday the military arrived and saved the city, which otherwise, I think, would before this time have been in ashes from end to end. So soon, so suddenly, can danger arise; so easily, so certainly, can the Lord set bounds to the wickedness of man, in the height of its rage, and say, "Hitherto shalt thou come and no further". I believe multitudes went to St George's Fields in the simplicity of their hearts, not aware of the consequences, not aware that many, with very different views, would avail themselves of the occasion, and meet with them.

'I preached on Wednesday, and had a tolerable auditory; but I cannot describe the consternation and anxiety which were marked on the countenance of almost every person I met in the streets of that day.

'I preached on Sunday forenoon from Lamentations 3:22: "It is of the Lord's mercies that we are not consumed." In the evening from Psalm 46:10: "Be still, and know that I am God."'

A publication appeared about this time which created a painful interest in the religious world, and more especially in the mind of Mr Newton and of some of his friends. It was entitled *Thelyphthora, or a Treatise on Female Ruin*, and the writer was the Rev. Martin Madan. Mr Madan was brought up to the bar, but afterwards going into orders became chaplain to the Lock Hospital, and was for some years a popular preacher amongst those who at that time were designated by the general name of 'Methodists', whether in or out of the Established Church. He was the intimate friend of Mr Newton, and related to Mr Cowper; hence the interest taken in the book by these individuals, and the frequent reference to it in their correspondence.

Mr Newton, in a letter addressed to Mr Cowper, dated July 2nd, 1780, gives his opinion of it in the following words: 'I have now read the first volume. It is specious, certainly, and well calculated to convince those who hitherto felt a conflict between their passions and their consciences. They are now at liberty. The violations of the seventh commandment, according to this writer are few indeed. A man may leave his wife or put her away — if she is cross or ill-tempered to a certain degree, of which he is the proper judge — without harm, only that he is answerable to conscience and to God for the justness of the cause. And all this with such plausibility of argument, such abundance of Scripture, such appeals to what Warburton calls the "Hebrew verity," that though I wonder any spiritual person should approve the book, I do not wonder that many should think themselves unable to answer it.'

Once more Mr Newton, writing to Mr Cowper and referring to this subject, says: 'Your epigram made us sharers in your laugh, but the occasion and subject summoned my muscles back to their pristine seriousness. I am afraid there will be many bundles of matches, and many families inflamed by them with the fire of contention. How can that be true in theory which if reduced to practice must be mischievous! Your dilemma (with three horns) will hold good. He that is happy with one wife will want no more, he that is not happy with one has one too many. Or, suppose we Sternholdize the thought —

'What different senses of that word, A Wife!
It means the comfort or the bane of life.

The happiest state is to be pleased with one,
The next degree is found in having none.

'You will perceive I am rummaging my budget for something to entertain you, but though I have ransacked every corner, I can feel nothing but palpable emptiness. Methinks harlequin is as unsuitable to my calling as to your situation. Yet I would admit him almost at any time (except when in the pulpit, etc.), provided he would furnish me with something for your amusement. Yea, if my talents lay that way, I would occasionally turn harlequin myself to please you. I think the attempt would extort a smile from you, whether you would or no. Be assured that we are most affectionately and unalterably yours,

J. AND M. NEWTON.'

After Mr Newton left Olney he ceased to keep a regular diary, and we have only occasional entries, which are chiefly suitable reflections suggested by the recurrence of the 'memorable days' of his life. Henceforth, therefore, we lose this source of information, and must make such use as we best may of the materials that are left us.

In September, Mr Newton writes to Mr Bull: 'I was invited to dine with one of my parishioners yesterday. It was the first invitation I had received from any who were not professedly serious. They have behaved well. I behaved poorly, for I could not at the first sight introduce the best subject. This is often a hindrance to me; but the Lord can give me further opportunity, and put a word in my mouth some time. Ah! it is a shame to seem so earnest and pressing in the pulpit, and then to be so cold and mealy-mouthed at table.'

Early in October, Mr Newton was with Mr Thornton at Ramsgate, and of that brief visit we find the following memorial:

A THOUGHT ON THE NORTH FORELAND LIGHTHOUSE
OCTOBER 4TH, 1780.

Thus on a height in safety I survey
That wide deceitful storm-vexed sea, the world;

How often there the thoughtless and the gay,
Are lost, on rocks, or on each other hurled!

Kindled by Thee, dear Lord, may I thus shine,
And timely warn them of each dangerous shelf,
Remembering well their perils once were mine:
I fear for them though now secure myself.

1781. Early in this year was published *Cardiphonia*, a series of letters in two volumes, being a selection from the actual correspondence of the author. He thus speaks of his object in giving them to the public, in the following words addressed to Mr Bull: 'I am glad *Cardiphonia* is at hand, to put you often in mind of me. You see me there in my best and in my worst. Or, rather, you see what I am, and you may guess what I would be. It seems likely to sell and spread, which I shall be glad of, if the Lord be pleased to accompany it with His blessing. If the letters are owned to comfort the afflicted, to quicken the careless, to confirm the wavering, I may rejoice in the honour He has done to me, and need not envy Johnson or Robertson. Surely I ought to prefer being useful to one soul, to the applause of twenty nations and ages. I hope I do.'

A good title to a book every writer knows is of no little consequence; and Mr Newton wisely availed himself of Mr Cowper's help in this matter. 'I shall be obliged,' he says, 'to your ingenuity to hammer me out a title and a motto — my name is not to be prefixed. Can you compound me a nice Greek word as pretty in sound and as scholastically put together as *Thelyphthora*, and as much more favourable import as you please, to stand at the top of the title-page, and to serve as a handle for an inquirer?' Hence the happy designation *Cardiphonia*, or utterance of the heart, and the motto, *Hæc res et jungit, junctos et servat amicos* [this unites friends and serves those who are united].

All reasons for the concealment of the names of the friends addressed by Mr Newton having through the lapse of time passed away, it may not be without interest to supply that information. Those of the first volume were written to the Earl of Dartmouth, the Rev. Thomas Scott, T. F. Barham, Esq., the Rev. Mr Rose (a clergyman, son-in-law to Mr Barham), the Rev. F. Okeley (a Moravian minister at Northampton), the Rev. Mr Powley (son-in-law to Mrs Unwin, and vicar of Dewsbury, Yorkshire), Mrs Gardiner, Miss Foster, Mr John Catlett (Mr Newton's brother-in-law). The letters of the second volume were addressed to Mrs Thornton, Mrs Talbot (widow of the Rev. Mr Talbot of Reading), the Rev. Mr Jones (curate of Clifton), the Rev. Mr Whitford (Independent minister at Olney), Mrs Place (a Moravian), the Rev. Mr Bowman (a clergyman in Norfolk), the Rev. John Ryland, Jr. (afterwards Dr Ryland of Bristol), the Rev. Dr Ford (Melton Mowbray), Miss Thorpe, Sally Johnson (Mr Newton's servant), the Rev. Mr Collins, Mrs Wilberforce, Miss Delafield (afterwards Mrs Cardale), Mrs Harvey, Miss Perry, and the Rev. William Bull.

Of this excellent work, its wide circulation, and its great usefulness, more will appear hereafter.

In his letters written about this time Mr Newton deplores the state of the times. Thus he says: 'The cloud grows darker, the flames of war are spreading wider, and difficulties seem increasing against us on every side. The Lord's hand is lifted up, and men will not see. Hitherto the nation is in a deep sleep, and professors, I am afraid, are sadly slumbering. I can hardly find anywhere around me (alas! that I cannot find in myself) a spirit of humiliation and prayer, in any degree answerable to the state of the times.' Elsewhere: 'What a mercy to know who is at the helm! Bishop Reynolds says somewhere; "Jesus will either be your pilot in the ship or your plank in the sea." This is good news, and therefore we need not fear for ourselves. But I would wish to be much affected for others.'

A general fast was appointed for February 21st, on which occasion Mr Newton preached a sermon from Jeremiah 5:29, afterwards printed, on the guilt and danger of the nation. He sent a copy of it to all his parishioners.

To turn now to another subject. Things had not gone on comfortably after Mr Newton left Olney. The curate who succeeded him, and whom the people at first preferred to Mr Scott, disappointed their expectations, and early in this year the latter received the curacy. This was a great gratification to Mr Newton — a revolution in their favour, he says, 'he could not hope for, but the Lord works wonderfully.'

At the close of the preceding year, at the suggestion of Mrs Unwin, Mr Cowper was induced to commence writing those poems which have made him so widely known, and so greatly loved. He sent a copy of his earlier productions to Mr Newton in the spring of the present year, requesting that his friend would write a preface to his book, and find him a publisher. The second request Mr Newton at once complied with, but he demurred to the former, feeling himself incompetent for such a task. To this Cowper replied, that not having the least doubt himself upon that score, and being convinced that there ought to be none, he neither withdrew his requisition, nor abated one jot of the earnestness with which it was made. 'I admit,' said he, 'the delicacy of the occasion, but am far from apprehending that you will therefore find it difficult to succeed. You can draw a hair-stroke where another man would make a blot as broad as a sixpence.'

Mr Newton accordingly wrote a preface; but Johnson, the bookseller, though he well knew and highly respected Mr Newton, looking at the matter from a trade point of view, thought that in certain quarters it might injure the sale. Johnson had shown himself to be a man of considerable judgment, and as in such a case he was supposed to possess experience as well, Mr Newton, though much to Mr Cowper's regret, consented to withdraw his preface. 'Not for containing anything offensively peculiar, but as being thought too pious for a world that grew more foolish and more careless as it grew older.' Southey thinks the step was an unwise one. When a subsequent edition appeared there was a change of opinion, and the preface was inserted.

As early as the spring of this year, Mr Newton, finding how acceptable *Cardiphonia* had proved to the Christian public, began to make preparations for two more volumes. It was not his purpose, however, to publish them during his life, and they appeared as a posthumous work.

In June he visited his old friends in Olney and its neighbourhood. Writing to Mr Bull some months before, he says: 'Come May! come June! that we may trot down to Olney, Weston, Newport, Bedford. Ah, wretched creature! will you dare to wish the time away? Rather wish every minute was an hour, while you have so much to do, and can so poorly improve the little space allotted to do it in. Well, I wish to wait patiently. May I improve the interval! June will arrive. Then if we shall be spared, be alive, well, and have money in our pockets, and the Lord's good leave, away for Bucks; and then I shall hope to share —

> A theosophic pipe with brother B.,
> Beneath the shadow of his favourite tree,
> And then how happy I! how cheerful he!'

The journey was accomplished in June, and Mr Newton speaks of it as having left a very pleasant savour on his mind. Thus Mr Cowper writes of it: 'Your visit was most agreeable here. It was so even to me, who though I live in the midst of many agreeables am but little sensible of their charms. But when you came I determined as much as possible to be deaf to the suggestions of despair; that if I could contribute but little to the pleasure of the opportunity, I might not dash it with unseasonable melancholy, and, like an instrument with a broken string, interrupt the harmony of the concert.' Not only did Mr Newton on this occasion enjoy the society of his friends, and seek as much as possible by kind and wise counsels to accommodate matters at Olney, but he was also diligent in using every opportunity to preach and to exhort.

We quote the following sentences from the diary, written August 4th, Mr Newton's birthday. After speaking of Mrs Newton having enjoyed better health than for many years past, he proceeds: 'My strength for service as yet remains firm, so that I can do the whole three times on the Lord's Day, and three or four times (and oftener if need be) in the week without inconvenience. I would have spent this day or much of it in retirement, but I could not. In company from morning till nearly night, and I see not how to avoid it. Oh that I could get Thee always before me, and converse with Thee not only in solitude but in crowds. Pity, pardon, and accept me. I am a poor creature, but I trust I am Thine, and to Thee I devote and resign myself again.'

There is no record of anything further as having occurred this year, except that in November Mr Newton printed an address to his parishioners, sending one under cover to every housekeeper in his parish. Mr Newton, it is evident, was induced to this address more especially because many of his parishioners habitually absented themselves from his ministry. It is a very judicious and affectionate appeal, in which, with considerable delicacy and tact, he endeavours to remove their objections and prejudices and to awaken them to a sense of religious duty.

In connection with some brief reflections suitable to the last day of the year, Mr Newton says in his diary: 'The Lord has not suffered me to decline, as to my outward profession and service. I still love His house, His people, His ways; and to publish His salvation is my pleasure. I am still supported in the work, and have still reason to hope that He does not let me speak in vain. My connections are comfortable, friends very kind, auditories large and attentive, with few discouragements in my ministry. I believe some think me diligent and spiritual; but I know myself to be chargeable with much indolence, vanity, and folly. I am ashamed of myself. Oh, what must I appear in the Lord's eyes! But my hope is founded on His mercy, blood and promises. The good Lord give me a word for the morning, and for the sermon to the young people in the evening. I have transferred my old custom of an annual sermon to them from Olney to London.'

1782. In the early part of this year Mr Newton was engaged in a work which to some might seem rather out of his line of things, but in which he evidently engaged *con amore* [with love or devotion]. The whole subject will be best understood by the following extracts from some letters to his friend Mr Bull. He thus writes, April 17th: 'Mr Clayton* lately called upon me, to tell me that many persons are seriously thinking of establishing a new academy, upon a liberal ground, for preparing young men for the ministry, in which the greatest stress might be laid upon truth, life, spirituality, and the least stress possible upon modes, forms, and non-essentials; that it must be at a moderate distance from London; that, in fact, Newport Pagnell was the placed fixed upon, for the sake of one Mr Bull, who lives there, and who, it was hoped, would accept the superintendency. He then said it was his request, and the desire of many of his friends, that I would draw up a plan for the formation of such an academy, and likewise that I would write to you upon the subject.

'The design met my hearty approbation, as it stood connected with Mr Bull, who I said appeared to me the most proper person I could think of to undertake it. As to my drawing up a plan, I half promised to write my thoughts of it — that is, I mean to tell Mr Clayton by letter how I should sketch out such an institution if I lived in Utopia or Otaheite [Tahiti], and could have the management of things my own way. If they can pick any hints worthy of notice from such an attempt they shall be welcome to them; but to draw a formal plan how an academy should be regulated in this enlightened age and country, and to hit such a medium as might unite and coalesce the respectable dissenters and Methodists who seem willing to promote this business, might savour too much of presumption in one who was never either at university or academy himself, but spent the time which other young men employ in study in the wilds of Africa.'

Again, under date May 25th: 'I expect many if not all the parties concerned will not much admire my plan. I have given my senti-

* The Rev. J. Clayton, of the Weigh House, London.

ments undisguised and at large, without much caring who is pleased or displeased; for as I live in Utopia, it is of no importance to me what the people who live at such a distance as London are pleased to think of me ... This will seem an awkward business all round to some persons. What apology can Mr Clayton make to many dissenters for applying to a clergyman for a plan of an academy? And what can the poor cleric say to some people in his line, for chalking out the plan of a dissenting methodistical academy? How will the staunch Tabernacle folks like his innuendoes against some of their popular, loud, powerful preachers? I think this poor speckled bird will be pecked at by fowls of every wing. But it is well that, though he does not wish to offend any of them, he is mighty indifferent as to their censures. If we act with a single eye, and are desirous to serve and please the Lord, we may be easy as to consequences. When the conscience is clear and the heart simple, neither the applauses nor the anathemas of worms are worth twopence per bushel.'

The sketch drawn up by Mr Newton was printed two years afterwards under the title of 'A plan of Academical Preparation for the Ministry, in a Letter to a Friend.' It may be added that the plan so originated was carried out, and an institution was founded at Newport Pagnell, and successfully carried on till the year 1848, when it was amalgamated with Cheshunt College. It was a means of introducing many excellent men into the gospel ministry, some few of whom were thus trained for the Established Church.

Mr Newton, after more than two years' experience, thus speaks of his position in London: 'If,' he says, 'the Lord had left me to choose my situation, London would have been almost the last place I should have chosen. But since it was the Lord's choice for me, I am reconciled and satisfied. He has in this respect given me another heart; for now I am fixed here, I seem to prefer it. My sphere of service is extremely enlarged, and my sphere of usefulness likewise. And not being under any attachment to systems and parties I am so far suited to my situation ...

'I preach my own sentiments plainly but peaceably, and directly oppose no one. Accordingly, Churchmen and Dissenters, Calvinists and Arminians, Methodists and Moravians, now and then, I believe, Papists and Quakers, sit quietly and hear me . . . It was my mercy to be satisfied with Olney while I was there; but when I came to London I left many trials behind me.'

It will be observed that Mr Newton speaks of his sphere of service and usefulness being enlarged. There are many notices in these pages of what he terms 'House-preachings'. He not only regularly expounded the Scriptures morning and evening at home, and when occasionally visiting amongst his friends, but he held monthly services of this character at several houses in or about London, and a register of them still exists. At Mrs Wilberforce's he gave a series of lectures on the *Pilgrim's Progress*, and also at Mr Neale's of St Paul's Churchyard. Here also, at a later period, a meeting was established by Mr Neale, in conjunction with Mr Newton, for prayer during the awful period of the French Revolution.

Such exercises as these — and they were by no means confined to Mr Newton — must surely have greatly contributed to the promotion of personal and family religion. The interest with which they were regarded shows that these professors were willing to make some sacrifice of time and convenience for the possession of such benefits. Alas! must we not say, *Tempora mutantur et nos mutamur in illis* [the times are changing, and we are changing with them]?

It appears that many strangers came from different parts to hear Mr Newton. The fact was that by this time his letters had made him generally known and appreciated in the religious world; and the author of *Omicron* and *Cardiphonia* had become an object of attention to many when they visited the metropolis. A new edition of the latter work was called for. One of his old correspondents, writing to Mr Newton, congratulates him on this circumstance, adding how much he had been benefited by the perusal of his letters. A communication from Wales, while furnishing a like testimony, informs the author that

Omicron was translated into Welsh. Mr Newton's old friend, Captain Scott, writes to him in a similar strain of the great acceptance of his work, both in England and Scotland, and begs that he will not let his proposed additional volumes be a posthumous publication.

Early in September, Mr Thornton, with his sister, Mrs Wilberforce, and his brother-in-law, Dr Conyers, being at Hastings, Mr Newton and Mr Bull were invited to join them. The two latter went down together, and Mr Newton thus writes to his wife: 'I hope my journey will prove for good — perhaps to myself a little air and change may be good for health; a little retirement may, if the Lord please, be good for my mind — I seem to need it. I cannot avoid living in a crowd and continual hurry in London, and the Lord is pleased to carry me through, yet it is desirable to be a little alone . . . Mr Bull sends his love. We have had three prayers upon the road, in which you were not forgotten, and two pipes, in which you would not have wished to share. A deal of chat, sometimes more serious, sometimes pleasant. Making rhymes and *rebuses* [representations of words in the form of pictures or symbols, often presented as a puzzle] with Tommy and such sort of play. Love to Mr Jones. I wish he may do good, much good, in Mary Woolnoth pulpit.'

'Last night I preached, and I suppose there were about a dozen strangers and townsfolk in the room. All seemed very sober and attentive; and perhaps the preaching of the gospel of old did not cause more wonder at Philippi than it does at this time in Hastings. They have neither Dissenter nor Methodist in the town or neighbourhood, and I suppose if we were not under Mr Thornton's wing we should be soon driven out of the place. As it is, all is very peaceable.' Speaking of this service, Mr Bull says: 'We had a delightful meeting last night. Mr Newton preached in Mr Thornton's house to about thirty.' It seems that services were held twice every day; in fact, morning and evening prayers, accompanied with exposition of the Scriptures, which were conducted by one or other of the ministers of the party. Mr Newton's stay at Hastings was very short.

11: LONDON
(1783–5)

Eclectic Society – Letters to Mrs Cunningham and Dr Ford – Letter from M. Apellius – Visits Olney, Newport, etc. – Mr Cowper - Diary – Liberality of Sentiment – *Apologia* – Lymington and Southampton – Letters – Cowper's *Task* – Letter to Mrs Newton – Eliza Cunningham – Usefulness – Mr Wilberforce.

We have no means of ascertaining whether or not the Eclectic Society, formed at the beginning of the year 1783, was the suggestion of Mr Newton; although from the deep interest he took in it, and from the fact that he attempted something of a similar kind so soon as he was settled at Olney, is not at all unlikely. He thus speaks of it in a letter, dated February 28th, to his friend at Newport: 'Our new institution at the Castle and Falcon promises well. We are now six members, and voted in a seventh last night. We begin with tea; then a short prayer introduces a conversation for about three hours upon a proposed subject, and we seldom flag . . . I think they are the most interesting and instructive conversations I ever had a share in.' After stating several questions, as subjects for discussion, Mr Newton adds: 'Thus far for the history of our Royal Society, which, perhaps, deserves that name more than that which meets at Somerset House; as with us, I trust, the members are all of the royal family, and the King Himself condescends to meet with us.'

Amongst these seven members were the Rev. John Newton, the Rev. Henry Foster, the Rev. Richard Cecil, Eli Bates, Esq., and probably the Rev. J. Abdy, the Rev. Basil Woodd, and Mr Bacon, the sculptor.

In a subsequent letter Mr Newton says: 'I believe our Eclectic Society has been increased, since I mentioned it last, by the addition of two members whom we value greatly, Mr Clayton and Mr La Trobe. Our number is now eight. We are all unanimous and pleased with each other. We are one as to essentials, and our smaller differences of sentiment are such as only conduce to give the conversation a more agreeable variety, and tend to illustrate our subjects to greater advantage. The spirit of the design is kept up, and every member seems to find it well worth his while to attend punctually. I hope I find some real advantage, and have reason to number it among my chief privileges. Help us with your prayers, that life and love, peace and truth, may flourish among us.'

It was according to the original design of the society that it should include two or three laymen and dissenting ministers. Subsequently the meetings of the society were held at the vestry-room of St John's Chapel, Bedford Row. There is an exceedingly interesting volume, edited by the Rev. Archdeacon Pratt, giving a history of the discussions of the society from 1798 to 1814, from the notes of the Rev. Josiah Pratt, carefully kept through the whole of this period. The book is full of most important and suggestive matter. Amongst some other great practical results the Church Missionary Society owes its origin to the discussions of this institution.

Frequent mention has been made in the preceding pages of Mr Newton's sister-in-law, Mrs Cunningham. She was now a widow, and it was arranged that she should reside with her relatives in London. It pleased God, however, so to lay His afflicting hand upon her that she was not only quite unequal to such a change, but was not even likely long to survive the attack. Before the illness of the mother, her daughter, Eliza Cunningham, had been received by Mr and Mrs Newton. In March, Mr Newton addressed the following beautiful letter to Mrs Cunningham:

'MY DEAR SISTER, On the receipt of your kind friend's letter last night, we felt something like Jacob, when he said, "My son is yet alive". Our sister is yet alive — and there is something in us which would wish to hope further (as he did) we shall see her again. But I dare not encourage such a wish. I know that the Lord can do all things, and that His will is right. Miss Cowie's account gave us no reasonable ground to hope for your recovery. But He to whom belong the issues from death can raise you, if He sees it best; but if He sees it best to take you home to Himself, shall I wish that I could resist and control His will? I must not indulge in such a thought; I dare not, and, by the grace of God, I will not. I commend, I entrust, and resign you into His hands, and there I would leave you. I am well satisfied that He will surely do you good.

'I told you your Eliza should be ours. This was a settled thing before we saw her; but she has made herself ours since, upon her own account, and has taken possession of a large room in each of our hearts. Her affectionate, obliging, gentle behaviour has endeared her very much to me. As to her health, though she has too much of a fever, I think she is better since she came. I hope she does not suffer much pain, but she is so very patient that I cannot be certain. My chief desire for her is, that the Lord may speak to her heart, draw her to Himself, and seal her for His own. And then whether she goes to heaven at the age of twelve or of a hundred and twenty is no great matter . . . You are always in our thoughts and in our prayers. The Lord bless you, yea He has blessed you, and He will bless you to the end! We shall meet again (and it will be a bonny meeting) before the throne, to sing the high praises of the Lamb that was slain.'

Mrs Cunningham died in the month of May.

Not only did Mr Newton excel as 'a son of consolation'; he also possessed the rare faculty of faithful yet loving reproof. His friendship was too genuine to suffer sin in a brother. Of this the letter we are about to quote is a striking illustration. It is long, but would be spoiled by any attempt at abbreviation.

In former pages there has been frequent reference to the close intimacy subsisting between Mr Newton and Mr Ford. The latter had laboured for twenty years with much devoted zeal and earnestness, consecrating his learning and talents to the promotion of the gospel in his parish of Melton Mowbray; but after that period, to the exceeding grief of his pious friends, his zeal abated, and the duties in which he had taken so much delight were omitted or discharged as matters of form. It is to be feared that his wit and conversational powers had proved a snare to him. He was led to associate with the world, and to imbibe its spirit. Deeply sorrowing, his neighbour Mr Robinson of Leicester, wrote to Mr Newton, who addressed his old friend in the following strain of remonstrance:

'MY DEAR DOCTOR,

'It has seemed long since we exchanged a letter, and for some time past I have been purposing and repurposing to write. Week after week has brought its new excuses for delaying, but a letter I lately received from Leicester has put an end to my procrastination. You will not wonder that our common friend, who knows my love to you, who has seen so many proofs of your kind regard to me, and who loves us both, should communicate to me some particulars of his late correspondence with you, and the occasion of it. And I think an attempt to describe the impression his information has made upon my heart would be quite unnecessary.

'There have been times (I owe this assurance not to my own vanity, but to multiplied proofs of your friendship) when the very sight of my handwriting in the direction of a letter has given you pleasure before you have opened it. If my present preamble should lead you to read this with a different emotion I am sorry. The change is not in me; I feel no abatement in the warmth of my friendship, nor have I knowingly done anything to cause an estrangement in your mind. Nor indeed do I doubt of your love; but I fear my silence would now be more acceptable to you than that frank simplicity with which I formerly used to open my whole heart to you. The event of our friend's writing affords me but little encouragement to resume the subject; but something, yea, much, is due to the Lord whom we serve, to my own conscience, and to the great regard I bear you; and something must be risked for such important considerations. Never, surely, did I feel a more earnest desire that the Lord would direct my thoughts and my pen than upon this occasion. His eye is upon me while I write, His eye will be upon you when you read. May He touch my heart and yours, and give a happy issue.

'Were I capable of listening hastily to rumours and hearsays to your disadvantage you might justly blame me; but, alas! I go upon grounds too sure to be contravened. I have a part of your own letter before me. It is not a tale-bearer, but my dear Dr Ford himself tells me, "That my zeal and activity have abated is most certain, if they are to be determined by the circumstances of my ministry. I neither preach so frequently, so long, or so loud as I have done, and have entirely omitted the kitchen meeting." My dear friend, can you really think you were ever too frequent or too earnest in the most active part of your ministry? Are the souls of men, the cause of truth, the honour of our Lord, become of less importance than formerly? Have the world or the devil beaten a parley, made a truce, withdrawn their snares, or discontinued their assaults, so that it is no longer needful for you to be earnest and frequent in warning every one, night and day, publicly and from house to house, as you once did? Were your services in the kitchen so burdensome, so tasteless, so useless, that you saw just reasons for omitting them entirely? and do you feel your omission justified by an increase of light, and peace, and blessedness in your soul since you have declined them? Ah! my friend, truths and facts remain in themselves just as they were; and there never was a moment in your life when your obligations to zeal and activity were stronger upon you than they will be in the hour when this letter reaches you. Bear with me, I have no right to throw a stone at you; while I weep for you I may tremble for myself. The snare in which you have been entangled has been spread for me, and it is not by any power, or wisdom, or goodness of my own that I have escaped it.

'I believe you sincere in saying, "When I take my turn to preach I do not know that I keep back any truth which I was wont to deliver heretofore." But at the same time I fear you are mistaken. I fear there are many important truths respecting the impropriety and danger of worldly compliances, the choice of our company, the fear and favour of man, the small, unsuspected beginnings, and the imperceptible advances of a spiritual decline, and the necessity of a close attention to maintain a walk with God, and a separation from the world, which are not so obvious to you now in the course of your preaching as heretofore. You will hardly find a heart to warn others against the things in which you allow yourself; or if you could, you might as well keep silence, for your warning would have no weight. You possibly continue to preach the general truths of the gospel with almost as little success, and therefore with as little offence to the world, as if we were to entertain them with fairy tales.

'The sight of Mr Mozeen revived in my heart a design of revisiting Melton, and I told him I would if I could in the course of the summer; but since the letter I lately received I must give up the thought till a warm and cordial invitation from you, to be a witness of that blessed change in your views and conduct, which I am daily praying for, shall make me long for wings to fly to you at an hour's notice. As things stand at present, considering what I have known and heard and seen at Melton in the past, my heart must be made of marble if I were capable of walking through the town without such emotions of distress as would engage the notice of every person who saw me. Your case reminds me of what Lucan says of Pompey, "*Stat magni nominis umbra*" [He stands the shadow of a great name] or, to keep to Scripture, the case of Samson. Alas! that there should be those who once saw you in your strength that can now rejoice to see you shorn, and say (I doubt not to the purport, if not in the words of the Philistines), "Call for Samson and let him make us sport."

'For as to the new connections, to which, I suppose, the change I lament may be, in part, ascribed, I am persuaded of two things.

1. That formerly, when they affected to despise you and treated you ill, your uniform, consistent deportment as a gospel minister struck them with a secret awe, and constrained them to reverence you in their hearts. 2. That now, though they profess a regard, and though I know how much it is in your power to make yourself agreeable in company, they secretly, and perhaps openly, if you were absent, triumph over you. In time past you have hurt their cause and pained their consciences, so that now they do not consider you as a friend, but rather as an enemy whom they have taken captive (whom I trust the Lord God of Israel will yet deliver out of their hands). They smile, while your poor people, your kitchen people, once so dear to your heart, must weep to see themselves like a flock forsaken of the shepherd. With you the enemies of the gospel will now observe terms of decorum; but I am pained to think what they who love you for the truth's sake must suffer from their taunts and reproaches.

'I hope Mrs Newton and I are the only persons in London who know of these things. The dearest friend I have shall not hear of them, in the first instance, from us. But love is suspicious, and sometimes when people say, "Have you heard lately of Dr Ford?" I think I see a meaning in their looks which they are unwilling to express.

'After all, I trust this dark cloud will one day be dispelled, and you will shine again, and live to be avenged of the enemy for the loss of your hair. Surely you love the Lord! Surely He loves you! You are fallen, but I trust you will arise. I am no prophet; I know not in what way He will recover you. The shortest way may seem hard, but it may be done. Humble yourself, my friend, before Him, and pray for the return of that Spirit which can make your bonds like flax burnt by the fire. Oh! break off these ensnaring connections at once, *Cito, citius, citissime* [quickly, more quickly, most quickly]. One bold, determined effort in the name and strength of the Lord will set you free. But if not, it seems probable to me that the Lord in mercy will free you Himself in a more leisurely and painful way. I expect trouble and grief of heart will sooner or later arise to you from these very connections to which you have unhappily attached yourself. You will meet with mortifications and disappointments which you are not aware of, which will make you feel it was an evil and a bitter thing to forsake the Lord, the fountain of living waters, for such muddy, leaking pits. Then you will say, "I will return unto Him from whom I have wandered, for then it was better with me than now."

'And now I close my painful task. The Lord knows every word I have written has been dictated by grief and love. I doubtless wish to hear from you, but if I have offended you do not write till you have quite forgiven me. We join in best love to dear Mrs Ford, love to Mr Mozeen, if you mention that you have heard from me.

'I am your afflicted but most affectionate brother,

JOHN NEWTON.'

Happily the good man saw his error, and made public confession of it, and Mr Newton, as we shall find, visited him again.

In June Mr Cowper wrote to Mr Newton, congratulating him on the commendations he had received from certain Dutch divines; and, without altering their imperfect English, we quote the following eulogistic sentences from a letter of M. Apellius, to which, we suppose, reference is made:

'I have read in my lifetime many and different writings with great pleasure and edification, but never did I read anything whereof the whole content and manner of proposing caused me such a pleasure and edification as those letters. I have upon good foundation been long persuaded of the matter therein expressed; but I never found them proposed with so much clearness, firmity of arguments, grace, and liveliness. That charitable moderation, without any indifferency about the truths and forms of Christianity; that penetrating insight in the entire corruption of man without legality; that extraordinary light in the blessed gospel, and the Absolute Dependency of Man from grace, without injuring the Law and our unalterable obligation to godliness; that great measure of holiness, accompanied with so much charity, about them that have remained backward, all which, and many things more, do exceedingly shine in these letters. As often I do read them, which I do repeatedly, I find that the Holy Spirit accompanies it with His gracious operations. You did many services to our Church, but if you had never done anything, nor would do for the future, with publishing of those letters, you have done so much that not only the present but all future generations, as long as any of these letters are spared, will hold themselves obliged to you.'

In July, Mr Newton once more visited the scene of his former labours, and was also at Bedford and Newport. In writing from Olney he says: 'I am now very busy amongst a people whom I have long loved, and who are glad to see me, and though I am going from house to house almost all day and every day, I shall hardly be able to see them all while I stay.'

Mr Newton further speaks of his visit in the following terms: 'I was very cordially received at Olney; the heats and animosities which prevailed when I was there last seem in a good measure subsided. There are, however, many who have left the church and hear among the dissenters; but I hope they have not left the Lord. Mr Scott has some, and some of the best, who are affectionately attached to him. He is a good and upright man, and a good preacher, but different ministers have different ways. He has the best intentions, but his natural temper is rather positive than gentle and yielding. I was perhaps faulty in the other extreme; but they had been so long used to me that a different mode of treatment does not so well suit them.'

Mr Cowper was at this time more than usually depressed, and the presence of so dear a friend aggravated his malady. Writing to Mr Newton in September he says: 'You know not what I suffered while you were here, nor was there any need you should. Your friendship for me would have made you in some degree a partaker of my woes, and your share in them would have been increased by your inability to help me. Perhaps, indeed, they took a keener edge from the consideration of your presence. The friend of my heart, the person with whom I had formerly taken sweet counsel, no longer useful to me as a minister, no longer pleasant to me as a Christian, was a spectacle that must necessarily add the bitterness of mortification to the sadness of despair.'

On the 31st December, on a review of the year, we have among other reflections the following entry in the diary: 'I have preached in peace, for the most part with liberty, and I have reason to believe with acceptance and usefulness. My connections have enlarged, my little name is spread, my books translated in Germany and Holland. Such honour for such a creature! Oh! to be suitably affected with the Lord's goodness and my own unworthiness.'

1784. Of the liberality of Mr Newton's views on the subject of Church and Dissent there could be no possible question. In letters written to a Presbyterian friend, at this time, about the true use of zeal in the great questions of sin and salvation, he says: 'But when zeal spends itself about the less essential matters of forms and names, about points in which the wisest and the best have always differed, I would, if I could, lull it fast asleep. How does Christ receive us? Does He wait till we are all exactly of a mind? Does He confine His regards, His grace, His presence, within the wall of a party? Is He the God of the Presbyterians or the Independents only? Do not some amongst you, and some amongst us, know with equal certainty that He has received them? Do not they, do not we, know what it is to taste that He is gracious? Does He not smile upon your ordinances and upon ours? Are not the fruits of true faith the same on both sides of the Tweed and in every corner of the land? And shall zeal presume to come in with its ifs and its buts, and to build up walls of separation? Yet many true believers are so much under the spirit of self and prejudice that they verily mean to do the Lord's service by substituting their own commands in the room of His. And they see no harm in saying, "You must think and act as we do, subscribe to my paper, and worship in my way, or else, though I hope the Lord has received you, I think it my duty to keep my distance from you."'

And again: 'What seems principally wanting both in Scotland and England is a dispensation of the Holy Spirit; without this I hardly see a pin to choose, among all the different forms and modes of Church government.'

Much else of a like kind is to be found in Mr Newton's writings. Yet at the beginning of this year he published his *Apologia*, being four letters to a minister of an Independent church by a minister of the Church of England; and who will deny that a man may be liberal in his views, give the right hand of fellowship to those who differ from him in non-essentials, yea, the heart of love to those of kindred spirit, and yet have an opinion, and a reason for that opinion, on these lesser points?

We know very well that Mr Newton was exceedingly averse to controversy. There was no pugnacity in his disposition. If he erred it was in loving too well, and not always wisely. But because Mr Newton was liberal and large-hearted, and because he often spoke of the *comparative* insignificance of the secondary matters of church government, there were those who impeached his probity by charging him with interested motives for continuing in the Church, and called in question the sincerity of his opinion respecting her ritual, discipline, and order. Hence the letters, hence the motto —

> Quid me alta silentia cogis
> Rumpere?' *

The *Apologia* is a defence of himself against these charges. Different opinions will probably be formed of the statements and reasonings which have place in all works of this class. Be a man Churchman or Dissenter, Presbyterian or Congregationalist, Baptist or Pædobaptist, we believe it is utterly impossible, when he engages in controversy, that he can altogether free himself from the many unfavourable influences which in such circumstances must affect him. There is of necessity an unconscious bias towards his own views, and

* Why do you force me to break a profound silence? (from Virgil's *Aeneid*, Book 10, Line 63).

a degree of prejudice against those from which he differs. There is, moreover, the unavoidable ignorance arising from his position. He cannot see both sides of the shield. The consequence is that there will too often be a real though an undesigned misrepresentation of an opponent's views. In a word, he must occupy his own standpoint, and see only with his own eyes, and therefore see and know but partially. Whatever of these defects may possibly attach to either Mr Newton's statements or arguments, we may surely say this much, that his letters are a sufficient vindication of himself, and are written with admirable temper. Mr Newton expressed his determination not to be drawn into controversy. Writing to his dissenting friend, Mr Bull, he says: 'I suppose I have been pretty well talked over by them (the dissenting ministers in London) by this time, but their verdict has not yet reached me, nor am I solicitous about it. I trust I meant well, and had no allowed motive for publication but a desire of being useful. I cannot expect that the high church folks, either on my side or on yours, will be greatly pleased, but I hope I have given them no just cause of offence.'

May returned again, and we do not wonder that, loving the country as he did, the budding of the trees in Charles Square should remind Mr Newton of the rural scenes which once he had so heartily enjoyed, and that he should express himself to a friend in the following terms: 'It pleases me to think that, though I am much and often surrounded with noise, smoke, and dust, my friend Mrs C. enjoys the beautiful scenes of rural life. Oh, how I long sometimes to spend a day or two among woods, and lawns, and brooks, and hedgerows, to hear the birds sing in the bushes, and to wander among the sheep and lambs, or to stand under the shadow of an old oak, upon a hill-top! Thus I lived at Olney. How different is London! But hush! Olney was the place once; London is the place now. Hither the Lord brought me, and here He is pleased to support me; and in some measure (I trust) to own me. I am satisfied. Come, I hope I can make a good shift without your woods, and bushes, and pastures.'

In autumn, Mr Newton escaped for a little time from 'the noise, and smoke, and dust' of London, and enjoyed a pleasant season at Lymington and Southampton. In the neighbourhood of Lymington he visited a Mr Etty. 'I was happy,' he writes, 'at Prestlands with Mr Etty. He told me that he was sixty-five years of age; that he has feared the Lord, and walked much in the way he does now for many years, but could never make an acquaintance to whom he could freely open his mind before I came to him.'

'I could tell you as much about Southampton, Mr Taylor, and Mr Kingsbury, etc., if I had time. I was very happy there. Preached in two churches on the Lord's Days, and frequently in the evenings in Mr Taylor's house. What with walking, talking, riding, sailing, and a little smoking, O Time, how pleasantly and how swiftly didst thou pass!'

Mr Newton undertook his journey, in great part, for the sake of the health of his niece, Miss Eliza Cunningham; and in writing to Miss Catlett, who was left at home, he gives the following more particular account: 'We have enjoyed a good measure of health and peace, and have met with nothing but kindness since we have been abroad. At Mr Etty's I had a pretty retirement, a summer-house, which was appropriated to me for a study. Underneath there is a grotto, lined with moss and shell-work, and a hermit in it; he is dressed in a friar's habit, and would almost make me ask his pardon for disturbing him; he looks so grave and so much alive, as if he was reading a paper that lies before him among several books upon a table. The walks in the garden were very pretty, so was the country round about. There are many things and pleasing likewise at Southampton. But I shall not be sorry when the time comes to leave them all, and return to Charles Square.'

We quote the following extract from a letter written by Mr Newton while at Lymington: 'When I was writing here yesterday I had a beautiful prospect of the Isle of Wight and the sea from the hermitage window. I am looking through the same window now, and can see nothing of them. But I do not suppose the Isle of Wight is sunk because I cannot see it. I consider that this is a thick, rainy morning, and I expect when the weather clears up the island will be visible again. Thus it is with respect to many great truths, which you and I have seen with the eye of our minds. There may be returns of dark, misty hours when we can hardly perceive them, but these should not put us on questioning whether we ever saw them at all. Faith and obedience are like the road we travel, the frames and feelings of our spirits are like the weather. Though the weather may often change, the road is always safe, and they who travel upon it will renew their strength as they go on, and at length surely arrive at the end of their journey, and possess the promised land.'

Another letter, written probably during this year, and addressed to Miss Flower, the sister-in-law of the elder Mr Clayton, contains the following striking passage on contentment with our lot. After speaking of being tantalized by her description of the country, Mr Newton proceeds: 'Were it June instead of November, neither the place nor the company should tempt me to wish myself there when the Lord appoints me to be here . . . It is reported of a certain King of Portugal that he presumed to say that if God had consulted him at the creation about the dispositions and motions of the planets, he would have contrived them better than they are. I suppose the poor man took the schemes and dreams of the astronomers of his day to be a just representation of the system. It sounds, however, like a blasphemous speech in our ears. We take it for granted that the sun, the moon, and Jupiter, and the rest are exactly where they should be, and move just as they ought. But if we are content that the Lord should manage the heavenly bodies without our assistance, we are ready enough to advise Him how He should dispose of our insignificant selves. We think we could point at twenty things in our situation that might be mended, and that we should serve Him much better than we do, if we were at liberty to choose where and how we would be placed. Thus we can gravely censure the vanity and folly of this King

Alphonso, without being aware that the thoughts we sometimes indulge are no less arrogant than his, and that we might with as much reason offer to assist Him in the government of the universe as in the direction of our own paltry concerns.'

The best of men are not perfect; and it may be just mentioned, as a part of this year's story, that there was a slight misunderstanding between Mr Cowper and Mr Newton, the former not having informed his friend of the work upon which he had been some time engaged. *The Task* was completed before any tidings of it reached London, and not only so, but for some reason or other Mr Unwin was referred to about its publication. It would appear that Mr Cowper was doubtful whether it would ever be finished, for he was greatly depressed while writing it; and he wished, moreover, to give Mr Newton a surprise. However, this misunderstanding was of short duration. Mr Cowper writes to Mr Unwin: 'I was very much pleased with the following sentence in Mr Newton's last: "I am perfectly satisfied with the propriety of your proceeding to the publication. Now, therefore, we are friends again." Now he once more inquires after the work, which till he had disburthened himself of this acknowledgement, neither he nor I, in any of our letters to each other, ever mentioned.'

During the year eight papers were contributed by Mr Newton to the *Theological Miscellany*. They are on important subjects, and characterised by the author's usual excellence. They will be found in the last volume of Mr Newton's collected works.

1785. From the time of the arrival of their niece, Miss Eliza Cunningham, Mr and Mrs Newton had been anxious about her health. She had won their affection by the remarkable sweetness of her temper, and they witnessed with exceeding joy the development of those religious principles in which she had been trained. It pleased God at the latter part of this year to take this dear child from them by death. The air and bathing of Southampton and its neighbourhood had proved on former occasions of much use in restoring her; and, with the hope that a like beneficial result would follow, their friends the Taylors invited Mrs Newton and her niece to visit them in the summer. During this absence Mr Newton was, as usual, frequent in his letters to his wife. August 10th he writes journal-wise; and, after speaking of the many with whom he had intercourse at home and abroad, of his Sunday services, his attendance at the Eclectic Society, and other matters, he adds: 'I long to hear that Eliza has been in the water, and how it agrees with her. The Lord can give it the virtue of the Pool of Bethesda, and He will if He sees it the best, upon the whole. I am sure He does all things well, and I have no doubt He will do well for her. I had a thousand times rather see her as she is than in full health and spirits, if careless and fond of dissipation, as is the case of most girls.'

In a letter written a week after the above date, Mr Newton thus gives expression to his unrelated attachment to his wife: 'If I could say with confidence that I hold you now in your proper place of subordination to Him who gave you to me, then I need not scruple to profess that your peace, your welfare, and your love, are dearer to me than all earthly things. The latter I can say with truth; I hesitate about the former. I fear you are too much my idol still. The good Lord pardon me in this thing. Do, my dearest Mary, pray for me — pray earnestly for me; and may He return all the good you can ask for me a thousandfold into your own bosom.'

In another letter the following interesting observations occur: 'If you should be asked to stay to the sacrament I should like you to do it if you choose it. It would be an impropriety in me to join with them, considered as a minister of the Establishment, otherwise I could cordially make one of their occasional communicants, but I see no impropriety in your being one. My wife and any of my people have my full consent "to eat of that bread and drink of that cup" with Mr Kingsbury and his people, and he and they shall be heartily welcome to share with us at St Mary Woolnoth. And I should not be sorry, but glad, if such testimonies of mutual love and consent in the great truths of the gospel could sometimes take place amongst those who are ranked under different denominations.' Mr Taylor was connected with the Independent church at Southampton, of which Mr Kingsbury was the minister.

After being six weeks at Southampton without deriving any essential benefit from the change, Miss Cunningham returned to London about the middle of September, and died in less than three weeks, being little more than fourteen years of age. Mr Newton published a brief account of this interesting young person, entitled, 'A monument to the praise of the Lord's goodness, and to the memory of dear Eliza Cunningham.'

In that little work Mr Newton beautifully says: 'The Lord sent this child to me to be brought up for Him; He owned my poor endeavours; and when her education was completed, and she was ripened for heaven, He took her home to Himself. He has richly paid me my wages, in the employment itself, and in the happy issue.'

We are told that after her return to London, when informed, at her own particular request, that she had not long to live, she said with an air of ineffable satisfaction, 'Oh, that is good news, indeed.' Being asked if she should wish to live, provided the Lord should restore her to perfect health, she replied, 'Not for the world.' And again, on the last day of her life, being questioned as to her state, she answered, 'Truly happy; if this be dying, it is a pleasant thing to die.' Addressing Mrs Newton, she said, 'Do not weep for me, my dear aunt, but rather rejoice and praise on my account.' She had something to say, either in the way of admonition or consolation, as she thought most suitable, to every one whom she saw. Writing to Mr Bull, Mr Newton thus expresses himself in reference to this event: 'The translation of our sweet Eliza was most comfortable, yea glorious. Blessed be the Lord, I can hardly name one of the many merciful dispensations with which he has favoured me in the course of my life which my heart is more satisfied with, or which calls more loudly upon my gratitude, than this last. A trial it doubtless was to part with such a child; but I have not been permitted for a moment to wish it had been otherwise.'

This year, like all others, brought with it many testimonials to the happy result of Mr Newton's labours. Thus, a correspondent from Devonshire tells him that the *Narrative* had been the means of his conversion. A friend writes: 'I cannot help acquainting you of the pleasure and profit I derived from your conversation on Tuesday evening. I thought before that I possessed some good degree of charity, but have since found upon examination that it was much of that kind that is entirely confined to a party.'

A curious letter also is still in existence, written by a German merchant, in which he relates how he and another friend many years before, on the introduction of Mr Whitefield, had visited Mr Newton at Olney, and what very happy hours they spent on that occasion. But not the least memorable circumstance of this year, as illustrating the benefits derived from Mr Newton's friendship, is the fact that Mr Wilberforce desired to make his acquaintance. We are told of the profitable results of this intercourse; how Wilberforce was impressed with the pleasing and unaffected manners of Newton, and how, upon hearing him afterwards at St Mary Woolnoth, he spoke of his whole heart being engaged in the service.

Mr Wilberforce must have known the character of Newton well before he thus sought him out as his spiritual adviser; his aunt, Mrs Wilberforce, and Mr Thornton, her brother, being so closely connected with both parties. Henceforth a friendship was formed between these distinguished men, terminating only with the death of Mr Newton.

It is said that Wilberforce, while yet a boy, was introduced to Newton; and that when Wilberforce was awakened to religious concern and sought the good man's advice, Newton told him that since their first acquaintance he had not ceased to pray for him. Thus the name of Wilberforce, as well as those of Scott and Buchanan, may be added to the number of those who were, in a measure, if not entirely, the fruits of Newton's pious efforts.

12: LONDON
(1786–9)

The *Messiah* – Oratorios – Mr Newman removes to Coleman Street – Buildings – Southampton – Concern about Mr Cowper – Mr Johnson and Botany Bay – Hannah More – Funeral of the Rev. Charles Wesley – Visits Northamptonshire and Buckinghamshire – Story of Ellis Williams – His trials – His faith – His usefulness – His death – Mr Jay – Mr Newton's Breakfasts – Thanksgiving Sermon on the King's Recovery – Diary – Southampton.

In the spring of the year 1786, Mr Newton published his *Messiah* – fifty expository discourses 'on the series of Scripture passages which form the subject of the celebrated "Oratorio of Handel."'These sermons were preached at St Mary Woolnoth in the year 1784–5, and published in April, 1786. The first sermon gives an account of the occasion of their delivery. 'Conversation in almost every company, for some time past, has much turned upon the commemoration of Handel, particularly on his oratorio of the *Messiah*. I mean to lead your meditations to the language of the oratorio, and to consider in their order — if the Lord on whom our breath depends shall be pleased to afford life, ability, and opportunity — the several sublime and interesting passages of Scripture which are the basis of that admired compostion.'

In connection with the general subject of such performances Mr Newton gives his opinion in a very just and striking passage at the beginning of the fourth sermon on the words of Malachi 3:1–3, 'The Lord whom ye seek shall suddenly come to His temple', etc.

He supposes a number of persons charged with treason, and awaiting their trial. The evidence of their guilt is conclusive, and there is no doubt of the result. But, wholly unaffected with the awfulness of their situation, their only care is to amuse themselves; and, amongst other devices, they make the solemnities of their trial, and the terrible sentence to which they are exposed, the subject of musical entertainment. In the meanwhile the king graciously sends them an offer of a free pardon, urging them to comply with its terms. But instead of doing so they in like manner set this message to music. 'Surely,' says Mr Newton, 'if such a case as I have supposed could be found in real life, though I should admire the musical talent of these people, I should commiserate their insensibility.'

At Lady Day [March 25th] of this year Mr Newton removed from Charles Square, Hoxton, to No. 6, Coleman Street Buildings, where he continued to reside till his death. 'Coleman Street Buildings,' he writes to Mr Bull, 'is about half way between London Wall and King's Arms Yard (where was Mr Thornton's counting-house). It is an airy, lightsome situation for the City; and No. 6, which we are going to, is a very good house. N.B., There is a clever snug smoking-room. I was providentially led to this house, and have it remarkably cheap. It is nearer to all my connections by a mile, and within seven minutes' walk of my church. I trust you will pray that the Lord, who has shown so much of His goodness at Charles Square, will afford us His gracious presence in Coleman Street likewise; for without Him a palace would be but a dungeon.'

In May Mr Newton was called upon to fulfil the painful duty of preaching a funeral sermon at St Paul's, Deptford, for his old friend Dr Conyers — a sermon which was a just tribute to a remarkably holy and single-minded man, and a faithful preacher of the gospel.*

This month of September found Mr Newton again at Southampton, or rather Portswood, which was henceforth for many years the place of his retreat in the summer, and where many pleasant visits were spent at the house of Walter Taylor, Esq. In one of his letters to Mr Campbell he says: 'Here are five churches, but no pulpit open

* See *Works*, vol. 5, p. 170.

to me, but Mr Taylor has opened his house and made room for five hundred hearers. I preach three evenings in the week while I stay. We are often full. My hearers are chiefly from the neighbouring villages, and seem willing to listen to the gospel if they had any one to preach to them; but, alas! in these parts, and many parts of the kingdom, the hungry sheep look up and are not fed.'

It was during this year that Mr Cowper removed from Olney to Weston — a change from a house with certainly very few attractions or comforts to a very pleasant residence in a delightful neighbourhood. This change was mainly effected by the kind intervention of Lady Hesketh. It led to a connection of a more or less intimate character with the family of the Throgmortons and others, whose religious sympathies were not altogether in accordance with those of Mr Cowper and Mrs Unwin. Some exaggerated reports of the intercourse and doings of his old friends had reached Mr Newton, and with a love jealous for the welfare of its objects he expostulated, perhaps without sufficient inquiry into the truth of such allegations. Mr Newton's course was perfectly natural, although it might be a little precipitate. No wonder he feared for his friend, lest in his peculiar circumstances worldly influences and associations should altogether extinguish those religious views and feelings which still remained — a glimmering light amid all the darkness of his despondency. The translation of Homer of necessity engrossed Mr Cowper's attention, and was to others as well as to Mr Newton a source of regret, from the particular point of view to which we have alluded.

Taking all these circumstances into consideration, together with Mr Cowper's self-exclusion from the ordinances of religion, Mr Newton's fear may be justified, even if we allow that it was in some measure needless and too strongly expressed. But surely when Southey finds in Mr Newton's conduct ground for charging him with unwarrantable interference, and for making insinuations of spiritual pride and direction (not confined, as he says, to the Romish priesthood), the biographer of Cowper manifests entire ignorance of the character of a man whose whole history belies such accusations.

It was towards the close of this year (1786) that our convicts were first sent to Botany Bay. We are told that, through Mr Wilberforce's interest with Mr Pitt, a Mr Richard Johnson was appointed chaplain to the settlement and further, that the Archbishop of Canterbury, Sir Charles Middleton (afterwards Lord Barham), and Mr Thornton, with many others, greatly approved this mission and were much interested in it. We may add that it was hoped it might be a means of introducing the gospel to the aborigines. Mr Newton had been for some time acquainted with Mr Johnson, and thus refers to the subject in a letter to Mr Bull: 'A minister who should go to Botany Bay without a real call from the Lord, and without receiving from Him an apostolical spirit, the spirit of a missionary, enabling him to forsake all, to give up all, to venture all, to put himself into the Lord's hands without reserve, to sink or swim, had better run his head against a stone wall. I am strongly inclined to hope Mr Johnson is thus called, and will be thus qualified. He is humble and simple-hearted. I think he would not have thought of this service had it not been proposed to him; for some time he wished to decline it, but he could not, he durst not.'

On this occasion the following lines were written by Mr Newton, headed:

OMICRON TO JOHNSON,
GOING TO BOTANY BAY.

The Lord, who sends thee hence, will be thine aid;
In vain at thee the lion, Danger, roars;
His arm and love shall keep thee undismayed
On tempest-tossèd seas, and savage shores.

Go, bear the Saviour's name to lands unknown,
Tell to the Southern world His wondrous grace;
An energy Divine thy words shall own,
And draw their untaught hearts to seek His face.

Many in quest of gold or empty fame
Would compass earth, or venture near the poles;
But how much nobler thy reward and aim —
To spread His praise, and win immortal souls!

1787. It was during this year that Mrs Hannah More was added to the number of Mr Newton's friends. She had read *Cardiphonia*, and was so deeply impressed alike with the truths it contained, and the manner in which they were presented that she sought the acquaintance of its author. Of the correspondence which grew out of this intimacy a considerable portion remains, proving the high regard which Mrs More entertained for Mr Newton's religious character, and showing her opinion of the agreeable and instructive letters which he addressed immediately to herself.

Mrs More writes to Mr Newton, November, 1787, telling him of the pleasant and quiet retreat she had found at Cowslip Green, and of the hope she had cherished of quiet spiritual progress under such circumstances. 'I am certainly happier here,' she says, 'than in the agitation of the world, but I do not find that I am one bit better; with full leisure to rectify my heart and affections, the disposition unluckily does not come. I have the mortification to find that petty and, as they are called, innocent employments can detain my heart from heaven as much as tumultuous pleasures.'

We quote the following sentences from Mr Newton's reply: 'We are apt to wonder that, when what we accounted hindrances are removed, and the things which we conceived would be great advantages are put within our power, still there is a secret something in the way which proves itself to be independent of all external changes, because it is not affected by them. The disorder we complain of is internal; and in allusion to our Lord's words upon another occasion, I must say, it is not that which surrounds us; it is not anything in our outward situation (provided it be not actually unlawful), that can prevent or even retard our advances in religion, we are defiled and impeded by that which is within. So far as our hearts are right, all places and circumstances, which His wise and good providence allots us, are nearly equal; such hindrances will prove helps; such losses gains, and crosses will ripen into comforts; but till we are so far apprised of the nature of our disease as to put ourselves into the hands of the great and only Physician, we shall find, like the woman in Luke 8:43, that every other effort for relief will leave us as it found us . . . When we understand what the Scripture teaches of the person, love and offices of Christ, the necessity and final causes of His humiliation unto death, and feel our own need of such a Saviour, we then know Him to be the light, the sun of the world and of the soul, the source of all spiritual light, life, comfort, and influence; having access by God to Him, and receiving out of His fulness grace for grace. Our perceptions of these things are for a time faint and indistinct, like the peep of dawn; but the dawning light, though faint, is the sure harbinger of the approaching day.'

During this year Mr Newton's remarks on the African slave trade were given to the world. We have spoken of this publication elsewhere. We may add that Mrs Hannah More in a letter to Mr Newton tells him how much she is pleased with his sensible, judicious, well-timed, and well-tempered pamphlet on the slave trade, and that in a letter from Bristol she had been informed that Mr John Wesley named it with great commendation in a sermon he preached on the subject. We also find that Mr Newton received a communication from Scotland speaking most highly of his writings, and stating that they had made his name 'savoury' in the most remote and distant part of the island, and concluding with a request that he would allow their reprint in that part of the kingdom.

1788. In April of this year Mr Newton attended the funeral of the Rev. Charles Wesley, who was buried at Marylebone Church. It was Mr Wesley's wish, expressed before his death, that his friend Mr Newton should be one of the eight clergymen who were to bear the pall. In a letter to his niece, Miss Catlett, he says that he felt it to be his duty to pay this mark of affection and respect to Mr Wesley, though he was himself unwell at the time, and it was to be a walking funeral, the wind being exceedingly cold and the snow falling.

About this time we have a letter addressed to Mr Johnson at Botany Bay — a very judicious and in every way excellent communication, which is, however, too long for insertion.

In August, Mr Newton was in Northamptonshire, and writes thus of his visit to Mr Bull:

'My Dear Friend,

'A great object with me was Creaton, where I preached twice on Wednesday. Surely the Lord dwelleth in that place. But who that judgeth by outward appearances would look for Him in so small and obscure a village? Yet that little village is more truly glorious than all the mountains of prey, than all the Babylons and Romes that ever existed, though a detail of the madness, tyranny, and profligacy of those cities engages the attention of the unlearned, and is dignified with the name of history.

'I have had eight doses from Dr Pulpit this week, am to take the ninth this evening. They agree perfectly well with me, only that their operation, together with the warmth of the weather, have left me a little in the lazy way.

'We intend visiting you and Mrs Bull on Tuesday next.'

Amongst Mr Newton's numerous acts of kindness there was no work of charity in which he took greater delight than aiding his poor brethren in the Church. Many sought his guidance and help in their various exigencies, and he often became the means of affording them valuable pecuniary assistance, both from himself, and as the medium of the bounty of others. One case we may mention as a sample of many. The story is interesting, as an exhibition of the manifold labours and heavy trials of a devoted servant of the Lord, and of the gracious interpositions of Providence on his behalf, and therefore we venture to give it in detail. The account is taken from letters to Mr Newton written in the years 1787 and 1788.

The good man tells Mr Newton that he is induced to write to him from having read his *Cardiphonia*. 'I am,' he says, ' a very little, insignificant curate of the Church of England, a native of Wales (my name is Ellis Williams), but notwithstanding my littleness, unworthiness, and insignificance, I am a man that has been highly favoured of the Lord, for I was made acquainted with the gospel pretty early in life, and have been now for upwards of seven years engaged in the important work of preaching it to others.

'The place where I live is called Clay-Hydon, in the county of Devon and diocese of Exeter. The gospel was strange to the people when I first came among them, and for a time I met with little success. At length some seemed under conviction, and I asked them into my house, for the better opportunity of conversing with them. They remained for family prayer. Presently it was noised abroad that the parson had prayer in his house morning and evening, and that without any book, and that all were welcome to come. Many did so, especially on Sunday evenings, and thus there came about a great revival in the place. Opposition arose, as a matter of course, but soon subsided, and enemies became friends.'

Mr Williams had a family, and his only dependence was his small curacy; but he makes no complaints, though he writes again to Mr Newton, asking if he can aid him in getting one of his boys into the Bluecoat School.

The next letter is an expression of heartfelt gratitude for timely help which Mr Newton sent the good man. 'Although,' he begins, 'I never saw you, yet I dearly love you in the bowels of Jesus Christ. I want to tell you a little of my history, what trials, what mercies, what kind acts of Providence have often appeared in my favour since I last wrote you.' He then goes on to say how bare he and his family were of clothes, but he felt assured the Lord would supply their wants. 'Little,' he adds, 'did I then know that the Lord was making use of you as an instrument in His hands to supply me in that respect, and so the five pounds came very seasonably to clothe me, that I might appear a little more decent in my Master's house and service.' Just after this Mr Williams relates how he was taken ill and laid aside from his work, and that, when he went to his apothecary to ask him for his bill, his blessed Lord and Master had been there before to turn the doctor's heart, and so he would take nothing from him, but frankly forgave him all; and yet again he speaks of help which came to him unsought at the time of his wife's confinement.

In February, 1788, he acknowledges a sum of ten pounds, which he says reached his 'unworthy hands last Monday night. The sight of your letter forced some tears out of my eyes, and I hope some gratitude out of my heart to my dear heavenly Father, and to you next as His instrument. What you sent was a seasonable supply indeed. When returning from visiting a sick person I was meditating how I should get through my difficulties. I owed more than the little I had to the butcher; I remembered that my three little boys wanted clothes, that my wife had told me the linen would not bear another mending, and finally that I owed five pounds to an old usurer. All these things weighed very heavily upon my mind, but I felt assured that the Lord would grant me assistance. As soon, therefore, as I came home I asked my wife whether any letter was come, and she with a smile answered yes, and gave it to me.'

Other letters followed containing further acknowledgments of Mr Newton's kind interposition on his behalf.

The course of this worthy man was cut short by fever caught in the fulfilment of his pastoral duties.

'I have sad tidings to relate to you,' says the Rev. J. J. Neucatre, a neighbouring clergyman; 'poor Williams of Clay-Hydon is now numbered among the dead. He died this morning at one o'clock. He preached four times last Sunday fortnight, and was taken ill on the Monday morning, and the fever increased so rapidly as to baffle both his physician and apothecary. Last night, his wife asking him how he was, he replied, "Oh, well, charmingly well. A few minutes more will land me safe in my Father's kingdom." On Saturday evening when he saw the putrid spots on his legs, he said, "Ah, it's over! Oh, my dear and beloved wife, and my dear children! What will become of them?" But on recollection he would now and then say, "Oh, what a God have I! how faithful has He been to me! He will provide for mine, since He is going to provide so well for me."

'His faith was prophetic, for this morning a respectable attorney in Wellington, the patron of the living, called upon me to begin a subscription for the widow and children.'

In another letter we find these sentences: 'The Sunday before he was taken ill, preaching in the afternoon at Hydon, which was his last sermon, he would not give over. He said twice or thrice, "My dear people, this may be the last time that we shall meet on earth. Forgive my warmth, my heart loves you. God knows how sincerely I desire your salvation and your advancement in holiness. I know not how to part with you. Oh, remember the Redeemer, remember Him; He is the glory of heaven — all its beauty centres in Him."

'On the Sunday preceding his death many farmers and others went to see him; he said to one of them: "Oh, Mr Blackmore, I am glad to see you here; this is heaven upon earth; I die in this way only believing that gospel which I have preached to you for nine years, and so happily will you all die, if you believe what I have preached to you." He never spoke of the affairs of the world but once, and that not above two minutes. Leaving a poor delicate wife without a house, without money, and without rich relations, and six infants, the eldest but ten, and the youngest on the feeble mother's breast, he bore away with a full sail, not casting one look behind, to the best of my knowledge. Oh, how often has his honest zeal to God made me blush! His rector is a Socinian, yet never would he yield an inch to accommodate, and in all companies his God and Saviour, and that religion which never was and never will be in fashion, were honestly confessed. Thus lived and thus died Ellis Williams, in the thirty-second year of a useful and laborious life, having seen many seals to his labours for God, having through grace changed a rude people into as benevolent and kind a people as most whom I know; and leaving behind him a name which will not soon be forgotten, and which well deserves to be held in remembrance.'

The expression of feeling at his funeral indicated the intense affection of his people. 'They cried out, they pressed about the grave's mouth, and in every possible way showed the depth of their love, and no wonder,' says his friend Neucatre, 'for his affectionate spirit, his fatherly love, and irreproachable life and behaviour, engaged the love of the good, and forced respect from all thoughtful people.

'The sphere of my dear and faithful brother's action was three parishes, which he faithfully and honourably served, and whose inhabitants (seven or eight excepted), are in unspeakable woe. The good rejoiced in his light; the evil reverenced him; never did a minister's light more shine before men; never was there a man more beloved, or more lamented in similar circumstances. God honoured him, blessed his labours, and gave him to see many noble witnesses go to heaven before him. He found Clay-Hydon a dark place, but has left it wonderfully abounding with zealous witnesses for God. I cannot tell half his worth, nor the loss the Church of God has sustained in his removal.

'My own distress is peculiarly great, because I am perplexed about what I shall do for his widow; it is true I can raise possibly twenty pounds hereabouts; "but what is that among so many?" I thought I would acquaint you with this lamentable tale, hoping that the Lord would by one and another answer the faith and hope of my dearly beloved brother and Christian friend.'

So great was the interest created by the destitute circumstances of the widow and her six fatherless children, that a thousand pounds was raised on their behalf, of which Mr Newton was the means of obtaining two hundred pounds in London. Mr Newton was requested to write an epitaph for this good man, to be inscribed on a plain stone in the churchyard of Clay-Hydon, a copy of which has been preserved.

Not in one, but in many ways Mr Newton endeavoured to fufil the work given him to do. 'Young ministers,' says Mr Cecil, 'were peculiarly the objects of his attention; he instructed them, he encouraged them, he warned them, and might truly be said to be a father in Christ, spending and being spent for the interest of His church.' The case of the Rev. W. Jay of Bath well illustrates this feature of Mr Newton's character. Mr Jay first visited London about this time. It was customary to hold a Friday morning service at Surrey Chapel. Thither Mr Newton sometimes went. 'After hearing me,' says Mr Jay (then quite a young man), 'he introduced himself, and spoke to me in the most kind and encouraging way: and invited me to his house.' He adds: 'On subsequent visits, whenever I could, I went to Mr Newton's breakfasts, when his conversation was very delightful and edifying. Nothing dull about him, but a good deal of pleasantry and wit, or rather humour.' It may be added here that Mr Newton was in the habit of receiving ministers and other Christian friends at his house to breakfast once a week, for prayer and the discussion of religious subjects. To the reminiscences of friends in connection with these meetings we are indebted for the preservation of many of the striking sayings of Mr Newton.

We are enabled through the kindness of a friend to give the following characteristic illustration: 'I was present,' says the late Rev. John Clayton, 'at one of Mr Newton's Thursday breakfasts, and observing that our host had been for some time silent, I challenged him to give his opinion on something or other. "Well," said he, "I will tell you my dreams if you like. I dreamed that I was crossing a sea. It was narrow but very rough. After long struggling with winds and waves I entered a still and beautiful harbour. I landed, and meeting a grave and affable person I said, 'Pray, sir, what is the name of this port?' He replied 'The Harbour of Comfort.' 'And what is that stormy sea which I have just crossed?' 'The Bay of Care.' 'I suppose this beautiful port can be reached sometimes without such trouble as I have had.' 'Oh no; it is the will of the Master of the port that it shall be reached in no other way. Through much tribulation you must enter the kingdom.'" "Surely, Mr Newton," said I, "you were making this beautiful comparison while you were silent." "No; it came to me in a dream the night before last, and when you rallied me I was thanking God for it." "I wish," said Mr Cecil, "that we could do awake what you do asleep.'"

There is very little to record of the year 1789. In April Mr Newton preached a thanksgiving sermon on the king's recovery. His text was 1 Thessalonians 4:16, 17, and he composed some verses suitable to the occasion.

To Mr Clayton, then about to settle as minister of a London congregation, Mr Newton gave the following valuable advice: 'You will soon find plenty of sparks – domestic, political, ecclesiastical. Don't take a pair of bellows to blow them, but stamp them out.'

Abundant appreciation of Mr Newton's character and labours found expression at this time. There is a letter from the Countess of Leven, at the close of which she says, referring to the visit of Mr Thornton and Mr Bull to Melville: 'I wish he (Mr Bull) would return, and bring you along with him, or that you would bring yourself, at any rate. Many a one in Scotland desires to see you, but pray do not come for one week only.'

Other letters from Scotland were received by Mr Newton from his old correspondent, Mr McIntyre. 'You will be glad to hear,' he says, 'more as a minister than an author, that there is an eager desire for your works through most parts of Scotland, and that, by the blessing of God on these writings, many sinners are reclaimed, many mourners are comforted, the doubtful confirmed in the truth, the weak strengthened, and saints enabled with more joy to walk in the ways of Zion.' Again he says: 'I would not wish to lose a line published, or, if possible, written by you.' Another of his Scotch friends states that a letter which Mr Newton had written to him had been universally admired, and was so worn by use that it was falling to pieces.

A gentleman, who was a stranger to Mr Newton, addressing him from America, informs him that since the Revolution, his works had become known there, and endeared the author to himself, and to thousands more who had read them with comfort and delight, and that an edition had been printed at New York. But perhaps the most remarkable and interesting expression of feeling of this kind was from a Baptist church at Whitchurch, in Hampshire. Such was the value set by that religious community on Mr Newton's writings, that at a church meeting they agreed to present a memorial to him, which is signed by the minister, three deacons, and several of the members. After offering their Christian salutations, they tell him that the work of God has been promoted amongst them, in great measure, by his writings, and that this circumstance has led them thus to address him. They desire, losing sight of lesser differences, to express their great satisfaction in his admirable exposition of the great truths of the gospel; and knowing the many discouragements of the faithful ministers of Christ, they consider it their duty thus to address him. The letter is dated October 18th, 1789.

It may be added that in the course only of the next few months he received further testimonies to the value of his writings from India, and again from Scotland and America. From other quarters nearer to home we find letters from religious inquirers, and from those who had derived benefit from his preaching or his writings. The narrative of his conversion still continued to be instrumental of good.

We quote the following brief passages from Mr Newton's diary, containing a general review of several preceding years. It was written on the 4th of August. 'Thirty-one years have today elapsed since Thou didst draw my heart solemnly to devote myself to Thy public service. Thou hast honoured me, Thou hast given me a tongue and a pen, many friends, hast made me extensively known among Thy people, and, I have reason to hope, useful to many by my preaching and writings. *Totum muneris hoc tui est* [This is all Thy gift]. It is of Thine own that I can serve Thee . . . I am a poor, unworthy, unfaithful, inconsistent creature, and I may well wonder that Thou hast not long ago taken Thy Word utterly out of my mouth, and forbidden me to make mention of Thy name any more.'

There still remain some memorandum books in which Mr Newton has entered what he calls 'travelling notes' — brief records of his journeys. Thus: 'September 2nd, 1789. Wednesday. Preparing to set off for Southampton with my dear Mary, and B. May the Lord make it beneficial to body and soul to me and mine. May we do and get good where we are going. May we aim at Thy will and glory, and return in peace to praise Thee with our family and people, whom I commend to Thy gracious care. Amen.'

Mr Newton tells us that on this occasion some of the churches at Southampton were open to him. Frequently he heard Mr Kingsbury, the Independent minister, and was generally occupied on sabbath evenings, and two or three times during the week, in addressing a large company at Mr Taylor's house. There were many pleasant walks and rural retreats about Portswood, among which may be especially mentioned the grounds of General — and Sloane's Wood: the latter was a favourite spot with Mr Newton. 'Spent near two hours,' he says, 'in Mr Sloane's wood, aiming to praise the Lord for His goodness, and to commend my future ways to Him.'

During this visit Mr Newton went over to Priestlands to visit his old friend Mr Etty. They reached London again October 2nd.

13: LONDON
(1790–2)

Death of Mr Thornton – Of Mrs Newton – Detail – Mr
Newton wonderfully supported – Van Lier's Letters – Mrs
Althans – Claudius Buchanan – Reflections on the Loss of Mrs
Newton – Rev. Mr Coffin – Journeys into Cambridgeshire, Bath,
Bristol, Southampton, etc. – Letter from Mrs More – Bibles for
Wales – Diary – Saturday-evening meetings – Doctor's Degree –
Letters on Political Debates – Journey to Northamptonshire and
Buckinghamshire – Baptismal Regeneration.

If the previous year was, as far as we know, uneventful in Mr
Newton's history, it was not so with 1790. Some few of his early
friends had passed away, and more recently he was called to mourn
the loss of Mrs Wilberforce, Mrs Trinder of Northampton, Mr
Barham, and Mr Symonds of Bedford — all dying within a very short
time of one another. But before the year closed the great and good
John Thornton, Mr Newton's 'best friend,' rested from his labours;
and not long after it was the will of God to sever that singularly
happy connection which had subsisted for so many years between
Mr Newton and his wife. But we must speak more particularly of
these last events.

Mr Thornton's death took place at Bath, after a short illness,
November 7th. During the illness Mr Newton thus writes to Mr
Bull: 'You know something of my peculiar obligations to him . . .
To him, under the Lord, I owe all my consideration and comfort
as a minister. It was a pleasure to me if I only saw him passing by. I
believe I shall see his face no more here; but, hereafter, oh what a
hope! what a prospect! But what is my private loss, compared with

that of the public! I think it probable that no one man in Europe, in private life, will be so much missed at first; but I trust his place will be well supplied, even by those of his own family.'

And now to speak of Mrs Newton. Her health had been for some months evidently failing. 'I have been watching,' says her devoted husband, 'with much feeling and too much anxiety my failing gourd, upon which a worm by the Divine appointment has been long preying.' Nevertheless, as the fatal issue approached, the good man possessed his soul in patience. 'Through the Lord's mercy,' he writes, 'my mind is calm and resigned. I have not one allowed wish to alter His appointment, were it possible. Instead of complaining that she is to be taken from me now, what reason have I for admiration and praise that she has been spared to me so long, when I have justly deserved to forfeit her every day of my life. How few in the married state live together upwards of forty years! Still fewer who preserve their mutual affection unabated for so long a term.'

On the 15th December, Mrs Newton was released from her sufferings, and the following are Mr Newton's words to Mr Bull three days after: '. . . I am supported, I am comforted, I am satisfied. The Lord is good indeed! I can think without regret of the day when the Lord first joined our hands (excepting when I reflect on my folly and idolatry); and now I feel not much more regret when I think of the day which separated us for a season. I trust we shall soon meet to part no more.'

At the close of his *Letters to a Wife* her husband has given an account of Mrs Newton's last illness, and his own feelings and views in connection with it.

We are told that a year or two before her death symptoms of cancer made their appearance, but that she bore her sufferings with much resignation, and even with cheerfulness.

'On Sunday, December 12th,' to quote the words of Mr Newton, three days before her death, 'when I was preparing for church in the morning, she sent for me, and we took a final farewell as to this world. She faintly uttered an endearing compellation, which was familiar to her, and gave me her hand, which I held, while I prayed by her bedside. We exchanged a few tears; but I was almost as unable to speak as she was.

'That evening her speech, her sight, and I believe her hearing, wholly failed. She continued perfectly composed, without taking notice of anything, or discovering any sign of pain or uneasiness, till Wednesday evening, towards seven o'clock ... I took my post by her bedside, and watched her nearly three hours with a candle in my hand, till I saw her breathe her last, on the 15th December, 1790, a little before ten o'clock in the evening ... I kneeled down with the servants who were in the room, and returned the Lord unfeigned thanks for her deliverance and her peaceful dismission.'

Then follows this important passage: 'I believe it was about two or three months before her death, when I was walking up and down the room, offering disjointed prayers from a heart torn with distress, that a thought suddenly struck me with unusual force, to this effect: The promises of God must be true; surely the Lord will help me, *if I am willing to be helped.* It occurred to me that we are often led from a vain complacence in what we call our sensibility, to indulge that unprofitable grief which both our duty and our peace require us to resist to the utmost of our power. I instantly said aloud, "Lord, I am helpless indeed in myself, but I hope I am willing, without reserve, that Thou shouldest help me." It had been much on my mind, from the beginning of this trial, that I was a minister, and that the eyes of many were upon me; that my turn of preaching had very much led me to endeavour to comfort the afflicted by representing the gospel as a *catholicon* [universal remedy], affording an effectual remedy for every evil, a full compensation for every want or loss, to those who truly receive it. It had been, therefore, my frequent daily prayer that I might not by impatience or despondence be deprived of the advantage my situation afforded me of confirming by my own practice the doctrine which I had preached to others. From the time that

I so remarkably felt myself *willing to be helped* I might truly say, to the praise of the Lord, "My heart trusted in Him, and I was helped indeed". Through the whole of my painful trial I attended all my stated and occasional services as usual; and a stranger would scarcely have discovered, either by my words or looks, that I was in trouble.

'Many of our intimate friends were apprehensive that this long affliction, and especially the closing event, would have overwhelmed me; but it was far otherwise. It did not prevent me from preaching a single sermon, and I preached on the day of her death. After she was gone my willingness to be helped and my desire that the Lord's goodness to me might be observed by others for their encouragement made me indifferent to some laws of established custom, the breach of which is often more noticed than the violation of God's commands. I was afraid of sitting at home and indulging myself by poring over my loss; and therefore I was seen in the street, and visited some of my serious friends, the very next day. I likewise preached three times while she lay dead in the house. Some of my brethren kindly offered their assistance, but as the Lord was pleased to give me strength, both of body and mind, I thought it my duty to stand up in my place as formerly.

'And after she was deposited in the vault I preached her funeral sermon from Habakkuk 3:17, 18, a text which I had reserved from my first entrance on the ministry, for this particular service, if I should survive her. I have reason to hope that many of my hearers were comforted and animated under their afflictions by what they saw of the Lord's goodness to me in my time of need. And I acknowledge that it was well worth standing awhile in the fire for such an opportunity of experiencing and exhibiting the power and faithfulness of His promises.'

Farther on he says: 'The Bank of England is too poor to compensate for such a loss as mine. But the Lord, the all-sufficient God, speaks, and it is done. Let those who know Him and trust Him be of good courage. He can give them strength according to their day; He can increase their strength as their trials are increased to any assignable degree. And what He *can* do He has promised He *will* do.'

That Mr Newton's attachment to his wife was excessive, as he himself confesses, almost idolatrous, there is ample evidence. It was a sort of lover's passion through life, never seeming to suffer abatement. It was, no doubt, greatly affected by the fact that such a connection had been in God's providence the chief means of his salvation and of his subsequent happiness and usefulness. Nor did the impression pass away after Mrs Newton's death. It seemed still to retain all its strength. The day became one of his memorial seasons, and for many years, on its return, he gave expression to his feelings in poetical pieces, which he termed 'anniversaries.' As late as the year 1800 he thus writes from Portswood to a friend: 'He must have a steady hand who can draw the exact line between overvaluing and undervaluing our creature-comforts. The latter was not my fault. Alas! I was an idolater, and I suffered for it. Now all is over. I can be thankful for the years 1789 and 1790. But I would not live them over again for the wealth of the Indies. Yet nothing in the singular history of my life is more wonderful to myself than the manner in which the Lord supported me through the trying scene, and at the close of it. Scarcely in any other way could I have known so much of the power and faithfulness of His promise to give strength according to the day, and of His all-sufficiency; for I had no more of what are called sensible comforts than usual, but still was supported I know not how; but I well know that if His arm had not been underneath me, I must have sunk like a stone in the water.'

It was during this year that, at the suggestion of Mr Newton, Van Lier's letters were translated by Mr Cowper. Van Lier was a Dutch clergyman residing at the Cape. He became acquainted with Mr Newton's writings, and corresponded with him. His letters contain an account of his religious history, which, as affording a striking illustration of the power of Divine grace, Mr Newton thought worthy of publication.

1791. Early in the year Mr Newton published a little work entitled *Christian Character Exemplified*, being extracts from the diary and letters of Mrs Margaret Althans. He consented to look over these papers, in the first instance, to oblige the husband of Mrs Althans; but he tells us that he soon found the employment peculiarly seasonable and profitable to him, quickening his feeling of submission to the Divine will, and of dependence upon God under his affliction.

This excellent little volume has passed through several editions, and some years since was added to the number of the publications of the Religious Tract Society.

Nor thus alone was Mr Newton's mind in a measure diverted from his great sorrow. Other work of special interest was also given him to do.

It happened about this time that amongst his hearers at St Mary Woolnoth, there was found one Sunday an intelligent and well-educated young man, who was anxiously seeking the way of salvation. He had informed his mother of his state of mind, and she having heard of Mr Newton had urged her son to seek his acquaintance. The next day Mr Newton received an anonymous letter from the same individual, detailing some remarkable circumstances in his history. He informed Mr Newton that he was born in Scotland, and though well educated, and in comfortable circumstances, was seized with an irresistible desire to see the world, and entertained the romantic purpose of travelling over the Continent on foot. Quitting his home under a false pretext, he made his way southward, supporting himself by playing on his violin, till he came to Newcastle, whence he sailed to London. There he was for some months in great destitution, but at length obtained a situation as clerk to an attorney. He states that he was not without impressions of religion during this period; but for three years he lived for the most part in the neglect of its great duties, till the conversation of a religious acquaintance in 1790 led him to serious thought. And, to quote the words of the writer, he proceeds: 'On the receipt of my mother's letter, I went the next Sunday evening to your church; and when you spoke I thought I heard the words of eternal life. I listened with avidity, and wished you had preached till midnight . . . Yet my sins do not affect me as I wish. All that I can speak of is a strong desire to be converted to my God. Oh sir, what shall I do to inherit eternal life? I see clearly that I cannot be happy in any degree, even in this life, until I make my peace with God; but how shall I make that peace? If the world were my inheritance, I would sell it, to purchase that pearl of great price. Tomorrow,' he concludes, 'is the day you have appointed for a sermon to young people. Will you remember me, and speak some suitable word, that, by the aid of the blessed Spirit, may reach my heart? Whatever becomes of me or of my labours, I pray God that you may prove successful in your ministry, and that your labours may be abundantly blessed.'

Mr Newton felt a deep interest in this anonymous communication; and unable otherwise to find out the writer, whom he was very anxious to benefit, he gave notice at St Mary's that if the person who had written to him anonymously on such a day were in the church, he should be happy to converse with him: 'I called on him,' says the young man, in a letter to his mother, 'on the Tuesday following, and experienced such a happy hour as I ought not to forget. If he had been my father he could not have expressed more solicitude for my welfare. Mr Newton encouraged me much. He put into my hands the *Narrative* of his life and some of his letters, begged my careful perusal of them before I saw him again, and gave me a general invitation to breakfast with him when and as often as I could.' 'Oh sir,' he says, addressing Mr Newton, 'what a seasonable gift were your books to a person in my situation! Next to the Oracles of Truth I consult them. They contain something suitable for almost every condition in life.'

The person referred to in this statement was the afterwards well-known Dr Claudius Buchanan. In the words of his biographer, Mr Buchanan found in Mr Newton an enlightened and experienced guide, a wise and faithful counsellor, and at length a steady and affectionate friend.

It appears that in early life Buchanan had been designed for the ministry. This purpose had still at times, in what he terms his 'unhappy years', often recurred to him, and now it revived in all its fulness. His natural talents and acquirements were already considerable, and his piety unquestioned; Mr Newton therefore felt quite justified in encouraging his wishes. His preferences were to the ministry in the Church of England, and the first thought was to seek the ordination for him at once; and Mr H. Thornton, who had become interested in his case, thought that object might be accomplished if he were willing to accept the chaplaincy of the colony of Sierra Leone. To this, under Mr Newton's advice, he cordially assented. This design, however, was relinquished, and Mr Buchanan became at first much depressed. But very soon all his fears were ended by the generous offer of Mr Thornton to send him to the university at his own expense; and thus unexpectedly he became a student at Queen's College, Cambridge, on Michaelmas Term, 1791. Thus was Mr Newton's heart cheered by being made an instrument of good, alike to a friendless but most worthy man, and through him to the Church of God.

In a letter written to Mr Bull in the month of March, Mr Newton, after speaking of his great loss, continues: 'My health and spirits are good; I eat and sleep well. I preach, write and converse as usual. I hope in spirituals I have been rather a gainer by my loss than otherwise. I think, likewise, that in the time of my trial, and since, there has been an additional blessing going forth in the public ordinances. The church is more thronged than formerly, and there seems an attention and earnestness in the hearers which is very encouraging.'

It was to be expected that such a man as Mr Newton would be constantly increasing the circle of his acquaintance; but it is only just to observe that while he attracted new friends we never find it was to the diminution of his affection for those who claimed an earlier interest in his regard. Thus, this year commenced a correspondence with the Rev. James Coffin and his family in Cornwall, which continued to 1801. These letters have been published, and have passed through three editions.

We find the following striking statement in the preface to this volume: 'The correspondence which is now for the first time presented to the public was commenced under very interesting circumstances. Our revered and beloved parents were first awakened to a sense of the importance of vital religion through the instrumentality of some of Mr Newton's works, which had been kindly lent for their perusal. Under much concern for their past ignorance, and hardly knowing what to think or do, they, in the fulness of their hearts, addressed their benefactor, though personally unknown to him, and stated without reserve the new position in which they found themselves, as light from the Sun of righteousness dawned upon them. The letter commencing the series will show how their communication was received, and how prompt and ready this servant of God was to come in and aid with his experience his spiritual children. An intimate and sanctified friendship was quickly formed, which continued till the death of Mr Newton in 1807.'

In this first letter Mr Newton, ever remembering with deep humiliation the circumstances of his early history, speaks in the following terms: 'Had you known me, you would not have thought so much apology necessary for writing. Indeed, I am not a person of such mighty consequence as you may suppose; when you write again, think of the poor wretch who wandered at the plantations without shoe, shirt, or friends; think of one who, like the man possessed by the legion, was a perpetual torment to himself, and mischievous to all about him; and correct the opinion you may at present form of me with these ideas. For I am the same person still; and though the Lord has dealt bountifully and wonderfully with me since, I have still equal reason to lie low in the dust before him, with my hand upon my mouth, and to say, "Lord, be merciful to me a sinner."'

In June, St Mary Woolnoth was shut up for repairs, and Mr Newton was absent from London for about four months. During this
period he made several excursions. June 21st he left home for Cambridge, where he met with Mr Simeon and many other friends. He
preached on two successive Sabbaths at Mr Simeon's church. Then
we find him at Yelling and Merton. 'I find Mr Berridge,' he says,
'very weak.' Mr Venn, too, was growing feeble, and Mr Newton observes of his old friends:

'They may teach me what to expect. No matter: I am in the Lord's
hands; I have had a favoured lot — a large share of all that is valuable
in temporal wealth. My Lord, teach me to resign and forego with a
good grace.'

Mr Newton went thence to Bedford, preached Sunday, July 10th,
twice at St Paul's Church, and worshipped with the Moravians at
night. On the 12th he reached home.

On the 15th he travelled south to Teston, in Kent, the residence
of Sir Charles and Lady Middleton. 'Kindness,' he says, 'within
doors; beautiful walks and prospects in the park.' Sunday morning
he preached at Teston, in the evening at Nettlested: and afterwards
had a long and interesting conversation with some who sought his
advice. Thence Mr Newton and his companion (Miss Catlett) proceeded to Dover.

'Friday, 23rd. Walked in the morning upon the beach. Remembered old times, and tried to praise Thee, my Lord. What a wretch
was I, and what misery was before me, when I passed Dover-on-the-
Sea the last time, which was in the year 1745. And oh, what mercy
and goodness hast Thou shown me since!

'At church to prayers in the forenoon. Wrote a long letter to Mr
Bacon. The rest of the day various. I seem rather out of my element
here. I have not wisdom or strength to attempt anything in a direct
way; nor do such occasions offer as I can skilfully improve. If I drop
a word, it falls like a spark to the ground, and meets with nothing to
kindle.'

Sunday he calls a vacant day. He heard at church, in the morning; at the Baptist meeting in the afternoon, and at Lady Huntingdon's at night. He returned home at the beginning of August, preaching at Langley by the way.

A third and longer journey was undertaken on the 6th of August; and Mr Newton, with his companion, visited Reading, Bath, and Bristol, and was a guest at Cowslip Green. While at this last place Mr Newton preached on the Sunday at Shipham, to the children of Mrs More's Sunday-school. 'It was a pleasing sight; the whole congregation were attentive, and I was favoured with liberty.' He officiated again in the afternoon at Wrington, and in the evening had 'a parlour preaching'. From thence Mr Newton went to Bath, where he preached, and saw Mr Jay. By September the 9th he reached Portswood, of which he speaks as a sort of second home, a journey's end, and therefore he adds: 'Here would I set up a special Ebenezer to my Lord.' He adds this note: 'In consequence of a desire I had formed, I walked to Mr Sloane's wood. Spent about two hours there in retirement. There I recollected some exercises of my mind in the same place when I was here last. There I set up my Ebenezer for answered prayer. For surely, though the Lord has seen it fit to remove the desire of my eyes since that time, I have good reason to say, He has heard my prayer. Did He not shield her from the excruciating pain which I expected she must endure, and at the idea of which my heart trembled? Did He not wonderfully support and strengthen me under my great trial, so that many could praise Him on my behalf? Has He not graciously preserved me to this hour? Does He not still afford me great comfort in my dear child and in my family, and still enable me to preach His good gospel? Praise the Lord, O my soul.' In a letter written to London, he says: 'I am now within my old circle, where I miss my dear in every room and every walk. But no matter. We shall meet again. For the rest, this is a delightful place, as you have heard me say, but this looks like a weeping day. It rains much, and the trees in the garden seem to drop tears upon me as I pass along.'

He preached at St Michael's — the only church offered to him while at Southampton — and returned home on Friday the 30th, and makes the following reflections upon these excursions: 'Oh, for a heart to praise the Lord! what mercies have I been favoured with in the last three months, in which we have travelled about seven hundred and fifty miles without harm or alarm, and always good news from home. The families I visited all in peace. Much kindness from friends: nothing to be called a trial. Many opportunities, and for the most part liberty of speech and spirit. Oh, make me humble and thankful.'

In reference to this visit Mrs More writes in September: 'I assure you your kind wishes and affectionate remembrance of the mountains of Mendip, and of the little hermitage at the foot of it, are returned with great sincerity. Your pipe still maintains its station in the black-currant tree, and that hand would be deemed very presumptuous and disrespectful which should presume to displace it; for my own part, the pipe of *Tityrus* [a shepherd in Virgil's first *Eclogue* who played on a reed pipe], though in my youthful days I liked it passing well, would now not be deemed a more venerable relic. And even the little sick maid, Lizzy, who gratefully remembers the spiritual comfort you administered to her, often cries out: "O dear! I hope nobody will break Mr Newton's pipe." . . . Patty and I remember you as we are trotting over the hills; she desires her affectionate regards, as do all the rest. You would enjoy the vale of cowslips in this renewed spring. We have everything of the golden age except the innocence. The garden is full of roses as in June, and an apple tree literally covered at the same moment with ripe fruit and fresh blossoms. Adieu, my dear sir. May the remainder of your peregrinations be prosperous! Pray remember that no one stands more in need of your prayers than your most obliged and faithful,

' H. MORE.'

How much Mr Newton's company was sought will appear from the following expressions in a letter from Scotland: 'When I was at Montrose I was informed that your church was under repairs. Now, dear father, is not this a time to visit your Scotch friends? How happy would thousands be to see you! All who know of you would be happy, except some Antiburghers. One of them at least is afraid, if you should come down, that some of their flocks might play the Latitudinarian, and run after you. Come, come, and break the bonds of bigotry — an object worthy your attention, worthy your exertion.' And thus does Buchanan mourn the absence of his friend: 'I long much for your return to St Mary Woolnoth. I was driven about from place to place; and, like Noah's dove, I fear I shall find no rest for the sole of my foot till my return to the ark.'

All are familiar with the story of Mr Charles of Bala coming to London to procure copies of the Welsh Bible, and how that simple incident was, in God's providence, the originating cause of that most noble institution, the British and Foreign Bible Society; but it appears from a letter written to Mr Newton at this time by good Mr Jones of Creaton that the want of Bibles in the Principality was felt, and that there was an earnest desire to supply it, as early as the year 1791. 'There are several thousands of poor families,' says Mr Jones, 'amongst the mountains in Wales without God's Bible in their houses. Is there any poverty like unto their poverty? But owing to a very wonderful revival of religion which has lately taken place amongst them, there is a loud and universal cry throughout the country for Welsh Bibles; but there are none to be had for money; and if there were, hundreds and hundreds of families must still go without for want of money to buy with. But Bibles they must have, for it is the will of God. A new edition must be printed; some to be given away, and the rest to be sold at a reduced price. Some of my countrymen have pressingly solicited me to undertake the work; but how can I go on without money? Was I possessed of a thousand pounds, most joyfully would I devote the whole of that sum to this blessed purpose, and would trouble no man. But I am poor and have no might, therefore I pray you, my dear sir, to direct and help me in this great work. This business has been of late so much upon my mind that I can hardly sleep at night. If you please to favour me with a line as soon as convenient you will greatly oblige me.'

Whether Mr Newton made any effort in this direction we know not; but we are quite sure that he would feel a real sympathy in the object of his friend at Creaton.

The above letter is introduced as showing how highly Mr Newton's influence was appreciated. It is also interesting as affording an illustration of the state of feeling which existed about the time of the origin of the Bible Society.

The 15th of December was especially observed by Mr Newton, and we find this record in his diary: 'On this anniversary of the day when my dearest was removed from me I have kept at home for retirement, and to take occasion for a review, for exercises of praise and humiliation. Much cause I have for both ...

'Now I have been enabled to live a year without her, and wonderfully supported, so that, though she is always present to my mind, and always will be, I have not known one uncomfortable day. Indeed, this has been a highly favoured year, in which I have scarcely met with anything that deserves the name of a trial. The affection and attention of my dear child and servants make home still pleasant to me. I was much abroad in the summer; but everywhere safety attended us upon the road, and kindness received us wherever we called. My health has been uninterrupted and my ability for public service continued to this day, though I am more than four months in my sixty-seventh year.'

He also wrote on this occasion the first of what he termed his 'Anniversaries', a memorial piece of thirty-eight verses which will be found at the end of the second volume of *Letters to a Wife*.

Mr Newton was entirely free from either the vanity or ambition which too often shows itself in some great and even good men; and so when the University of New Jersey conferred on him at this time the degree of Doctor of Divinity, while grateful for such an expression of respect, he refused to appropriate the title: 'I have been hurt,' he says in a letter to Mr Campbell, 'by two or three letters directed [to] Dr Newton. I beg you to inform my friends in Scotland, as they come in your way, that after a little time if any letters come to me addressed to Dr Newton I shall be obliged to send them back unopened. I know no such person, I never shall, I never will, by the grace of God ... So far as this mark of their favour indicates a regard to the gospel truths which I profess, I am much pleased with it. But as to the title itself, I renounce it heartily. The dreary coast of Africa was the university to which the Lord was pleased to send me, and I dare not acknowledge a relation to any other.'

It was therefore no pleasure to Mr Newton to receive a work by the Rev. David Williamson of Whitehaven, dedicated to him with the addition of this title to his name. This book chiefly consisted of sermons, of which Mr Newton expresses great approbation. The *Lectures on Liberty* contained in the same volume were not so much in accordance with his views. His strictures on them will be found in his *Letters on Political Debate*, in the sixth volume of his works, p. 586, etc.

In June, Mr Newton left London for five sabbaths. After visiting his old friends in Northamptonshire and Leicestershire, he at length reached Olney, and took up his abode with Mr Bean at the vicarage. On the 1st of July he preached twice in his old pulpit, and spent the whole of the following week in visiting and receiving friends.

In a letter written to a clerical friend immediately on his return, Mr Newton, after speaking of his journey, thus expresses himself about certain points in connection with the ritual of the Church of England: 'Although a passable Churchman, I cannot undertake to vindicate every expression in our baptismal service. Our Reformers, though they did great things, yet they only made a beginning; if permitted, they would probably have done much more. Some persons who had a share in Church councils in Edward the Sixth's time, though they could not wholly prevent the Reformation, had influences sufficient to impede and embarrass it. They would not accept the Scriptures alone, as the sufficient rule of faith and practice, but prevailed to superadd the Fathers of the first six centuries. Afterwards Elizabeth with her *semper eadem* [always the same] forbade all further alterations. But the gospel purity was soon corrupted, and some of the Fathers were but mothers (old women) in divinity. However, their authority gave sanction to several expressions and sentiments which the Scripture does not warrant, particularly with regard to baptism. The Sacraments are of Divine institution, but I do not think either of them confers grace *ex opere operato* [from the mere fact of having been administered]. The rubric tells us gravely that those who die in infancy may be saved if baptised; I believe they may be and are saved whether baptised or not; for I cannot think that the salvation of a soul depends upon a negligent or drunken minister, who cannot be found when wanted to baptise a dying infant. In the homilies, however, they speak more to the purpose. The Fathers, or some of them, did indeed speak of baptism and regeneration or the new birth as synonymous; but while Scripture, experience, and observation contradict them, I pay little regard to their judgment.'

14: LONDON
(1793–7)

Early in the year 1793 appeared a new edition of *Omicron's Letters* and of the *Experience of Mrs Althans*.

Mr Cowper, as of old, frequently corresponded with Mr Newton. And to show how his much-loved friend was still remembered, we may quote what Mr Cowper writes in April of the present year:

'MY DEAR FRIEND, Had it not been stipulated between us that, being both at present pretty much engrossed by business we should write when opportunity offers, I should be frightened at the date of your last; but you will not judge me, I know, by the unfrequency of my letters, nor suppose that my thoughts about you are equally unfrequent. In truth, they are not. No day passes in which you are excluded from them.'

Strangely forgetful of God's benefits as are even the most thoughtful, and needing often to chide themselves in the language of the Psalmist, yet we believe few were less guilty in this respect than Mr Newton. Nearly half a century had passed away since the time of his great deliverance; but on its date, the 21st of March, he thus writes to a friend: 'On this day, forty-six years ago, I was pumping for life, and expecting every minute that the ship would sink, or the next wave would wash me overboard. Yet, by help obtained from the Lord, I continue to this day. What has God wrought!' Nor was there a day in his life, as he repeatedly says, when the events of his early history were not more or less in his thoughts, and the occasion of humbling and grateful remembrance.

In April, Mr Newton mentions to Mr Bull that his new work, *Letters to a Wife*, was finished. 'I am not,' he says, 'a proper judge of a work in which I am so nearly concerned. In some respects it will be new; in some parts it will be amusing; but oh, that it may be useful! I am to be pitied if I have employed a chief part of the winter in picking straws . . . I trust you will continue to pray for us. This mutual prayer is one valuable branch of the communion of saints. This clause as it stands in our creed, is repeated daily by many who know no more of the meaning than a goose does of algebra. Nor should we have been wiser than they, if the Lord had not condescended to be our teacher. May all the praise be ascribed to Him by you and by your very affectionate friend and brother,

JOHN NEWTON.'

There was but one opinion as to the more than ordinary value of Mr Newton's previous writings. Not so unanimous, perhaps, was the view entertained of the *Letters to a Wife*. Yet let it be remembered that in giving these letters to the public Mr Newton was in great part actuated by the same spirit — a sincere desire to promote the glory of God — which constrained him to lay bare in his *Narrative* those details which mere worldly wisdom would have induced him carefully to conceal from public view.

In August, Mr Newton visited Hampshire. On his way to Southampton he spent a week at Heckfield with his friend Mr Ambrose Serle. Speaking of him to one of his correspondents on this occasion, Mr Newton says: 'He is a first-rate man, not only for solid experimental religion, but for natural and acquired abilities and general information.' Mr Serle was the author of the *Christian Remembrancer*, and of *Horæ Solitariæ*. Before the time of which we are writing he was Under-Secretary of State to the Earl of Dartmouth, and afterwards one of the commissioners of the Transport Board.

During the visit Mr Newton regularly attended the Independent chapel at Southampton in the morning, and preached in Mr Taylor's house in the evening. No church was open to him.

Mr Serle wrote to Mr Newton while at Southampton: 'Accept my best thanks for your welcome and obliging letter, and for the favour of your company, with which you had the kindness to indulge me. It must stand high among those circumstances of my life which I trust, in gratitude to the Author of all my mercies, will never be forgotten. Allow me to thank you for the acceptable present of books to me and mine. May God bless all your labours with abundant success to His glory and the good of souls.'

On Mr Newton's return homewards his friend conveyed him to Reading. There he met a Mr Ring, afterwards well known and much esteemed in the religious world.

'Tuesday, 24th,' he says, 'in the evening, by Mr Ring's desire, we had a meeting in his drawing-room of about forty people. I spoke from Romans 12:1, 2. I thank Thee, my Lord, for the hope that it was a good time.'

On September 26th he says: 'I am willing to hope, my Lord, that Thy providence led me to Mr Ring's, and that the visit, by Thy blessing, will prove seasonable and useful. Reward them with Thy best blessings for their kindness to us.'

'Friday, 27th. Took leave, not without mutual regret, of Mr and Mrs Ring. Set off in the coach at seven, and arrived at No. 6 about one. Found all well and in peace at home. Especially I praise Thee for the liberty and opportunity afforded of preaching Thy good gospel.'

'Mr and Mrs Ring,' says Mr Serle, 'called upon me, thanking me most cordially for their introduction to you, and expressing the high degree of happiness they had received in your company; so that I have thanks on both sides, and consequently a great deal of pleasure for myself. I believe, with you, that there is a great work carrying on at Reading, and I rejoice in Mr Cadogan's success, and pray for its continuance and increase. There are, to my knowledge, some gracious souls in Reading, and I rejoice to hear of their most cordial and delighted acceptance of your ministry among them . . . You are often with us even now.'

Soon after Mr Newton's return home Mr Bull was in London, and makes the following remark in a letter to his son: 'I came home to dinner (at Mr Neale's), and Mr Newton came here to dine with me. He looks very old, and has got exceedingly fat since I saw him last, but he is full of piety, holiness, and heavenly-mindedness. I shall dine with him next Saturday. He says he has found out that both he and I have a great deal too much indulgence, and therefore he will not sleep after dinner any more.'

On the 20th of December, Mr Newton writes to Mr Bull: 'My dear friend, I thank you for your kind letter, which I accept as a full compensation for any or all the censures I may meet from snarling critics' (referring to his *Letters to a Wife*). 'I cannot expect that my publication will be approved by those who have not feelings to qualify them for understanding it. But yours is not the only encouragement I have received.'

In the course of this year a long letter was written to Mr Newton by Dr Robbins, a Congregational minister residing at New Plymouth, America, giving a very interesting account of a great revival of religion there, and of the avidity and delight with which Mr Newton's books were purchased and read under these circumstances. We may also quote, as belonging to this period, a striking portion of a letter addressed to a friend, who had been awakened through Mr Newton's instrumentality, but who still fell short of an entire and assured trust in the Saviour: 'I long to hear that you are entered into the peace and liberty of the gospel. I trust you will in time; and I am sure you would while you are reading this letter, if you could but take the Lord's word as readily and as cordially as you do mine. From the kind things you say of me, I cannot doubt but that if you thought I was able to save you to the uttermost, you would be satisfied of my good will. Why, then, will you not believe Him who has both promised and is able also to perform? Why will you rather listen to an enemy who grudges your peace, and who, you know beforehand, was a liar from the beginning? But you want to be better first. Depend upon it, you never will till He makes you so, and then you will think yourself worse. I should think the more sick you are, the more thankful you should be that you are invited to an infallible Physician. You do, indeed, apply, but then you would tell Him how to prescribe for you. I suppose Dr Walker would not attend upon a patient who should insist upon choosing his own medicines, especially if he should object to every medicine that was either unpleasant to the taste or in its operation, for there are few efficacious medicines that are otherwise. Dangerous and inveterate diseases are seldom cured by cakes and comfits.'

1794. February 28th was a day appointed for a general fast; and Mr Newton preached on the occasion at St Mary's from Hosea 6:1, and printed his sermon.*

So many were the claims made upon Mr Newton, that nothing but the greatest economy of time could have enabled him to satisfy the growing demands of a correspondence that had become, to his fullest conviction, a means of very great blessing, and so, on his part, a matter of solemn duty. Indeed, on one occasion, at the close of his life, upon a friend speaking to him of the profit and refreshment he derived from his letters, 'Yes,' he said, 'the Lord saw I should be most useful by them.' And, be it remembered, Mr Newton wrote letters long and 'matter-full', and instructive or comforting in the highest degree. That time has gone. Let us be thankful for the fruits it has left us. To Mr Campbell he says in April: 'I have about sixty

* See *Works*, vol. 5, p. 250.

unanswered letters, and while I am writing one I usually receive two; so that I am likely to die much in debt.'

Amongst the many correspondents of Mr Newton we find reference this year to the Rev. John Aikman, of Edinburgh. Mr Aikman, early in his religious life, was engaged with the devoted men who about this time were seeking to awaken a deeper religious feeling in various parts of Scotland. He afterwards became a settled minister in Edinburgh. He was a man of great piety and usefulness. His acquaintance with Mr Newton, as in so many other cases, was through the writings of the latter. But the circumstances were peculiar, and we give them as related to us, more than thirty years ago, by Mr Aikman himself. Conversing with him about Newton, Cowper, and Bull, the good old man told us, with deep feeling, how great were his obligations to the author of *Cardiphonia*. 'I was returning,' he said, 'to Jamaica, where I was engaged upon one of the plantations, and wishing to take out some books for the use of the people there, amongst others I selected was Newton's *Cardiphonia*. Its title struck me, and I supposed it was a novel.' He went on to say: 'Looking over the books on the voyage, I took up this, and soon found it was something very different from what I had thought; and that book was in God's providence the means of my conversion.' Thus wonderfully did God work through His servant.

Towards the end of June, Mr Newton made an excursion into Cambridgeshire. 'Saw many friends in Cambridge, and preached there, and visited Yelling and Bedford, returning home July 24th. 'It was', he says, 'very pleasant. We were chiefly at and round about Cambridge, at no time more than sixty-two miles from London. We saw many friends, and received much kindness. I preached while abroad in ten churches, nine of them in different places, besides many house-preachings. I found in most of these parishes active, faithful ministers, and attentive congregations. The gospel certainly spreads in the Establishment. And,' he adds, 'I seem to have completed my desire (in four summers) of visiting my old friends, among whom I have formerly preached Thy gospel, excepting those at too great a distance, in Lancashire, Yorkshire, etc. And, as now I enter my seventieth year, I mean to be no more far or long from my proper post, unless by an express call of duty from Thee. I would now wait for my dismission with patience, submission, and hope.'

We have been favoured with the copy of the following unpublished letter written by Mr Newton while at Cambridge to Mrs Onslow:*

'MY DEAR MADAM,

'I shall be glad to hear that you and Mr Onslow are both benefited by change of air, and that every pain and indisposition is sanctified. It has pleased God to favour me, with remarkable exemption from pain and sickness of body for many years past. But I have a sick soul labouring under a complication of disorders, each of them in their nature mortal and incurable by any physician but One. I had often heard of Him, but my prejudices prevented me from applying to Him till I was brought very low indeed. At length necessity compelling (it was a happy necessity), I went to Him, and He readily undertook my cure. It is now the business and pleasure of my life to procure Him more patients. I tell thousands in a year how much they need Him, how gracious and skilful He is, but I can prevail on very few to go. There is none like Him. He welcomes all who apply. No one miscarries under His hand, and He neither expects nor accepts any fees.

'He prescribes me medicines. These are the means of grace, in which I am to be found waiting, and the trials which He allots me when He sees they are needful. He likewise appoints me a regimen. He bids me beware of the world, its vain customs, and false maxims. He says the air of the world is unwholesome and infectious; and I have often found it so, and yet am prone to breathe it more than is necessary. For want of strictly observing his cautions when I have sometimes

* A daughter of Nathaniel Hillier, Esq., and the wife of the second son of Earl Onslow.

seemed tolerably well in the morning, I have brought on a relapse before night. He bids me be very careful of my temper, and says that pride, positiveness, anger, levity, and many other wrong tempers will certainly aggravate my disease. I always find His words true, yet I am too apt to neglect them. It is of His mercy that I am not worse. It is my own fault that I am no better. Oh, that I had hearkened more attentively to Him! I am frequently almost ashamed to apply to Him any more; but to whom else can I go?

'You, my dear madam, have suffered many things, and you still suffer — I trust not in vain. I wish I could follow the advice I would give to you. Let us pray for grace to be earnest and hearty. Many things seem to call for our attention: but one thing is needful — absolutely so. It will signify but little a hundred years hence whether we were sick or well, rich or poor, surrounded by friends or by enemies in June, 1794, so that we are possessed of the one thing needful as the balm of the present life and a passport to a better ... Dear Catty is well. We unite in love and respect to Mr Onslow, yourself, and your children. May the Lord's best blessings rest upon you all!

'I am your very affectionate and much obliged,

JOHN NEWTON

CAMBRIDGE, 28th *June,* 1794.'

In a letter written also in the course of the year to Mr Campbell, we have the following observations on dreams: 'I have known more instances than one of dreams resembling Mrs Tooley's, and they are worth recording when verified by the event; but this is not always the case. Dreams are to me a sufficient proof — First, That we are surrounded by invisible agents, and liable to impressions from them when our senses are asleep, and perhaps when they are indisposed by nervous disorders, but not when we are in perfect health or distinctly awake. N.B. It is a great mercy that some of these agents are under restraint, or we should be scared by dreams, and terrified by visions every night. Second, I infer from dreams that there is a power belonging to the mind adapted to the unseen state, which, though dormant when we are awake, is active in sleep. Then we seem to perceive by intuition. We are engaged in scenes we had no consciousness of before, and yet we know all that is going forward, take a part in the business, and are engaged and interested as if we were quite at home. This appears very wonderful to me. I think we know very little of our own powers at present. Third, Though some dreams are important, perhaps monitory, perhaps prophetical, as I believe that mentioned in my narrative was, yet there is so much uncertainty in their general character, that we should be cautious of laying much stress upon them at any time. I had once a young lady a month at my house, who had the singular faculty of dreaming that she heard a sermon every night; and she usually told us the text, the heads and much of the discourse at breakfast. The preacher was sometimes one whom she knew, and sometimes an utter stranger. But when she married she lost her gift; and, poor thing, she has since met with many things which she never dreamed of.'

In another letter, addressed to Mr Coffin, we find some strictures on the writings of Jonathan Edwards: 'I know not whereabouts in *Cardiphonia* I recommended Edwards on *Free Will*, nor what I said, nor why. I was younger then than I am now. I do not now recommend it to your farmers, nor even to yourself. Mr Edwards was an excellent man, but some of his writings are too metaphysical, and particularly that book. If I understand it, I think it rather establishes fatalism and necessity than Calvinism in the sober sense. I could object likewise to his book on *Original Sin*, though there are many excellent things in it. I am thankful that the Scriptures, which are designed to make us wise unto salvation, and the gospel, which is designed for the poor, are not encumbered with metaphysical subtleties. The first Adam brought death and woe into the world by sin; the second Adam repairs all the mischief with respect to those who believe in His name. These positions are plain; they are revealed by the highest authority, and universally confirmed by fact, experience, and observation. What need we more? Mr Walker, of Edinburgh, observes somewhere, that the gospel is *too good to be believed, and too plain to be understood*. I think this witness is true.

'Now I am grown old I am cautious of recommending books. I advise everybody to study the Scriptures with prayer, to draw from the fountain-head, and to examine and try the writings of men by the infallible standard, and not to pay too implicit a regard to the sentiments of great authors or preachers. The best are defective, and the wisest may be mistaken.'

1795. Mr Newton touchingly observes: 'My friends drop off like leaves in autumn.' Mr Bowman died in 1792, and in July Mr Romaine ceased from his labours. Mr Newton preached a funeral sermon for this excellent man from John 5:35: 'He was a burning and shining light.' 'Mr Romaine was fifty-eight years in the ministry, an honourable and useful man, inflexible,' he says, 'as an iron pillar in publishing the truth, and unmoved either by the smiles or the frowns of the world. He was the most popular man of the Evangelical party since Mr Whitefield, and few remaining will be more missed.'

Mr Buchanan's university course was now completed. He had received ordination, and became curate to Mr Newton — only, however, for a few months; for Mr Newton, though he seems long to have anticipated this arrangement, was willing to relinquish his services on his appointment, early in the following year, to be a chaplain of the East India Company. 'I saw his call clear,' says Mr Newton, 'and gave him up without reluctance, though he was to me as a right hand.'

We find about this time considerable mention in Mr Newton's correspondence of the works of Mr Riccaltoun, of Hobkirk, in Scotland. He thought very highly of them. 'I admire him,' he says, 'as the most original thinker I have met with. He has confirmed and enlarged my views of gospel truth.' The book contains essays on Human Nature, the Plan of Salvation, and a treatise on the Epistle to the Galatians. The author of this work was no longer living, and his son — a very worthy man, with a large family — was much encumbered by engagements which his father had contracted. Mr Newton was anxious to do something for him, and, amongst other efforts, wrote a letter to the *Evangelical Magazine* on the subject.*

After speaking of Riccaltoun to one of his friends, and saying that he believed he had been instrumental in the sale of nearly a hundred copies, Mr Newton speaks in terms of strong approval of Fuller's *Calvinistic and Socinian Systems Compared*. 'The author is a Baptist minister, a plain man, unlearned, and even illiterate when he first set out, but of a strong capacity and application. It is an answer indeed: I think strictly unanswerable; nor have any of the party (I think) attempted a reply. It is at once a beautiful summary of Christian doctrine, and the best-conducted book of controversy that I ever met with.' And so in a letter to Mr Campbell: 'The great learned doctors dodged Dr Priestley about in Greek and Latin to little purpose: it was reserved to Mr Fuller to cut off this great Goliath's head.'

In another letter written soon after to the same correspondent Mr Newton thus gives his views on the subject of Toleration: 'I think the Roman Catholics in Ireland were long treated much like Israel in Egypt. I do not consider their toleration in any way connected with religion; and as a political measure I highly approve it, upon this principle, that I am glad of liberty to worship God according to my light, and therefore am very willing that others should have the same liberty. Toleration, if considered as a matter of favour, is an insult upon conscience, and an intrusion on the prerogative of the Lord of conscience. I should be glad of a toleration to eat, if I might not eat without it; yet I should think it hard if I could not breakfast or dine without the leave of Parliament.'

On his memorial day (December 15th) Mr Newton speaks of his great loss in these words: 'And now, after five years' separation, she

* It may be observed here that during this and the two previous years Mr Newton contributed several papers to this periodical. See the list of them, *Works*, vol. 6, p. 436, etc.

is as present to my mind as when she first left me. What a constant call have I for gratitude and humiliation! She was the dearest of all earthly objects to my heart. But, alas! what returns did I make! How often, through my depravity, was she a hindrance and a snare to me!' He wrote on this occasion the last of his 'anniversaries,' or pieces *in memoriam*. We may give the closing verses:

> Then let me change my sighs to praise,
> For all that He has done,
> And yield my few remaining days
> To Him, and Him alone.
>
> I hope to join her soon again
> On yonder happy shore,
> Where neither sorrow, sin, nor pain,
> Shall ever reach us more.

Early in the year 1796, Mr Newton tells that he cannot write so much or so readily as formerly; that he is soon weary, and his sight begins to fail. Nevertheless, in his letters to Mr Coffin and his family, written about this period, we find some characteristic illustrations of his treatment of several topics of interest and importance. Thus in February of this year he makes the following observations on *lowness of spirits* in a letter to Mrs Coffin: 'I wish you to come, not only for the pleasure I hope for from your company, but upon your own account, for two reasons. First, I hope the change of air and exercise will do your spirits good. Sometimes when nervous people come to me, distressed about their souls, and think *that* is their only complaint, I surprise them by asking if they have no friend in Cornwall or in the north of Scotland whom they could visit; for I thought a ride to the Land's End, or John o' Groat's House, might do them more good than all the counsel I could give them. Now if a trip from us to you might be salutary to weak nerves, why not a ride from you to us? Secondly, you would not only breathe different air, but you would see new faces: you would talk with new people: you would meet with cases which you would find to be very much like your own. You would likewise have plenty and variety of preaching, which is not amiss for a stranger, and for a season; though I am afraid this over-plenty gives many who live in London a spiritual surfeit. By one or other of these means, or all taken together, I hope, with the Lord's blessing, you would return to Linkinhorne improved in health and spirits, and thereby stronger in faith and more comfortable than when you set out.'

Then again, two months later, in writing to the husband of the same friend: 'We have talked at times a good deal about the path that leads through the wilderness to glory. She would travel on more pleasantly if she was not often teazed by a rude, unreasonable fellow called *Unbelief*. I have fought him more than once, and more than once I have almost driven him away; but he still returns, especially when he sees she is alone; for he is a coward, and keeps at a little distance when she is in good company. I have some fear that he will go in the same coach with her to Bridport, and perhaps to Linkinhorne; but I know One who can, and I believe will, send him packing in due time.'

And Mr Newton thus wisely speaks on the subject of Providence: 'Mrs Coffin has told me of an offer made to place her son in the academy at Woolwich. She asked my advice, and I could not honestly say that I quite approved of it. If I saw you with one of your little boys in your hand, and should ask, "What is your highest wish for your child?" I think you would say, "To meet him at the right hand of the Lord in the great day," or to that purpose . . . If a man is "called", *being a soldier*, perhaps he might safely abide in his calling, as Colonel Gardiner and other good Christians have done; but I question whether it is becoming our profession, for a believer, especially a minister, to place his son deliberately in the school of slaughter, to be trained up in the art and practice of hurrying sinners in an unprepared state into eternity. This offer was not of your seeking, but it came to you unexpectedly, and therefore looks like an opening in providence; but I often consider providential openings as temptations or tests put in our way to prove our sincerity.'

Addressing Mr Coffin, he urges upon him the importance of *extempore preaching*. 'The great aim of preaching,' he says, 'should be to make an *impression*, and this is more likely to be effected by speaking to your hearers than *reading* to them.' Again: 'Digest your thoughts beforehand. There is no harm in having a slip of paper to remind you of your principal heads and texts; but even this in a little time you will be able to lay aside.' And he adds: 'Mr Scott (the Rev. Thomas Scott) is perhaps the most ready and fluent extempore preacher amongst us. Yet when he agreed with me on other points, he still insisted that he should never be able to preach without a book.'

Mr Newton tells us at this time of the Lord's goodness to him at home and abroad: 'We still jog on, much as usual, at No. 6 and at St Mary's. Heart-peace, house-peace, and church-peace are great blessings. I am favoured with them all. It is true there is an inward warfare, but there is peace at the bottom. It might make a coward bold to be assured of victory while upon the field of battle . . . My church is full and crowded, my auditory peaceful and attentive; there are many eminent Christians among them; a general seriousness is upon the face of the congregation; some, and as times go, many, are successfully awakened, and we have particularly a fine show of young people springing up, and increasing in numbers and graces, like willows by the watercourses. In a word, the blind receive their sight, the lame walk, the lepers are cleansed, the deaf hear, the hungry are fed, the burdened are set at liberty.'

On the 19th of August, Mr Newton left home for a six weeks' absence.

A very pleasant week was spent at Reading. Mr Newton was daily engaged in morning and evening exposition or preaching, and in religious converse with his many friends. He says: 'The Lord has many people in Reading, warm-hearted, upright, and loving.'

The tradition is still preserved that on one of these occasions, at the house of Mr Ring, Mr Newton, speaking on 1 Corinthians 15:10, 'By the grace of God I am what I am', uttered himself — in brief — to the following effect: '1. I am not what I ought to be. Ah, how imperfect and deficient! 2. Not what I might be, considering my privileges and opportunities. 3. Not what I wish to be. God, who knows my heart, knows I wish to be like Him. 4. I am not what I hope to be — ere long to drop this clay tabernacle, to be like Him, and see Him as He is. 5. Not what I once was — a child of sin and slave of the devil. Though not all these — not what I ought to be, not what I might be, not what I wish or hope to be, and not what I once was — I think I can truly say with the apostle, "By the grace of God I am what I am."'

On the 26th he and his companion reached Portswood. 'I am surrounded,' he says, 'by woods, lanes, prospects, kind friends, and what want I more?' And here he tells us he enjoyed, as on previous occasions, many pleasant seasons of retirement, and was occupied with his accustomed round of religious services.

When Mr Buchanan went to India, Mr Newton engaged a Mr Benamor to be his curate. To him Mr Newton was much attached, and had been chiefly instrumental in bringing him forward. 'He was able and ready as a preacher, humble, spiritual, and devoted as a Christian, beyond the common standard at his years. I was ready to call him Seth, and thought the Lord had given him to me in the room of Buchanan. But a few days before I left London he was suddenly taken with a bleeding of the lungs, which terminated his life below in about a fortnight.' This sad news Mr Newton received while at Southampton, and he writes: 'Sunday, September 4th. News that dear J. Benamor went home to Thee on Friday evening last. Before he died he said, "Thou, my Lord, dost all things well." I desire to say so likewise — yea, to think and believe so from my heart. Thy will be done. I preached in the evening from Psalm 126:5. Notwithstanding the enlargement my friend has made, the place was very full. I suppose there were more than two hundred people. O may Thy blessing accompany the Word — that they that have not known Thee may seek Thee, and that Thy people may be confirmed and comforted.'

On Friday, 30th, he gave a farewell address from Philippians 1:27, and reached home on Saturday, October 1st.

December 15th was not forgotten by Mr Newton. But he wrote no memorial verses. He says to a friend: 'I have no anniversary for you this year; though it was on my mind for three months beforehand I could hit upon nothing; and I have been led to think I have written enough upon the subject. After acknowledging in my last that the Lord had healed my wound, what can I with propriety say more?'

In the spring of 1797, Mr Wilberforce published his well-known and admirable book, *The Practical View of Religion*. Mr Newton's impression of its value was so great, and so deeply was he interested both in the author and his work, that he says: 'I can scarcely talk or write without introducing Mr Wilberforce's book. It revives my hope that, ripe as we seem for judgment, while the Lord raises up such witnesses for His truth, He will not give us up, as we justly deserve, for a prey to our enemies. His situation is such that his book must and will be read by many in the higher circles, to whom we little folks can get no access. If we preach they will not hear us; if we write they will not read. May the Lord make it useful to the great men both in Church and State.'

In the autumn, Mr Newton and his niece paid their annual visit to Reading and Southampton. In a letter to Mr Bull we have the following account of his labours at Reading: 'The people are hungry; the Lord made me able and willing. The time was short, so we made the most of it. I never preached so often in an equal space; five times in the church, twice in Mr Young's school, every morning at Mr Ring's, and every evening in a large room of one or other of our friends. I have found good individuals in many places; but perhaps I have nowhere met with a body of professors so compact and united, so lively, and yet so solid, judicious, and free from wild-fire as the bereaved people at Reading.* The two dissenting ministers, likewise, Mr Douglas and Mr Holloway, are such as I have seldom seen. They were generally present with their wives at all our meetings, when not engaged themselves. I stayed with them a fortnight, and left them with regret.'

At Southampton the time was spent, as on former occasions, in constant preaching and expounding, in religious converse, and in letter-writing. Old scenes were revisited, and the woods and walks about Portswood were still the places of silent prayer and praise, of hallowed remembrances, and of renewed consecration. On the 13th September Mr Newton reached home.

Mr Campbell kept his friend fully informed of the itinerant work in Scotland, and Mr Newton replies in October: 'I thank you for your letter of September 8th, which gave great pleasure to me and to my friends at Southampton. Give my love to Messrs. Haldane and Aikman, and tell them that I rejoice in their zeal, their acceptance, and in their success. Why should not the Orkneys and the Highlands deserve attention as much as the islands of the South Sea? . . . The gospel ministers in our Establishment are mostly confined to their parishes, and cannot do much abroad; but the Congregational dissenters are stirring in most parts of our kingdom, and associating with a design to spread the good news amongst the villages in their respective neighbourhoods, which are woefully neglected in many places. Indeed we cannot expect those who have no concern for their own souls should be careful for the souls of their parishioners. I fear but few of them, comparatively, have either the will or the skill which the shepherd's office requires; and therefore, though I am a mighty good churchman, I must bid God speed the labours of all who preach the truth in love, whether in meetings or barns, in the highways or in the fields. It is better people should be dissenters or Methodists than heathens.'

* Referring to the Rev. W.B. Cadogan, who died in the month of January preceding.

Mr Newton was again happy in finding a suitable curate to supply the place of those he had lost. Speaking of his absence he says: 'Mr Gunn fully supplied my place at St Mary's. He pleases the people, and he pleases me. Though very popular, he is very humble, and remarkably punctual and attentive. The Lord has granted my desire; and though he seems more obnoxious than any of us to the clergy in general, the Lord Bishop of London licensed him to my curacy without the slightest hesitation.'

In November, Mr Newton writes again to Mr Bull, and speaks thus of his health and ability to preach: 'I am certainly favoured with a measure of health and strength not common at my years. I never could preach with more ease and liberty than at present. I thank the Lord I am as well as an old man can be. I think and I hope that the Lord bears testimony to the work of His grace at St Mary's more than ever, which makes health doubly valuable. The church is often nearly full on a Wednesday, quite crowded on the Lord's Day, and we have a large and increasing number of inquiring young people . . . Oh for grace to retire at his bidding, like a thankful guest from a full table! I have had a long and highly-favoured day. But the night cometh; pray for me, that my decline of life may not be stained with foolishness, impatience, jealousy, or anything that might disparage my profession or ministry.'

December 19th, Mr Newton preached a sermon at St Mary Woolnoth on 'the day of general thanksgiving to Almighty God for our late naval victories'. It is stated in the advertisement to this sermon 'that the preacher, considering himself as standing on the verge of an eternal state, thought it might not be improper to avail himself of the occasion to attempt at least, in a more public manner, to rouse the careless to a serious consideration of the awful state of the times, and to offer some hints for the consolation and encouragement of those whose eyes affect their hearts, and who are continually supplicating mercy for themselves and their fellow-sinners.'

15: LONDON
(1798–1807)

Work of God in Scotland – The times – Mr Newton's Servants – Southampton – African children – Death of the poet Cowper – Letter to Mr Bull – Fragmentary Memoir of Cowper – Affliction of Miss Catlett – Mr Newton's Distress – Journey to Reading on her account – Particular – Her gradual recovery – Journey into Essex – Mr Newton's decline of health – Dr Carey – Letter – Marriage ceremony – Mr Bull to Mr Newton – Hornchurch – Last entry in diary – Feebleness – Miss Catlett's Marriage – Mr Newton still preaches – Gradual Approach of Death – Account of his last months – Death – Epitaph – Funeral Sermons.

We have several letters to Mr Campbell this year (1798). Mr Newton rejoices in the continued progress of the work of God in the North. 'A fig', he says, 'for forms and names, if the truth is preached and sinners converted.' Yet on the subject of itinerancy he thinks, and very justly, that there should be some regulation and order: 'That every man *who thinks himself* qualified to preach has therefore a warrant to go forth is a position productive of many bad effects on our side of the Tweed.'

Of the times Mr Newton thus writes in April: 'If we take the report of *sense*, the times are dark indeed. But what says *faith*? What would become of us if the Scriptures were not true? and if they are true, there must be such times, because they are foretold, and not one jot or tittle can fail. Perhaps *dark* times are the *brightest*, for they are usually seasons when the Lord's people are stirred up, and when many who would not hear Him in prosperity are glad to seek Him. I think the gospel is spreading amongst us, and I hope the prayers of the true remnant will so far prevail that our enemies will not be permitted to swallow us up . . . I know that He doth, and will do all things well. And when you and I shall meet on one of the green and flowery mounts which Dr Watts speaks of, we shall see it more clearly. Till then may His peace rule in our hearts.'

In the month of July, Mr Newton and his companion, Miss Catlett, set off for Southampton, taking Reading and Wallingford in their way, and arrived at Portswood on the 28th, and returned September 19th.

While from home, Mr Newton devoted his leisure to a life of Mr Grimshaw of Haworth, which he had commenced two years before. The profits of this work were devoted to the use of the Society for the Relief of the Poor Clergy. It was published in February of the next year.

In November, Mr Newton had an attack of illness, which seemed to assume the character of a slight paralytic seizure, but he soon entirely recovered from it. 'Means,' he says, 'were used, and the prayers of my affectionate people and friends prevailed for a blessing on them.'

The feelings of Mr Newton towards his domestics were of a character somewhat unusual perhaps even in Christian families. They were more to him than servants. During their long residence with him they had become friends; they were beloved for Christ's sake, and the attachment was mutual. Even Mr Newton's more intimate friends to some extent shared in the same feelings, while the servants who loved their master loved those who loved him. And thus Mr Newton writes at this time to one of his correspondents: 'Phoebe is drooping, and I think will not hold out long; Crabb is very asthmatic; Sally but so-so. Perhaps one young, healthy servant could do as much as all our three; but then we live in love and peace, and bear each other's burdens as much as we can; and for their past services, especially in the time of my great trials, from 1788 to 1790, I shall always think myself more obliged to them than they can be to me, and I hope nothing but death shall part us. Pray for them, for they all love you and Mrs Coffin.' And in a postscript, added to the letter three days later, he says:

'Phoebe went quietly home yesterday, rather more suddenly than we expected, aged sixty-four. She lived sixteen years with us in London, and though she was not a hired servant, nor slept often in the house, she was as one of our family fourteen years at Olney. She was ignorant and could not read; but she knew she was a sinner, and I trust she knew the Saviour, and is now with Him. She never could say much about herself. She was an honest, faithful, careful, and affectionate servant, and in losing her I think I have lost a valuable friend; but for her own sake I am glad she is gone. She was a great sufferer.' Shortly afterwards, writing to the same friend, he says: 'Phoebe's place is well supplied by a niece of Crabb; we took her up at the age of ten years, a helpless orphan, liable to fall into bad hands. She is now a good servant, of about twenty-one years of age, and *she likewise* thinks she has reason to love us.

'I think Mrs Coffin will remember Miss Hillier.* She is in a dying state, but she is very comfortable, and though possessed of a good fortune, rejoices in the thought of leaving all behind her. The Lord has inclined her, unasked and unthought of by me, to do what affords me great pleasure. If I ever wished for more than I have, I think it was for the sake of Crabb and Sally, who, if they survive me, will scarcely be fit for another service, especially after we have lived so long together in a way perhaps almost peculiar to ourselves. I have done what I prudently could for them in my will but I thought it too little. Miss Hillier has made provision for building and endowing eight or nine almshouses. She often came to our house; our maids were respectful to her, and she liked them; but neither they nor I had the least expectation that she would appoint two of the houses for them. This provision, with what I shall leave them, will be quite enough — they may

* Miss Hillier was sister to Nathaniel Hillier, Esq., of Stoke Park, near Guildford. The family possessed property in Buckinghamshire, and Miss Hillier fitted up a small chapel, and left an endowment for the preaching of the gospel in the village of Bow Brickhill. We find also that Mr Hillier annually sent to Mr Newton a considerable sum of money to bestow on such cases of necessity as might come under his notice.

live like ladies. And now I hope I can say from my heart I have no desire to be richer than I am this day, and by the grace of God I will not. There was a house designed for Phoebe likewise, but the Lord has called her to a better mansion — a heavenly. We all jog on in our old way. The Lord heaps blessings and mercies upon us, and enables us (I trust) to see His hand in them, and to seek His blessing in the use of them. May He dwell in your heart and in Mrs Coffin's, in the hearts of your children, your men and maid-servants; and may His blessing be upon all that you have in the house and in the field.'

In reference to the principal topic of the above letter, it may be stated that there are still in existence more than a hundred letters addressed by Mr Newton to his servants, but chiefly to Elizabeth Crabb — just such letters as would proceed from the pen of one who utters himself as Mr Newton does here. It were well if at the present there were more of this mutual feeling of kindness and concern in Christian families.

In July, Mr Newton once more visited Reading and Portswood. While he was at Southampton his friend Mr Bacon (the sculptor) died, and he thus refers to this event: 'The 8th. Informed of the death of dear Mr Bacon. I was dumb, I opened not my mouth, because Thou didst it. Wrote immediately to Mrs Bacon. The Lord comfort her.' Elsewhere he says: 'Though the Lord has given me many friends, he was my particular intimate; but I shall not miss him long.' Reaching home on the 11th of September, Mr Newton writes: 'Came safe to No. 6, at five. Found all well. Lord, accept my poor praise, and let the uncertain remainder of my life praise Thee.'

Mr Newton told one of his friends that his legs, eyes, ears, all admonished him that he was growing old apace, that his recollection greatly failed him, though seldom in the pulpit; but that it was not true that he was ill at Southampton. 'Miss *Report* is a talking baggage, and tells lies all over the kingdom. She said I was ill at Southampton, and that Crabb was sent for to me. All this was utterly false. She had the assurance to tell Mr Serle so, from whom

I suppose Mrs Gardiner heard it. My health was never better than while we were abroad; we had not a finger-ache between us.'

There is an interesting statement respecting Africa in a letter to Mr Campbell in October. Twenty African boys and girls had been brought over for instruction, and after five years were sent back to the coast of Guinea. Mr Newton says: 'Last week I was at Clapham, and saw the twenty African blackbirds. The girls were at Battersea, out of my reach. When I went into the school I said *Lemmi*, which is, being interpreted, How do you do? Two or three answered *Bah*, that is, I thank you; by which I knew that they had some knowledge of the language of Sherboro', the scene of my bondage. I am told the boys come forward apace, behave well, and seem very happy, and especially when they see Mr Macaulay.'

1800. On the 30th of March Mr Newton preached a sermon at St Mary's before the Lord Mayor and City authorities for the benefit of the Langbourn Ward Charity. The subject was the constraining love of Christ. The sermon will be found in the sixth volume of *Works*, p. 492, a truly excellent discourse, clear, full of gospel truth, and powerful in its appeals to the conscience.

It is well known to all who are even slightly acquainted with the life of the poet Cowper, that he left Weston in the year 1795 to reside with his relative Dr Johnson, in Norfolk. Mr Newton's interest in his afflicted friend could not suffer the least abatement. He heard of him through Dr Johnson, and sometimes he wrote to him. Dr Johnson speaks, in a letter in May, 1798, of a plan he had of taking Mr Cowper to the sea-side. 'I assure myself,' he says, 'of your prayers, my dearest sir, that it may be for good', and adds: 'Oh how am I indebted to you for the kind and affectionate instruction contained in your last letter! I envy my old acquaintance John Wright, who can see you and hear you when he pleases.' In July, 1798, Mr Cowper himself wrote to Mr Newton a short letter, but, alas! full of the most melancholy views of his own case. So again in April, 1799, in reply to one from Mr Newton. This last sad note — for such it is — concludes thus: 'Adieu, dear sir, whom in those days (before referred to) I called dear friend with feelings that justified the appellation. I remain yours, WILLIAM COWPER.'

In January of the present year Dr Johnson tells Mr Newton that Mr Cowper's spirits are much as they were, his bodily health not altered for the better. 'Our dear friend allows me to say that he has not forgotten you, and wishes, though "infinitely wretched", to live in your remembrance.' Dr Johnson expresses his best wishes for Mr Newton and Miss Catlett; and adds: 'Poor, dear Mr Cowper! Oh that he were as tolerably comfortable as he was, even in those days when dining at his house in Buckinghamshire with you and that lady, I could not help smiling to see his pleasant face, when he said, "Miss Catlett, shall I give you a piece of cutlet?"'

On the 25th of April of this year Mr Cowper was released from all his sufferings. It might be imagination — and yet why should it not be fact? — when his devoted relative says of his appearance after death: 'The expression with which his countenance had settled was that of calmness and composure mingled as it were with holy surprise.' Mr Newton preached a funeral sermon for his beloved friend from Ecclesiastes 2:2, 3.

He was at Southampton from the middle of July till the 10th of September. Hence he wrote to Mr Bull, on the 1st of August:

'MY DEAR OLD FRIEND, Though the flame of our affection is not much supported by the fuel of frequent letters and converse, I trust it still burns brightly, for it is fed from a secret, invisible, and inexhaustible source. If two needles are properly touched by a magnet they will retain their sympathy for a long time. But if two hearts are truly united to the Heavenly Magnet their mutual attraction will be permanent in time and to eternity. Blessed be the Lord for a good hope, that it is thus between you and me. I could not love you better if I saw you or heard from you every day.

'The almanac tells me that if I live till Monday next I shall enter my seventy-sixth year. I believe you will pray for me on that day. My writing days seem almost over; I cannot well see to write; but I make an effort to send you one letter more, which may probably be the last you will receive.'

These words occur in his note-book: 'September 9th, went to the wood, my Bethel, perhaps for the last time. Thou, my Lord, knowest, and I wish to refer all to Thee.' It proved to be so. He never visited Southampton again.

Some of Mr Newton's leisure moments at Southampton were employed in commencing a memoir of Mr Cowper; but the time for such work was passed now, and its few pages remain at once a monument of affection for his friend, and of feebleness on Mr Newton's part, for his was no longer 'the pen of a ready writer'. It, however, contains some important statements, and is the document from which we have already availed ourselves in the course of this narrative.

A month or two later, writing from London, Mr Bull says, in reference to this effort: 'Mr Newton talks of writing a life of Cowper, if ever he is able, but that I do not expect;' and again, in August, 1801: 'He thinks he could remember enough to make a tolerable memoir .. . He is too infirm — has many things in his head, but is almost dark, and his memory imperfect.' All, therefore, that remains is the fragment of sixteen pages commenced at Southampton.

Mr Newton's attachment to his niece, Miss Catlett, was very great. She had grown up under his care from her early childhood, had become truly pious, and was in many ways a great comfort to him: 'The best substitute,' he says, 'for the loss of Mrs Newton the nature of the case would admit.'*

The year 1801 is memorable for the commencement of a long and heavy affliction, with which it pleased God to visit her.

'Since the removal,' says Mr Newton, 'of my late dear partner I have had a long halcyon season; my path has been comparatively smooth till lately, but now I have a trial indeed! It is His pleasure

* Twenty-one letters addressed to Miss Catlett while at school will be found in Newton's *Works*, vol. 2, p. 287, etc.

to touch me in a tender point. Oh for grace and strength according to my day! My dear Miss Catlett, my Eliza, who has been long, by the Lord's blessing, the staff and comfort of my old age, is at present laid aside. She is in a deep melancholy. In all that concerns herself she is quite deranged; but I thank the Lord she is mild and quiet, and can pay some attention to what passes around her. She expects to die every hour, though her bodily health is not amiss; and she thinks that the moment after death will sink her into the pit without hope, for that all her religious profession was but hypocrisy, and that now the Lord had detected her, and cast her off for ever.'

How much Miss Catlett had been to Mr Newton is evident from the following statements made by him. After speaking of her truly Christian character, he continues: 'I sensibly miss my dear secretary, for my eyes are now so dim that I write with difficulty, and cannot easily read my own writing, nor a letter from a friend unless written in a large hand and with black ink. The poor likewise will miss her greatly. To them she was an assiduous and benevolent friend. She delighted to follow her Lord in going about doing good.'

Mr Newton was, however, sustained even in this heavy affliction. Yet though religious principle thus triumphed, and the good man bravely bore up under this great trial, his sensitive nature was not the less affected by it. Mr Bull saw him under these circumstances, and says: 'He is almost overwhelmed with this most awful affliction. I never saw a man so cut up. He is almost broken-hearted.' Yet Mr Bull adds, a few days afterwards: 'I was at Mr Newton's church. He spoke as loud and as well as I ever knew him, but his faculties rather fail him.'

In the month of May, Mr Newton took his niece to Reading to be under the care of his medical friend, Mr Ring. And he writes thus to Mr Bull of her situation there: 'The cottage where she lodges is a delightful spot. There my dear Eliza is under the care of faithful Crabb. There she has every advantage that fine air, extensive prospects, convenient walks, and the best medical advice can afford, and there she must be for a season, till we see more of the Lord's will. She is in safe hands. A letter from you now would be a great charity. Collect all the prayers for us that you can; and may the Lord bless you and yours, in your heart, house, ministry, and make you a blessing to many.'

Day by day — often greatly depressed, and as often greatly comforted — Mr Newton's time was divided between religious service, converse with Christian friends, and anxious visits to the cottage. We have such entries as these: 'At times very weak and depressed, but Thy mercy, my dear Lord, upholds me. Oh for gracious submission! Found dear E. very bad indeed; but in Thy wisdom, love and power, there is help. Support us both, and hear the many prayers offered for us. Give us patience and submission to Thy will.' 20th. Tea at the cottage. My dear seems worse in her spirits than before. Oh for faith and patience to await the issue which I trust shall be for Thy glory, to our good, and the good of others.' 'Sunday, 24th. Preached at Nettlebed. My mind much discomposed; but may it please Thee to bless my poor attempts.' '25th. Dear E. much the same. Only it rejoiced my heart and excited some thankfulness to Thee that she had been found upon her knees. Thou who hearest the cry of the young ravens graciously hear the faint breathings of Thine afflicted child.' 27th. Dear E. no better, will not take her medicines. O Lord, I am distressed; be Thou my helper.' 'Saturday, 30th. A peaceful night, some liberty in speaking from Amos 3:3. But at times my anguish and anxiety are great. My gracious Lord, I thank Thee for my support. Oh leave me not a moment to myself.' June 1st. Another trying visit to the cottage.' 'Tuesday, 2nd. Took leave of our dear friends and hearers from Acts 20:32. Removed dear E. to Mr Ring's. My poor heart full of anxiety. Lord support us.' 'Wednesday, 3rd. Left Reading. Thy good providence brought us home in safety. Dear E. bore the journey without inconvenience, but is otherwise grievously afflicted.'

Miss Catlett appears after this time to have grown worse, and in Mr Newton's diary, December 15th, after referring to the loss of Mrs Newton, he goes on: 'For ten years my loss was made up, so far as the nature of the case would admit, by the attention and affection of my dear adopted daughter. Thou didst send her to me when she was little more than five years old. Thou gavest me a parent's heart for her, and didst so bless my endeavours to bring her to Thee, that my wages were a rich reward. But this year it has pleased Thee to require of me, as Thou didst Thy servant Abraham, to resign my Isaac, my beloved child to Thy sovereign, wise, and holy will. She is now in Bethlehem; and though I have many causes for thankfulness for alleviations, my trial, Thou knowest, is great. I trust, however, that she likewise is Thine, and that Thy name is indelibly engraven upon her heart. O my Lord, bow, I beseech Thee, my will to Thine. Keep in my mind Thy voluntary humiliation and suffering. Thou hast given me a desire to lie before Thee as clay in the hands of the potter; let Thy grace be sufficient for me.'

The editor may be allowed to introduce in this place a touching circumstance of which he has heard his father speak in connection with Miss Catlett's confinement in Bethlehem Hospital.

It was Mr Newton's custom to walk every morning at a certain hour to the hospital, and to look up to the window of the poor patient's ward, and for each party to make an understood sign of recognition. Mr Newton was of course never alone on these occasions; and Mr Bull, the son of his old friend, being then on a visit at Coleman Street Buildings, several times accompanied Mr Newton to the spot. Pointing to the window, he would say, 'Do you see a white handkerchief being waved to and fro?' — he could not see himself — and being satisfied the good man returned home.

1802. In the diary under date March 21st, 'that awful, merciful, never-forgotten day', Mr Newton says, at the close of his entry: 'I pray for the relief of my dear child; but desire to say from my heart, Not my will, but Thine be done.'

In June, Mr Newton informs his friend Mr Bull of a great improvement in the state of his beloved niece. Her derangement continued, but its most painful symptoms had mercifully passed away.

At the commencement of the letter containing this account Mr Newton says: 'My poor weak eyes will try to thank you for your letter, but they will not allow me to write much at one sitting.' We find similar complaints of the decay of his memory; 'yet it is wonderful,' he adds, 'when I am in the pulpit I can recollect any passage of Scripture I want to introduce into my sermon, from Genesis to Revelation.'

Miss Catlett seems to have gradually recovered, and in September was so much better as to take a journey with Mr Newton. Having visited Billericay, they proceeded to Southend. The next day Mr Newton writes: 'My Lord, Thou dost sweeten our trials with many mercies. Give me faith, hope, and patience to wait for more!' 'Saturday. Still all peaceful and quiet. My soul, praise the Lord. Two or three walks with dear E.' 'Sunday, 12th. Heard Mr Austin twice at the little chapel. A small place and company indeed; but he is a good man, and preaches the truth in love.' 'Tuesday, 14th. I thank Thee, my Lord, for another peaceful day and night. Another walk with dear E. Oh, this ungrateful unbelief! Lord, pardon and help me against it.'

Having returned to Billericay, Mr Newton preached twice; on the latter occasion it was a house-meeting. 'Friday, 24th, to Mr Smith's at Hornchurch.' 'Saturday, application made to the ministers of Hornchurch and Upminster for a pulpit, but refused.' 'Sunday, 26th. Two house-preachings.' 'Monday, 27th. I thank Thee, my Lord that though my feelings are too often painful, yet Thou dost enable me to speak to others.'

At the close of the year Mr Bull was with Mr Newton at the house of a mutual friend. Mr Bull says: 'Before we parted we made him speak, which he did for fifty minutes, on "I, if I be lifted up from the earth, will draw all men unto Me." But his understanding is in ruins. Yet its very ruins are precious, and the bits you pick up retain all their intrinsic value, beauty, and richness.'

Notwithstanding his infirmities, Mr Newton did not lose his popularity. He says in his diary, on the memorable 15th of December: 'People still crowd the church, and are still attentive. May I not hope that Thou art still in the midst of us? If so, how ought I to rejoice, and willingly submit all my times and circumstances to Thee, as a blood-bought sinner!' And still he continued to receive assurances of the usefulness of his writings. Amongst others, there is a very interesting communication from a member of King's College, Cambridge, who expresses himself in terms of gratitude, reverence, and affection for Mr Newton's writings, which once, he says, he despised as nonsense and enthusiasm.

This year we find him in correspondence with Dr Carey, who sent him an account of the progress of the mission in India. Mr Newton, in some of his letters to Buchanan, shows how very high was his opinion of Carey. From misapprehension or prejudice, Dr Buchanan had expressed himself slightingly of the Baptist missionaries. This grieved Mr Newton, and he wrote him a kind but faithful letter, telling him in substance that it was easy for him from his superior and favoured position to look down upon these devoted men who were bearing the burden and heat of the day, and adding: 'I do not look for miracles; but if God were to work one in our day, I should not wonder if it were in favour of Dr Carey.'

1803. In January, Mr Newton wrote the following letter to Nathaniel Hillier, Esq.: 'My Dear Sir, The weakness of my eyes must be my apology for a shorter letter than my heart would otherwise dictate. I thank you for your very kind favour of the 1st instant. My heart says Amen to all the prayers you mention. May the Lord bless you, Mrs Hillier, and the children with the best blessings for time and eternity, and fulfil the desire He has put into your heart to shine to His praise as a light in a dark world. May you have the comfort of the Lord's presence with you in secret, in your family, in His ordinances, and in all the wise and holy dispensations of His providence. For I know that no situation in life can exempt those He loves from changes and trials. He appoints us this wholesome discipline to preserve us from the snare of the fowler, and from the noisome, pestilential air of this vile world. My health is remarkably good, considering I am this day half way through my seventy-eighth year. My spirits are tolerable, and I am still enabled to preach as formerly.

'Now my eyes wish me to leave off . . . Your two pensioners under my roof desire me to present their duty and thanks. The Lord grant that if we meet no more upon earth we may meet before His throne of glory.

'I am, my dear Sir, your affectionate and obliged,

JOHN NEWTON.'

In June, Mr Newton paid another visit to Mr and Mrs Smith at Hornchurch. 'Kindness,' he says, 'waited to receive us at the house. It is of Thy goodness and influence that I have such friends. I praise Thee for them, and I pray Thee to bless and reward them. I trust my heart was simple in referring this visit to Thy will. And as Thou didst not prevent me, I humbly hope Thou wilt do us good while we stay, and make me some way useful to those with whom I may converse.'

'Sunday, 26th. Preached twice in the family. Lord, I love them that love Thee.' 'Wednesday, 29th. My thoughts much exercised about the awful times. In the evening visited some poor cottagers, who I hope, from what I hear, are precious in Thy sight, for Thou art gracious to many whom men overlook and despise.'

'Friday, 8th July. My eyes and other hindrances prevent me writing regularly. We are still preserved in peace by Thy mercy. Yesterday Thy providence called me very unexpectedly to Aveley, and by the very door of the houses where I spent much of my early life in sin and folly. Little did I think then for what gracious purpose I was spared . . . I usually expound in the forenoon a chapter or two to Mrs Smith, etc. The Lord command a blessing.'

'Friday, July 15th. Returned home in safety. The Lord bless my dear friends. Own what Thou didst enable me to say or do amongst them, and pardon what was mine, sin and folly.'

In October, Mr Newton, at the earnest wish of Mr Bull and his son, conducted the service when the latter was married at St Luke's Church, Old-street Road. Mr Newton was really unequal to the task, but his great love to those who were so interested in the occasion induced him to consent. The editor has often heard his father say that Mr Newton, who sat during the ceremony, quite lost himself in the midst of the service, and exclaimed: 'What do I here?'

In the very same month Mr Campbell coming to London, called on Mr Newton. He found him attempting to read. Being told who he was: 'Stop a little,' he said, 'till I recollect myself.' Then, after a short silence: 'I am glad to see you. I am very feeble; I never experienced before what it was to be seventy-nine.'

Mr Bull having been on a visit to London in the summer of 1804 writes thus to Mr Newton after his return home: 'I think of you daily, with the most sincere affection and love. I feel much for the burden of age and infirmities you sustain; but I must and do rejoice in the great love of Jesus, which sustains you under them. Many pleasant interviews have we enjoyed in the house of our pilgrimage; but there is one interview yet to come, better than them all together. I trust, through grace — rich, free, all-sufficient grace — we shall, ere long, meet to part no more — for ever.'

In September, Mr Newton again visited his friends at Hornchurch. The journal is no longer in the good man's handwriting, but, as we suppose, in that of Miss Catlett. It only contains a list of the names of the friends he met and of the texts from which he spoke. Still Mr Newton continued his ministry; and in the pulpit he lost little of his old animation. He was heard with pleasure and profit by those who had long rejoiced in his instructions.

November 20th, Mr Serle, writing to him, speaks of a welcome letter he had received — 'welcome, because I always rejoice to see or hear from you;' and then adds: 'The Lord has spared your precious and useful life to His Church for many years. We know not how to part with you yet. We pray for your longer and longer detention from the glorified part of the Church above. And though the Lord can, and undoubtedly will, raise up faithful labourers to gather in His harvest till the whole be completed, yet it is a trial of heart and of faith to lose those whose places may be sooner filled, than their rich and ripe experience can be supplied, especially to those of their people who can, through grace, digest the meat of the word as well as relish the milk of it.'

1805. It is somewhat painful to copy, as we must now do, the last entry in Mr Newton's journal. It consists but of two lines; and it is singular, yet most appropriate, that it should be on the 21st of March, the day of his 'great deliverance.' 'Not well able to write; but I endeavour to observe the return of this day with humiliation, prayer, and praise.'

In September, Mr Bull was supplying the pulpits of the Tabernacle and Tottenham Court. While writing, he received a visit from Mr Newton, and when his old friend was gone he continued his letter thus: 'Mr Newton is very feeble — had great difficulty getting out of the coach. I was obliged to lift him with all my strength. He was most affectionate, and said he would not have come so far for many people — only for me. He wished me to come and dine with him tomorrow — to be there at nine, and stay till seven.'

Mr Bull accordingly spent the following day with Mr Newton. It was, however, in some respects painful. The good man was strong in his opinion that he was as capable as ever of preaching, and defended his position with some warmth. But Mr Bull says: 'Everybody else shakes his head and laments that he preaches at all.'

We believe it was in the course of this year that Miss Catlett, having quite recovered, was married to a very excellent man, Mr Smith, an optician of the Royal Exchange. He still resided with Mr Newton at Coleman Street Buildings.

Though now more than eighty years of age, Mr Newton continued to preach regularly, although he could no longer see to read his text. His memory and voice sometimes failed him; but it was remarked that at this great age he was nowhere more collected or more lively than in the pulpit. He was punctual as to time with his congregation, and preached every first Sunday evening in the month on relative duties. Mr Alderman Lea regularly sent his carriage to convey him to the church, and Mr Bates sent his servant to attend him in the pulpit. This friendly assistance was continued till Mr Newton could appear no longer in public.

Mr Newton's approach to death was singularly gradual. The loss of sight, and of hearing to a great extent, combined with much bodily feebleness and frequent depression of spirits, rendered the last two years of his life a striking contrast to all that it had been before, and there is consequently very little to record. The active brain had lost much of its power, and the busy hand all its cunning. Some of his friends fearing he might continue his public work too long, Mr Cecil said to him at the beginning of this year: 'In the article of public preaching, might it not be best to consider your work as done, and stop before you evidently discover you can speak no longer?'

'I cannot stop,' said he, raising his voice. *'What! shall the old African blasphemer stop while he can speak?'*

'In every future visit,' adds Mr Cecil, 'I perceived old age making rapid strides.' At length his friends found some difficulty in making themselves known to him; his sight, his hearing, and his recollection exceedingly failed; but, being mercifully kept from pain, he generally appeared easy and cheerful. Whatever he uttered was perfectly consistent with the principles he had so long and so honourably maintained.

Mr Newton appeared for the last time in the pulpit in October, 1806 — a little more than a year before his death. His first public sermon was preached for the benefit of the sufferers from the battle of Trafalgar, when his faculties were so far gone that he was obliged to be reminded of the subject of his discourse. When he could no longer preach, he usually sat in the pulpit to hear his curate, as deafness accompanied the other infirmities of age. The last time he attempted to speak in his church was in the reading-desk, just before the death of his curate, the Rev. Mr Gunn, which happened December 5th, 1806.

1807. And now we have arrived at Mr Newton's last year. Mr Campbell constantly saw him at this time, and has carefully chronicled the symptoms of gradual decline in his valued friend. From his memoranda we quote the following statements:

'January 14th, found Mr Newton looking worse; his feet and legs so swelled that he could not walk across the room without help.'

'February 10th. Mr Newton was now confined to his bedroom, not having been down stairs for three weeks. He said: "I have comfort from the Word — there is much comfort in it, could we take it."'

'May 28th. Calling in the evening, I found him very weak. I sat by his side about ten minutes, repeating in his ear passages of Scripture; but he spoke not a word, or took any notice of me. At last he recollected me. After prayer with him, he thanked me, and shaking my hand, he wished every blessing might attend me.'

After a long absence in Scotland Mr Campbell writes again: 'December 14th. Visited Mr Newton this evening for the last time. He was very weak and low — more than usual. He took little notice of any present. After going to prayer with him, he stretched out his hand, shook mine, as if he thanked me, but he said nothing.' A person present mentioned that the last time he had called on Mr Newton, he remarked to him how useful he had been by his writings — that Mr Newton replied: 'I need none of these sweetmeats.'

For some months before his death Mr Newton was confined to his room. Sometimes he would speak with his usual pleasantry, even of his expected dismission. 'I am,' said he, 'like a person going a journey in a stage-coach, who expects its arrival every hour, and is frequently looking out at the window for it.' And at another time, to the inquiry how he was, he replied: I am packed and sealed, and waiting for the post.' Mr Jay visited him near the closing scene. He was hardly able to speak, he however said to him: 'My memory is nearly gone; but I remember two things: that I am a great sinner, and that Christ is a great Saviour.' adding: 'Did you not, when I saw you at your house in Bath, desire me to pray for you? Well, then, now you must pray for me.'

We quote the following particulars from Mr Cecil: 'About a month before Mr Newton's death, Mr Smith's niece was sitting by him, to whom he said, "It is a great thing to die, and when flesh and heart fail, to have God for the strength of our heart, and our portion for ever. I know whom I have believed, and He is able to keep that which I have committed to him against that great day. Henceforth there is laid up for me a crown of righteousness, which the Lord, the righteous Judge, shall give me at that day."

'At another time he said: "More light, more love, more liberty. Hereafter I hope when I shut my eyes on the things of time I shall open them in a better world. What a thing it is to live under the shadow of the wings of the Almighty! I am going the way of all flesh." And when one replied: "The Lord is gracious," he answered: "If it were not so, how could I dare to stand before Him?" The Wednesday before he died, being asked if his mind was comfortable, he replied: "I am satisfied with the Lord's will."'

'Mr Newton', says Mr Cecil, in his funeral sermon for him, 'gradually sank as the setting sun, shedding to the last those declining rays which gilded and gladdened the dark valley. In the latter conversations I had with him, he expressed an unshaken faith in eternal realities; and when he could scarcely utter words he remained a firm witness to the truths he had preached.'

On the evening of Monday, December 21st, Mr Newton died, in his eighty-third year. He was buried in his church of St Mary Woolnoth, in the vault which contained the remains of Mrs Newton and his niece, Miss Eliza Cunningham.

He composed the following epitaph for himself, which he wished to be inscribed on a plain marble tablet in the church. He requested that no other monument and no inscription but one to this purport might be attempted for him. Thus to the very last would he commemorate the great grace of God so signally manifested towards him.

JOHN NEWTON,
CLERK,
ONCE AN INFIDEL AND LIBERTINE,
A SERVANT OF SLAVES IN AFRICA,
WAS,
BY THE RICH MERCY OF OUR LORD AND SAVIOUR
JESUS CHRIST,
PRESERVED, RESTORED, PARDONED,
AND APPOINTED TO PREACH THE FAITH
HE HAD LONG LABOURED TO DESTROY.

HE MINISTERED
NEAR XVI YEARS AS CURATE AND VICAR
OF OLNEY IN BUCKS,
AND XXVIII AS RECTOR
OF THESE UNITED PARISHES.

ON FEBRY. THE FIRST MDCCL HE MARRIED MARY,
DAUGHTER OF THE LATE GEORGE CATLETT,
OF CHATHAM, KENT,
WHOM HE RESIGNED
TO THE LORD WHO GAVE HER,
ON DECR. THE XVTH MDCCXC.

On Thursday, December 31st, Mr Newton was buried, the service being conducted by the Rev. H. Foster, about thirty ministers, with many other friends, being present. Mr Cecil preached the funeral sermon on the following sabbath from Luke 12:42, 43. Many other ministers both in and out of the Establishment testified their respect to the memory of this good man by funeral discourses at their places of worship.

16: GENERAL REVIEW

Mental Endowments – Strength of mind – Misstatements – His mind eminently practical – His character – Humility – Simplicity – Reasons inducing the publication of his *Narrative* and other works – Newton's loving and tender spirit – His friendships – Benevolence – Regard for Children – Catholicity – Strong faith – Fidelity to God – Spirit of prayer – His ministry, preaching, and pastoral duties – Conversational powers – Writings – Conclusion.

We have thus brought to a conclusion the history of a remarkable and most instructive life; and we venture to hope that the anticipations we indulged at the commencement of this volume have been, at least to some extent, fulfilled. For ourselves we must acknowledge that much as we always loved and venerated the name of John Newton, these feelings have been greatly increased by the work which has engaged our attention. It is, therefore, with no grudging pen, however unequal it may prove to the task, that we would still occupy a few more pages in attempting to inscribe the following memorial sentences, and so to bring together, as to one focal point, some of the scattered lights of our narrative.

First, then, to speak of Mr Newton's character. We do not think that his talents were of the highest order, but they were far above mediocrity, and he had the invaluable faculty of always turning them to the best account. He was unquestionably a strong-minded man. He possessed great determination of purpose, with singular earnestness, diligence, and perseverance in all he undertook. To this, notwithstanding the defects of his early training, he mainly owed the large amount of scriptural and general knowledge which he acquired, and his clear and decided views of revealed truth. Hence also the steadfastness with which, under God, he held on his way through so long a life. His judgment was, for the most part, thoroughly sound and trustworthy. We say for the most part, for his kindly nature did in some instances overcome his vigorous judgment. It is greatly to mistake Mr Newton's mental constitution to connect this quality of strength with aught that was hard and insensible, and, in phraseology we care not to repeat, to speak of him in terms which, so far from being correct, are more than an exaggeration — are an actual contradiction of the facts of the case. That a man of strong affections, ever ready to welcome the approach of kindness and confidence in others, responding with self-denying alacrity to every claim of temporal or spiritual necessity, with nothing cold or phlegmatic in his nature, but with everything genial, social, and loveable about him — that such a man should be wanting in all sensibility and tenderness is simply an impossibility. To give such a description of Mr Newton's character is only to draw a fancy picture, and not to give us a real likeness.*

It may be proper in this place to observe that the conduct of Mr Newton when about to enter the ministry may appear to some readers to be wanting in that decision of character to which we have referred. He seems now inclined to the Church, and again ready to join the Nonconformists. The truth is that, while his predilections were certainly towards the Establishment, yet his views of Church government were not at that time very decided; and, therefore, if only his cherished wish of entering the ministry could be fulfilled, he was ready to sacrifice all inferior considerations to that object.

It may be further observed that Mr Newton's mind was eminently *practical*. He was naturally averse to all that was speculative and controversial. He grasped and held with firmness the palatable truths, but he was impatient of the discussion of all matters he could not clearly understand, or which he deemed of secondary importance.

Mr Newton's own peculiar circumstances and tendencies had made him a very diligent student of the human heart in all its workings:

* See Sir James Stephen's *Essay on the Evangelical Succession*.

and hence he became very skilful as a moral anatomist, and thus greatly successful as a guide and helper of those who were the subjects of spiritual ignorance or distress, and many sought his advice.*

We have referred to Mr Newton's mental endowments; but it was his *goodness* rather than his *greatness* that rendered him so especially attractive — the abundance of the grace of God that was in him. In this respect we believe Mr Newton to be pre-eminent, justifying the eulogy of Mr Jay, who speaks of him as one of the most perfect instances of the spirit and temper of Christianity he ever knew — equalled only by Cornelius Winter. Some men excel in one virtue more than another; but Mr Newton's character was beautiful in its entireness. It rested on a solid foundation, the initial Christian grace of *humility*, and of this grace he was a most striking example. Mr Newton never for a moment forgot that by the grace of God he was what he was. Hence the frequent allusion to his former miserable and guilty state, in his diary, in his letters, his converse, his preaching. No day passed without the mingled feelings of self-abasement and gratitude which his circumstances awakened. If the thought of pride ever arose in his mind, it was at once suppressed. He would say that on such occasions he had only to mix a little Plantain sauce with his more savoury diet, and the evil was at once checked.

Closely connected with this endowment was the remarkable *simplicity* of Mr Newton's character. At Liverpool, Olney, London, he was the same. He never assumed anything. His wants were few, his mode of life unostentatious, many of his habits almost primitive. A friend belonging to the higher social circle invited him to his house, telling him he 'should have his dish of tea while they dined'. It was this simplicity which enabled him to secure his appointed times of devotion; and to the same feeling, too, we may probably in great part attribute the fact that he was never too proud to acknowledge his obligations.

* See Newton's letters to Lord Dartmouth, *Cardiphonia*, i. 61 (Letter 13).

We believe, also, that in these features of character, combined with an earnest desire to promote the Divine glory, we may discover the true reasons which induced Mr Newton to publish the details of his early life, his *Cardiphonia*, and even his *Letters to a Wife*. Very justly does Sir James Stephen say that it was not from that voracious vanity, that canine appetite for sympathy of any kind, that will exhibit its faults and vices rather than not exhibit itself at all; nor from the loathsome affectation of thus winning the praise of humility and candour, that Newton thus exposed his past history to the world. But not so justly does the essayist add, that 'his mistake was in transferring to the press the language of the oratory; that, insensible to the proprieties of places and times, he did not perceive that Truth herself ceases to be true, unless she shapes her discourse to the apprehension of her audience: that, as a straightforward sailor, who with a skin as thick as the copper sheathing of his ship, he laid bare the recesses of his conscience with as little squeamishness as he would have thrown open his ship's hold and overhauled her cargo.'

If this witness be true, then how strange that the Christian public should have received his *Narrative* as they did; that wise men, men of thought and feeling as well as good men, should have thought it a book eminently calculated for usefulness, and urged its publication! To how many souls did it prove a blessing! If the view of Sir James Stephen be right, does it not condemn at the same time the *Grace Abounding* of John Bunyan, the *Confessions* of Augustine, yea, the inspired record of like utterances of David and of the apostle Paul, and every religious biography which contains similar discourses?

Another element in the character of John Newton will only more fully show how alien to his nature were the insensibility and hardness so strangely attributed to him. He was a man of a most *loving* and *tender* spirit. He was attracted as by a necessity of his nature to every spirit congenial with his own, and there he at once, persistently and frankly, bestowed his affections, and registered the names of all such friends in the list of those he remembered before God.

There must have been something marvellously winning about Mr Newton to attract a circle of friends alike numerous and excellent. He was surely no common man who could count in that number such names as Lord Dartmouth and Wilberforce and the Thorntons, Charles Grant and Ambrose Serle and Mrs Hannah More, with the *élite* of the clergy of all denominations. And these were not casual, but life-long friendships.

But Mr Newton's love stretched itself beyond these limits. To do good to all as he had opportunity was ever felt by him to be his privilege and his duty. In the use of every possible means, and in all places, in the pulpit and the parlour, in the chamber of sickness, at home and abroad, he was ever engaged in this blessed work. He never counted that an interruption, how busily soever he might be employed, which called him from his studies to minister to necessities of those who sought his aid. 'He was peculiarly distinguished,' says a recent writer, 'for his tenderness and compassion. He literally wept with those who wept, and rejoiced with them that rejoiced. The law of love was in his heart, and the language of it on his lips.'

There is yet another aspect in which this amiable and loving temper appears. We have seen how the humblest of those connected with him were the objects of his Christian regard; how he ever sought the temporal and spiritual welfare of his servants; but the *young* especially had a warm place in his affectionate heart. Witness his great love to his nieces, the series of letters addressed to Miss Catlett, and the delight which all young people found in his society. How often has the editor of this volume heard his own father speak of Mr Newton's affection for him when a child. It may seem a trivial circumstance to record, but it well illustrates this statement. Many years since, the editor happened to be amusing some little ones by making small paper boats, 'Ah,' said his father, sitting by, and showing great interest in the matter, 'Mr Newton used to make just such boats as these to please me when I was a child, and I have never seen any like them since.' 'I charge you,' says Mr Newton in one of his letters to his friend Mr Bull, 'I charge you upon your allegiance that you bring Tommy (his son, then eight years of age) with you when you come to London. Venture not into my presence without him. We shall find some auger hole in which to put him.' Mr Jay, too, relates that once a little sailor-boy with his father called on Mr Newton. He took the boy between his knees, told him that he had been much at sea himself, and then sang him part of a naval song.

Mr Newton's heart was as *large* as it was loving. How many are the proofs of his *catholicity* which this volume affords! Of narrowness, sectarianism, bigotry, he seemed utterly incapable, and he beautifully showed how a man may love the particular denomination to which he is by conviction attached, and yet possess a charity that can embrace all who without its pale are agreed in the great fundamentals of Christianity.

In Mr Newton's Christian character the essential elements of *faith* and *love* were strikingly manifest. His faith in the atoning work of Christ was simple and unwavering; and his gratitude for the mercy of God bestowed upon him, the 'chief of sinners,' was the ever-abiding feeling of his heart. But here we would especially speak of Mr Newton's *faith in the overruling providence of God.* In all circumstances his soul stayed itself upon the Lord. Thus in the perils of the deep he possessed his soul in peace. When he had come to the settled conviction that it was the will of God he should be a minister he waited for six long years, convinced that God would, in His own time, open the door of admission; and at length he gave up a comfortable income, and went to his curacy of Olney, with £60 a year, believing that the Lord would provide. He lost all his little property soon after, but no murmur escaped him. He still trusted in the Lord; and his trust was not put to shame. On the death of his wife, the object of the fondest affection man ever entertained towards woman in such a relation, his faith assumed the form of *perfect repose.* He glorified God in the fire. He went on with his work, trusted, and was not afraid. We find also the same spirit of entire resignation in the fearful calamity which afterwards befell Miss Catlett, then the staff and prop of his old age.

Mr Newton was eminently *faithful* to the trust which the Great Master had committed to him. Quietly and perseveringly he worked on in his own appointed sphere. It was not given to him to evangelise like Whitefield or Wesley, and, trumpet-tongued, to arouse the masses; but in another way he laboured to build up and edify the Church, and to influence perhaps a yet wider circle. To these ends he preached, wrote, talked, lived.

And what in all this was the great secret of Mr Newton's power and steadfastness? Unquestionably it was his *spirit of prayer*. From the commencement of his religious history we find him cultivating this holy habit. It was ever his 'vital breath.' Thus waiting on the Lord, he continually renewed his strength, and all that he attempted was made to prosper in his hand.

Such was Mr Newton's character, such the graces that distinguished him; and thus it was that he came to be a man revered and loved better and more widely than most of his fellows.

We must, however, pass on to speak very briefly of Mr Newton's various *work*. And first, of his *ministry*. That ministry was eminently useful. His preaching can hardly be called popular, in the usual sense of that term. He was not eloquent. He had neither grace in his manner nor music in his voice to recommend him. His sermons were not the fruit of great study; indeed, his preparation for the pulpit was too often very imperfect. Yet not only in the country, but at St Mary Woolnoth, and year after year, Mr Newton preached to large, often to crowded congregations, consisting, in many cases, of advanced and intelligent Christians, who hung upon his lips, and who returned to their homes conscious that they had been fed with the bread of heaven.

What then, it may be asked, was the source of Mr Newton's power in the pulpit? It might perhaps suffice to say that he was possessed in large measure of the two great elements of all such power. His whole soul was in sympathy both with the truth and with his hearers. He spoke that which he believed, and because he believed; and he spoke with the conviction that it was the great truth of God he was uttering. He appealed to sinners with the loving compassion of one who had been in like peril with themselves, and who longed that they might share in his happy deliverance; he was a restored prodigal, and they too might be reconciled to their Father. Again, in addressing his fellow-travellers to the heavenly Canaan, he gathered lessons from the stores of his own rich and varied experience, and thus 'showed them all the way' which his God and their God was leading them through the wilderness. It must further be remembered that striking illustrations, happy turns of thought, racy and telling expressions, often enriched Mr Newton's extempore discourses. Then zeal, earnestness, and a winning affection breathed their spirit through all he said. And, finally, if there was often less of the *direct* preparation of thought and study than might have been desirable, there was ever the preparation of devout and earnest prayer, and that to an extent perhaps not very common. Of the great acceptance of Mr Newton's *'house-preaching'* we have the fullest proof. Here he seems to have been peculiarly happy.

Of his printed sermons Mr Jay (no mean judge) says: 'Some of Mr Newton's published sermons are exquisitely natural, simple, and intelligible, and easily remembered, and would be much better models for young ministers than such as abound with abstruseness and pomp and finery.'

It may be added that in all Mr Newton's *pastoral visits* and *religious intercourse* there was a savour and a power which have seldom been equalled. While he lived at Olney, where he had better opportunity for the fulfilment of this work, he was indefatigable in its performance — perhaps almost to excess.

Mr Newton's *conversational powers* were remarkable. He possessed all the elements which are essential to the exercise of this happy faculty. In no little measure he had wit, humour, ready thought and expression, with cheerfulness, social and kindly feeling, all pervaded by the purity and benevolence of real piety. 'As he had much good-nature,' says Mr Jay, 'so he had much pleasantry, and frequently emitted sparks of lively wit, or rather humour; yet they never affected the comfort or reputation of any one, but were perfectly innocent and harmless. Sometimes he had the strangest fetches of drollery. One day by a strong sneeze he shook off a fly which had perched upon his gnomon, and immediately said: "Now if this fly keeps a diary, he'll write — To-day a terrible earthquake." At another time, when I asked him how he slept, he instantly replied: "I'm like a beef-steak — once turned, and I'm done."'

It would be tedious to give even a tithe of Mr Newton's striking sayings. Good as they are in their proper place and setting, yet apart from these they lose much of their point; and when gathered together, like crowded gems, the reader is but dazzled by their glare. Already we have given many illustrations in the course of our narrative. Let two or three additional examples now suffice.

When on one occasion a question arose as to the priority of faith or repentance, Mr Newton asked: 'Are not the heart and lungs both equally necessary to the life of a man?' 'Yes, surely.' 'Well, then, tell me which of these began to play first? This resembles the point you have been discussing.'

Referring on another occasion to the apostle's expression, 'that we may present every man perfect in Christ,' he observed: 'This is not sinless perfection. The more grace a man has the quicker sensibility he has about sin; nor is it the perfection of an angel, but of a child, who has all the parts of a man, but is not a man. A perfect Christian is one who has all the parts of a Christian — the head, the heart, the hands, if we may so speak — he has faith, love, humility, and the like.'

Again, he speaks thus of the Christian in the world: 'A Christian in the world is like a man transacting his affairs in the rain; he will not suddenly leave his client because it rains, but the moment the business is done he is off. As it is said in the Acts, "Being let go, they went to their own company."'

Once visiting a family who had suffered a great loss by fire, 'I found,' he says, 'the mistress of the house in tears.' I said, "Madam, I wish you joy." "What, do you wish me joy of the fire?" "No, I wish you joy that you have treasure laid up which the fire cannot reach." This turn stopped her grief. She wiped away her tears, and smiled.'

Mr Newton used to give the following illustrations of the doctrine of predestination, for the purpose of showing the manner in which simple-minded Christians will see their way to truths about which the more learned often lose themselves in misty speculation: 'When some preachers near Olney dwelt on the doctrine of predestination, an old woman said: "Ah, I have long settled that point; for if God had not chosen me before I was born, I am sure He would have seen nothing in me to have chosen me afterwards."'

When once urging religious decision upon a young person, he observed: 'The method appointed for the attainment of the blessing is the most simple imaginable. It is only ask, and you shall receive. But then we are not to give a runaway knock at Wisdom's gate, but humbly and patiently to wait till it is opened.'

Finally, a word or two of Mr Newton as a *writer*, and here chiefly of his *Letters*. Upon these his usefulness while he lived and his posthumous fame mainly depend. His diligence in this department was prodigious, and he was quickened in it by the knowledge that it was not in vain. Without attaining to the elegance of style by which his friend Cowper was so signally characterised, and without traversing the wide field of literature and general knowledge which would have given a greater variety to his productions, yet in easy, flowing language he utters all his heart, and gives the fruit of his large experience for the instruction, the guidance, and the comfort of those whom he addressed. Some of these letters are just the expression of an ardent Christian friendship written to those who were in sympathy with their author in the great things of religious truth. Very beautiful, in the best sense, and very edifying are these productions. In addition to their deep piety they are so wise, so rich in kindly feeling, often so ingenious in their illustrations and modes of expression, that we do not wonder that they were greatly prized by those to whom they were addressed, or that when published they became universally popular.

Were we to seek, in one word, to characterize the whole of Mr Newton's life-work, we should say its whole aim was utility; and could any man set before him a nobler purpose? Thus did John Newton 'serve his generation according to the will of God, and fall on sleep'. He rests from his labours, and his works do follow him. Happy the man who by God's help lived such a life, and left such a memorial behind him, and happy all they who in their measure are enabled to follow his example.